# Carried Away

*by the same author*

*Just Looking: Consumer Culture in Dreiser, Gissing and Zola*
*Feminist Destinations and Further Essays on Virginia Woolf*
*Shopping with Freud*
*Still Crazy After All These Years: Women, Writing and Psychoanalysis*

# Carried Away

The Invention of Modern Shopping

RACHEL BOWLBY

COLUMBIA UNIVERSITY PRESS

NEW YORK

Columbia University Press
*Publishers Since 1893*
New York    Chichester, West Sussex

Copyright in the name of Rachel Bowlby © 2001
First published in 2000 by Faber and Faber Limited in Great Britain

Library of Congress Cataloging-in-Publication Data

Bowlby, Rachel, 1957–
    Carried away: the invention of modern shopping / Rachel Bowlby.
        p. cm.
    Includes bibliographical references and index.
    ISBN 0–231–12274–8 (cloth : alk. paper)
        I. Title.
HC79.C6 B69 2001
306.3'082—dc21                                              00–056123

Casebound editions of Columbia University Press books are printed
on permanent and durable acid-free paper.

Printed in the United States of America

c 10 9 8 7 6 5 4 3 2 1

# Contents

# 1  The Haunted Superstore

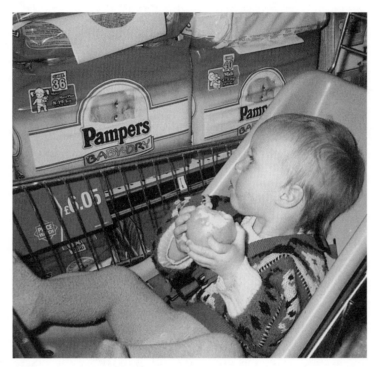

Safeway, Lewes, East Sussex, 1995.

*Saturday, 21 September 1996; IKEA, Purley Way, South London*

It is late in the afternoon and the lines of wide carts loaded up with flatpacks of future furniture stretch back from the row of checkouts. Back and back, right into the warehouse section, they bump up against the people still trying to pick out their own cardboard packages and happily oblivious, as yet, to the fate in store for them.

But gradually the news is getting through. The computers are down; all the purchase transactions are having to be done manually. The prospect of a handwritten receipt from IKEA seems quaintly unreal. Nobody, nothing moves, forwards or backwards. Nobody protests. Nobody seems to be talking to anyone else, passing the time in complaint or chat. We all stand sullenly by our carts, keeping our places, half-heartedly trying to decode the announcements. And nobody walks out, back through the store or out past the checkouts, leaving their cart behind.

We just can't leave now. These carts bear the tangible results of an afternoon's hard work. It may have been fun at the time, but now the prospect of going home empty-booted obliterates that from view. If we let go of the goods, we would have nothing to show for all this time and effort. And we are attached to these things already. This big brown box contains what a joyous, newly verbal two-year-old, still trailing clouds of consumerly innocence, is already proudly calling 'my IKEA bed'. Here we are, voluntarily trapped inside a store that we are unable to leave. Why did we come here in the first place? What is keeping us here? Is our behaviour perverse, a stubborn refusal to give up? Or is it calmly rational, suffering the short-term frustrations and making the best of a bad situation? In this IKEA world there isn't much to choose between the two, or much to choose at all.

*

The checkout come to a dead halt is a long-standing nightmare for retailers. For decades, self-service stores of all kinds have sought to ease what they recognize as that difficult moment when customers finally emerge from the dreamier delights of trolley-filling to reach the point of purchase. There, reality intrudes in the form of the monetary transaction, and the trance of the aisles is broken by a slow line at the checkout. For supermarkets, barcode technology was the godsend of the 1980s; but shut down the computers, and chaos – slow despondency – is come again.

IKEA with the computers down might be a comic vision of a late twentieth-century nightmare. We are familiar with tales of shopping as exploitation, addiction, false allure. As we wait, the frame for pondering the experience is already there for us: the store that you can't get out of as a microcosm of this consumer world, where shopping is endless and always, everywhere the same. One IKEA is much like another, each as reproducibly 'Swedish' as the next, from Leeds to Groningen and from Paris to New Jersey. For critics of over-consumption, the over-stark contrast between movement and stoppage, dream and reality, that the stores seek to parry is ever present – not the avoidable contingency or the dreaded emergency, but the staple metaphor of shopping as hellish confinement.

Consumer culture lends itself to images of unconscious imprisonment. The deluded are unaware that their desires are for worthless or superfluous things, or that they are shaped – if not entirely created – by the skills and tricks of advertising and other forms of presentation. They do not know that there is a better and freer world than the shopping world in which they find themselves; for them it has no exit, nor do they seek one.

Opposite dark pictures like these stand their mirror images: shopping as freedom of choice, pleasure, material progress. Instead of confinement, darkness, hidden controls, shopping in its positive guise appears as sheer heaven or, more prosaically, as the proud symbol of modern mobility. People are no longer restricted to their traditional horizons, whether geographical, social or psychological; consumer choice epitomizes their liberty to move away from old constrictions, to indulge the freedom of new desires and demands and to take on different identities as they wish. This is also the dream world of shopping's own self-images, its beautiful stores and its glossy advertisements, where people's desires are treated as forever open to change and fulfilment.

This book is about some of the strange shopping histories that lie behind the ironies of that peculiar IKEA afternoon, when all the options of shopping were jammed as immobility and impasse but the customers could not bring themselves to leave.

*Supermarket, anywhere, around 1999*

Here you are in the middle of the things. You are half-way through your list. You steer your way smoothly up and down, putting out your hand to take something at intervals, and placing it in your trolley. You know what you want, what it looks like, whereabouts it will be. You see different categories of product, differences between labels and brands and sizes that enable you to home in quickly on what you are seeking. This, not that. When you have finished, the seventeen items you have expertly selected from among the twenty thousand or so different possibilities are checked through one by one. A job has been efficiently done.

Here you are in the middle of the things. You have been here for quite a while. Twenty minutes, maybe half an hour. You came in to get something for tonight and thought you might as well stock up a bit while you were here. Everywhere around you are colours, letters, figures, pictures, all made to attract you. This and that. There is always something new or something on offer. If something appeals, you'll pick it up, perhaps put it back. But your mind is not really on what you're buying or looking at; you're thinking of other things. You will be here for some time, and eventually you will depart, with the same seventeen things.

What is the difference between the two? None, from the point of view of the receipt, which lists everything both shoppers buy in all-informing detail. To all supermarket intents and purposes, they are one and the same person; and maybe they are. In another life, on another day, the first shopper might easily slip into becoming the second; and the second, when pressed, might find herself or himself acting like the first.

The first shopper thinks of herself as in control, taking what she wants and only what she wants. The second shopper sees herself as comfortably susceptible to all the attractions of the place. The first shopper knows about the second and regards her with a certain affectionate scorn. The second shopper knows about the first and thinks she is missing out on the pleasure of shopping. Both, as well, partly share the other's opinion of them. And the first would also confess that she gets a certain pleasure out of her efficiency, while the second would declare that she also uses the time in the supermarket productively, unwinding the rest of her day as she drifts. Both, at times, when in a particular frame of mind, become the other one. The first is sometimes waylaid by a striking new product, while the second rushes urgently past, blind to everything but the two or three things she came in for.

Both, in one way, are figments or manufactures of the marketing imagination. Once upon a time, in the 1960s, it was principally the second shopper who featured, and she was dim and dazed, a childlike housewife passively picking up brightly coloured things she had no thought to resist. Nowadays the shopper is viewed positively, as the rational planner who knows what she wants and competently makes her selection. The upgraded version of the second shopper, meanwhile, is no longer seen as necessarily stupid, but as someone who simply enjoys what others regard as a chore. These characters, and others too, and mixes of all of them, have filtered into shopping consciousness, to become the cartoon versions or templates of how we regard our own behaviour. Like the products surrounding us, images of shoppers supply the background to the way that we experience and talk about whatever it might be that we are doing when we shop.

Some may see themselves as more involved or more detached than others, and certainly there is every possible gradation of difference between people's individual consumerly practices and ways of thinking. For what it's worth, shopping seems to be a part of everyday life in which people positively enjoy discussing their own peculiarities, as well as other people's, and often with much more subtlety than is shown by official psychologists of consumer behaviour seeking to make predictable sense of shopping. But even when people identify themselves as non-shoppers, or anti-consumers, there is no getting away from the surrounding wash of consumerly ways of representing human choices and feelings, in which we are all immersed.

On the one hand, there is a semi-technical language, derived from the big academic business of consumer psychology, that has entered everyone's vocabulary for describing or experiencing their own behaviour. Solemnly or ironically or both, with a knowing mixture of mastery and susceptibility, we refer to 'loss-leaders' and describe our 'impulse purchases' or avoidance of them. Marketing language may also be applied more widely. The 'sell-by date', heralded as an important breakthrough for food retailing in the early 1970s, moved out of the store in the 1990s to be used in relation to anything passé; now the expression has probably passed its own. We can speak the marketing language, we know what is being done to us; but this same language also shapes our understanding.

On the other hand, arguments about shopping and consumption involve much more than the situations in which actual buying takes place. Thirty or forty years ago, the phrase 'consumer society' usually suggested a deluded, essentially female population: the unresisting victims of manipulative advertising and vulgar, alluring displays. The implication might have been that too much of their life was shopping; but the consumers of 'consumer society' were not represented as being anything other than shoppers. Now, in a remarkable rhetorical turnabout, the consumer has been elevated to a status of exemplary good sense in areas extending far beyond shopping itself, with the name implying not a situation of vulnerability or delusion but quite the contrary. The consumer has ceased to be seen as part of a jellyishly susceptible mass, having become instead an individual endowed with rights of which, by implication, his or her previous incarnations had been deprived. She (or he) is no longer a fool, but the model of modern individuality, the one who, as patient or passenger or parent, demands and gets the deal to which, implicitly, she was always entitled but that she was never granted before.

In the course of this process, the consumer has lost her sex. 'He or she' is rhetorically removed from the picture of real shopping, where men and women remain readily distinguishable. In terms of perceptions of shopping (and women), the shift is crucial. Ceasing to be seen as passive, exploited and dim, the consumer has ceased to be seen as female.

## The department store and the supermarket

Though it wouldn't be obvious from a glance at the customers in IKEA today, the history of shopping is largely a history of women, who have overwhelmingly been the principal shoppers both in reality and in the multifarious representations of shopping. This history began to gather momentum in the middle of the nineteenth century, when department stores entered the world. Their splendid new buildings and permanent exhibitions of lovely new things brought middle-class women into town to engage in what was historically a new activity: a day's shopping. They were places of leisure and luxury, offering women the image of a life that they could then, in fantasy if not in substance, take home with them. So after the frustrations of IKEA, and before we embark upon the intricacies of the supermarket's many small histories, let us dwell for a moment in the more leisurely spaces of its principal predecessor as a revolutionary new idea in shopping.

The department store offered an experience of aristocratic grandeur to every woman customer. There, she could act the queen and be treated like royalty. Department stores flattered women into seeing themselves as part of a beautiful environment; they fostered a sense of perpetual and limitless desire for things, in a kind of socialized abandonment. Loosened longings blended and unfixed existing social differences: new shopping instincts made no distinction of class, just as anyone might look like a lady.

In the nineteenth century was the department store; in the twentieth century was the supermarket. Department-store shopping was leisured, middle-class, metropolitan. Supermarkets and self-service, the great retailing innovations of the twentieth century, came from the opposite directions. Instead of luxury, they offered functionality and standard products; instead of the pleasures of being served, consumers could congratulate themselves on saving money by doing the work themselves. Food shopping was associated with necessity and routine, whereas department stores had promoted a sense of goods that engendered new desires and possibilities, out of the ordinary. It was the difference between going shopping – an open-ended, pleasurable, perhaps transgressive experience – and doing the shopping, a regular task to be done with the minimum expenditure of time, labour and money.

But in many ways, department stores and supermarkets belong together. Both are large-scale institutions, selling a vast range of goods under one roof and making use of modern marketing principles of rapid turnover and low profit margins. Both rely on economies of scale through their large selling areas, and through direct buying in bulk from producers or manufacturers. Both were taken, when they first appeared on the scene, as emblematic of contemporary developments not only in marketing, but in social life more generally: cities and leisure in one case, suburbs and cars in the other.

Both came to be represented in terms of magic and enchantment, seen as either pleasurable or insidious. Department stores, and supermarkets in their later developments, dazzled with their lighting and displays of goods – so beautiful, or so much. Like the supermarket, the department store presented a new kind of indoor retailing space, which was *open*, with goods on display for looking at, and with no sense that customers had to come in with a definite intention to buy. Both were thought to produce in their female customers states of mind removed from the normal: the collective ecstasy of the nineteenth-century crowd of women in front of an array of heavenly new fabrics, or the hypnotic trance of the 1950s housewife numbed by the muzak as she glides along the aisles.

Yet the differences between the two kinds of store count far more than the similarities in their respective mythologies. First, in what they sell. The department store offered everything and anything, though with a concentration on clothes and furnishings. The supermarket is associated with something the department store did not always sell: food. Whereas the department stores were represented as bringing the glamour of fashion to the middle classes, supermarkets brought cheap food to 'the masses'. In one case, luxury items are offered to a class aspiring to an image of affluence and a sex aspiring to an image of beauty; in the other, necessities are made available to all.

The department store is European; the supermarket is American. The association in the first case is false, in the sense that department stores appeared in the United States at more or less the same time as in Paris or London or Berlin. In the second case, it's right; but the contrast functions to reinforce other distinctions. The department store is considered to be feminine, frivolous, French and fashionable; in its Parisian form, it is one of the emblems of nineteenth-century modernity for Walter Benjamin's retrospect in the first part of the twentieth. The supermarket, massive and materialistic, figures as an American invention subsequently exported to Europe; and it was.

The department store was called (by Emile Zola) 'the cathedral of modern commerce';[1] it was also a 'palace' for the middle classes. As a cathedral, it took over from religion; it had its consecrated building, and its own rituals and festive seasons in the form of designated times for sales and events in relation to particular themes and product groups: linens, toys, oriental rugs; autumn and spring fashions; winter and summer sales. The plain checkout visible at the end of each supermarket aisle hardly offers itself as an altar, though the uproar in the early 1990s in England about Sunday opening may suggest that the weekly shopping trip is indeed in some sense a symbolic replacement for the traditional family ritual.

As a palace, the department store offered a spectacle of opulence accessible to anyone who cared to enter and participate in an image of the aristocratic life. In the first American supermarkets, the show was less a planned or beautiful display than a performance or stunt. This was later to appear as a markedly dirty trick. In the 1960s, at the height of consumerist protests against exploitation by the big food corporations, the supermarket took on dramatically negative appearances, as a 'jungle' or 'trap', both giving titles to influential books of the period.[2] The images imply primitive aggression but also a space of confusion or imprisonment from which you cannot escape. Where the department store invites you in, the supermarket grabs you and won't let you out.

The differences between the images of the two kinds of store are today much less clear than they were. Supermarkets sell many kinds of product apart from food. Like department stores in their heyday, they try to present themselves as places for comfortably spending some time, with refreshments and rest rooms provided. Not the least remarkable feature of IKEA is that it seems to combine, in almost parodically differentiated sequence, the two forms of shopping, in history and experience. It is both department store and supermarket, both leisure and work, the one and then the other as though in artificial textbook separation.

First you walk through the suggestive displays of room settings and pause, looking to your eyes' content, trying out the chairs and pulling open the chests of drawers. There is no buying or selling here; this is shopping as possibility – the sight and feel of things, the embedding of desires and plans. After passing through all the different areas – ending, in true 1990s fashion, with the designer office furniture – you come to the café, where you can stop to gather your strength for the second part. Next, to ease the transition, an area of kitchen goods, plants, bed linen: a conventional, bright, self-service space with lots of small things you can pick up and put on your cart. Then the warehouse area where you find the boxes that contain whatever big-ticket items you have chosen from the room displays earlier on. It is for you to locate them, transport them home, and put them together; by doing the jobs yourself, you are saving costs on distribution and labour. This last lap reminds you in all its functional bareness that IKEA is giving you the best of both worlds, the leisurely indulgence of shopping and then the money-saving minimalism of the work and time you put in yourself.

These two versions of modern shopping, as labour or leisure, the pleasurable or the functional, are installed as co-present orientations in the minds of shoppers, as much as in the layout and self-presentation of shops themselves. At IKEA on that unusual afternoon, it was easy enough for once to pinpoint a moment when shopping shifted its meaning decisively from enjoyment to imposition. But much of the strangeness of shopping and consuming can come from the difficulty of knowing, experientially or otherwise, the difference between shopping's delights and its demands.

*Division Street, Manhattan, 1929*

The French writer Paul Morand, strolling in midtown Manhattan one evening in 1929, finds himself in a part of the Garment District for which he was not prepared:

No-one had mentioned Division Street to me. I went

along it by chance. Imagine a ghost-dance put on in the middle of a deserted street, in winter. Not a soul left; the city cleaned up as though by machine guns or a plague; and one after another, hundreds of small shops violently lit up with electricity, peopled with stiff and smiling dummies dressed in the most violent manner and throwing themselves this strange party. There are outfits for workers there and outfits for Park Avenue, copies of Worth and five-dollar dresses intended for the Saturday night dance; all backgrounds are mixed up, all the social classes disappear in this instant ready-made luxury for all.[3]

In this passage, different images of modern shopping meet in the night, and clash. In one way, Morand points to a familiar story of the social extension of fashion. Clothes that look like aristocratic originals are now available alongside recognizably lower-class things, so that the 'quality' ceases to be immediately distinguishable. The windows show the mixing of the classes not as a condescension from higher to lower, luxury reaching down and blending in the middle, but as a juxtaposition of two extremes, which thereby lose their distance. The cheap dress for the working girl is there in the same street as the copy of the Worth designer gown. The light of modernity shines out in the new magic of electricity, presenting a fairy-tale show of fashion for all.

Behind this picture, though, is another image, of strangeness and vague aggression, spectres of the night. Morand finds himself off the map, the only survivor in a world in which everyone has been killed by attacks of war or illness, the people replaced by a new population of dead-alive dummies, whose perfect self-containment destroys his own. There is something 'violent' in the artificial lighting and the look of the clothes. The mannequins leer with a life of their own, making the shop window alien and unfamiliar. The spectacle lacks all recognizable order, abolishing ancient class differences with a luxury that is incongruously 'instant': it takes no time and is not connected to a past or a future.

The shop window is cast ambiguously in two roles. It is a performance, a dance or a party, manifestly put on and surreal; and it is also an indication of something beyond itself – a change in the mores of fashion and society. Morand is not himself there as a potential shopper but as one who contemplates the signs of another shopping world as he looks into and beyond it. He is an outsider – to the glass, to the mannequins, to the street, to New York – and he has no interest in the window's objects in their normal mode, as showing things that a passer-by might wish to stop and buy. He is at a distance from the scene, and it is this position that gives him the perspective of a commentator on a social phenomenon: he is not a casual window-shopper. But he is affected by the picture that he sees, as something that haunts and threatens and assaults. He is alone with window displays that have taken on a disturbing life quite independent of their original function of advertising their merchandise.

Paul Morand visited New York just before the Wall Street Crash of 1929, and a year or two before the first American supermarkets came 'crashing' into the world, as the headlines put it at the time. Though Division Street may have taken him aback, he had no idea what was around the corner, as self-service retailing became the arena for the next great social change in shopping. As a result, the ghosts of shopping have changed, appearing differently to us now if we should ever look back to glimpse them in the shadows of the supermarket aisles.

The coming of the supermarket modified the image of earlier kinds of shopping. In the later twentieth century, the department store can be romanticized in the slow-motion time of a shopping that is no more, as opposed to a supermarket world that is brash, impersonal, routine. Published in 1993, Madeleine St John's novel *The Women in Black* sets its comedy of new beginnings and happy endings in a Sydney department store of the 1950s. Ian McEwan's *The Child in Time* (1987) begins with a child's abduction in a London supermarket, but later drifts back to a memory, two generations before, of a courtship across the counter in a provincial department store. Where the supermarket can be the scene of urban aggression, the department store acquires a kind of childhood innocence of simple, old-fashioned pleasures and values. In McEwan's novel, the department store is in another, simpler world from a contemporary nightmare, and the two are kept separate in time and space and in the novel itself.

That seemingly familiar present space of the supermarket has its doubles and disturbances. And though we may be perfectly lucid about the cons and the contradictions, we rarely think twice, or even once, about our supermarket selves, so oddly adapted to choosing and refusing, seeing and disbelieving, desiring and ignoring, listing and drifting. This book looks at some of the smaller and larger stories that surround the invention of self-service shopping, attempting to recover a sense of the peculiarity of supermarkets and the selves they have made or imagined for their customers. Pre-war debates about how to attract the elusive customer with beautiful packages and shop-window displays are revived, alongside angry post-war polemics about the supermarket's exploitation of 'mindless' female consumers. Abandoned gondolas and forgotten shoppers are dusted off and brought back into view. Spectres and dreams of shoppers and supermarkets past emerge once more, to cast a different light on our current arguments about shopping.

Speculations about the survival of shopping's history and its proper or possible forms of evidence are not new. But none is so striking, perhaps, as this anticipation of a posthumous shopping life and private life by Frank Pick, Vice-Chairman of London Passenger Transport, in 1936:

When the writer . . . goes to his tailor or shoemaker or outfitter he leaves behind him a curious record; – the size of his collar, or his shoes, or his vest, the dimensions of his clothes and shirts, with a history of change over the years which is illustrated graphically, if not altogether flatteringly, in the diagrams of this book. His choice or taste again is preserved, for a snippet of every cloth he buys for coat or shirt or pyjama is methodically stuck in the record which, from a survey, should show whether that choice or taste had grown more cultivated or had followed the vagaries of fashion. His rise in fortune or the reverse is revealed by the prices paid. One can picture some imaginative author building up a life history, detective-wise, out of these scanty indications which might be a foretaste of the skill of the recording angel in that last day of judgement.[4]

You were what you wore – but no more. Today, the 'imaginative author' might do some detective work with computerized records of expenditure, but the textural idiosyncrasies would be absent. The writer would probably wear ready-made garments and patronize different shops; there would be no bodily history, no tangible 'snippets' to make up 'a history of change over the years'.

Pick is introducing *The Home Market*, a book of social statistics for use by advertisers; he hopes that, beyond its immediate uses, it will fulfil the same memorial and historical functions as the clothing records. He regards it as 'a happy circumstance that this by-product of advertisement is to be saved and published in this convenient form, for how many facts about the market are lost for want of a similar care and appreciation?'[5]

I have come across my own shopping corpses and relics in many different places – in the trade literature of old marketing books and magazines, and in imaginative literature and critical writing from the United States, Britain and France. Mostly, the trade books are themselves discarded and forgotten, lying unread in university libraries or picked up in second-hand bookshops here and there. They are not considered valuable items for anyone. For contemporary business studies, for the most part, old salesmanship and marketing literature is simply regarded as out of date; only the libraries with the storage space or the copyright obligation have kept it available. And as far as buyers go, older versions of subjects like consumer psychology and retailing practices only slip into the realms of the currently purchasable when they verge on the arty: illustrated 1950s books on window display will cost you dear, but a manual on salesmanship a hundred years old can be yours for a dollar. And this remains true despite the surge of academic interest recently in the history of consumer culture, which has been one of the enabling backgrounds to the writing of this book.

Across the different languages, cultures and periods of this shopping history, I have sought to point out some of the continuities and connections, and to tell a few forgotten stories. But I have also tried to keep sight of the other image of modern shopping that Morand saw in the windows of Division Street – something unfamiliar and unsettling, not nearly as simple or uniform as custom has made it seem.

## 2  The Mobile Shopper

'Any window given over to the specialized display of a single item of merchandise – particularly sporting merchandise – is important enough to be worthy of a good deal of attention to be given to its planning. This example reflects some obvious care taken over the design and construction of the central decorative unit and the small cutout figures. The properties are helpful, and the whole display is well arranged, even though it actually shows a relatively small amount of merchandise for its large area.'

From *Display for the Man's Shop, Style for Men*, The National Trade Press, 1938.

In a fictional diary published in 1913, there is a passage that could claim to be the last word in shopping:

I did however make numerous purchases in the little shops of Florence. Shirts, walking sticks, items for travel, leather goods, luxury stationery. The whole lot is displayed on the tables and armchairs of my two sitting rooms. (I have, at the Carlton, a suite with ten windows overlooking the Arno, dining room, smoking room, bathroom as big as the bedroom; the number of staff has been doubled, on my floor.)

Spent the afternoon and the evening undoing these parcels, pouncing, scissors in hand, on the strings, sending the papers flying around on to the carpets, intoxicating myself with the smell of newness on all these finely made things, sometimes kissing them, and dancing for joy in the cluttered apartment. I don't think I will ever tire of buying luxury articles – with me it has the force of a vocation. I am reminded of the welcome I used to give my toys, those great big cases painted blue, all full of the latest new things from Paris and Nuremberg, which would reach me around the middle of summer, in December, there, where we lived. Those toys that my father caused to come for me from another hemisphere, where Christmas was celebrated in the snow. I haven't changed.

In a day or two I'll share all of it out among the hotel staff.[1]

To connoisseurs of the literature of shopping, this might well come as something of a revelation or an epiphany. Here it is, the very shoppingness of shopping, the consummation of consumption – in one of their aspects, at least.

But let us first disentangle some of the elements of the phenomenon. The 'numerous purchases' of luxury objects are bought for the sheer pleasure of buying them, at that moment, at that time. As objects, they have no connection with a plan or a need that prompts their acquisition, and no connection with either a future use or a future life: they are simply going to be given away. The moments of buying and of unwrapping together make the whole pleasure of shopping. They take place between two different kinds of semi-anonymous urban space: the shop and the hotel room. In the shop, the buyer can put on different identities in public, according to how she presents herself, or what she buys. The hotel room, a private enclosure, is itself available for purchase. Here the guest can act out parts for himself, become his own temporary person of no fixed abode or self.

Consumption is at once ecstasy and waste: not just the packages but also the things they contain are for throwing out or passing on, but meanwhile there are exorbitant private pleasures to be got from sniffing and seeing and touching. This multi-sensual enjoyment is linked to memories of childhood and Christmas, themselves associated with a fabulously simple global economy in which all the toys of one hemisphere are sent for the especial gratification of one child in the other. Childhood was assuredly a time when you had it all, and when the whole world was made for you. Consuming now is a way of getting out childish things again, only to toss them away once more, playfully all the while.

A few pages on, the narrator tells of a 'nouvelle crise de boutiquisme', a 'new boutiquing crisis', and complains that the French language has no equivalent for the English word 'shopping' (p. 104). And now let me say something about the identity of this unusual narrator. He – for it is a he – is the creation of another he, Valéry Larbaud, the French writer who among other things was an early promoter and translator of the writings of James Joyce. The *Journal intime* is purportedly written by one A. O. ('Archie') Barnabooth, the richest man in the world. American though he is, Barnabooth's name was invented when Larbaud visited London in 1902; it is supposed to be a combination of Barnes – as in, town on the south side of the Thames – and Boot's, the chain of chemists. For what it's worth, on this visit an aristocratic friend of Larbaud's allegedly went one step further than the fictional Barnabooth by hurling money out of the window.[2]

The situation of the diary is that Barnabooth has sold off all his property – houses and estates, also a yacht and an enormous automobile called Vorace, presumably the original gas-guzzler. He is spending his time travelling round Europe, the pure tourist-consumer, wondering what to do with his life, and engaging in prolonged exchanges with slightly older male friends from European countries that he meets up with. These encounters are always ostensibly by chance – one turns up in Italy in Vorace, which he has bought; another steps into an adjoining train carriage in a province of Russia; the first one again spots him in front of a shop window in Bond Street – and so on. But they have the effect of making Europe seem like a giant hotel lounge where the same few people are always somewhere in the vicinity, at the same time as the world figures for all of them as a map of possible roads and railways, at once miniature and infinite, on which they are free to move wherever they like from one moment to the next. At the end, having toyed with the idea of settling in London, Archie decides for no apparent reason to accept an invitation to return to the South American country where he was brought up, and the diary of itinerance and speculation comes to a close.

Throughout the book, shopping sprees are related to the narrator's situation as one who has divested himself deliberately of his property. He sees himself as a 'free man' now that he no longer suffers from the burden of his *propriété immobilière*, his immobile property (p. 88) – in other words the things that stay where they are, like land and houses. Property, especially as it figures in discussions with the Europeans whose families have held landed estates for generations, is like a physical burden carrying the further weight of its many obligations; to be free of one is to be free of the other. Shopping figures as the antithesis of property in this sense, in that it represents a pure mobility of selves and objects. One moment you are this, have this; the next you move on. In this slide from the compulsory to the compulsive, there are no duties, no continuities, no consequences and no history, only a succession of shopping instants.

In one way it is like living the life of pure fashion. For the moment when fashion is fashion, it has no past and no future. The 'latest' fashion, *la dernière mode*, is also the 'last': for now, there could be no other. The gratuitousness of the things that shopping buys – the disjunction of buying from needing or wanting its objects – is parodied here in the way that Barnabooth doesn't just have no particular use for what he has bought, he almost immediately gets rid of it. The desire is simply *to shop*, not to shop *for* anything in particular.

Because of this narrative premise – the hero not just as a wanderer, but as ultra-rich millionaire who has given up his fixed property, his 'immobiles' – Barnabooth can come to personify a series of oppositions between new and old worlds, new and old wealth: America and Europe; tradition and modernity; stability and mobility; the absence of change and perpetual change. The journal is scattered with records of self-conscious discussions about modern times and modern literature and ideas between Barnabooth and his European friends, one of whom is a bona fide breakaway French landed aristocrat, whereas Barnabooth, when he gave up his goods, was – like the name of his yacht – a *parvenu* with no heritage. There is a part of him that wants, or at least has wanted, to buy himself a Scottish title and found a dynasty, just as another part wants to marry a working-class girl and thereby, as he sees it, make amends to the people for his wealth (he all but does this with a dancer from a small town in England whom he gets as far as proposing to in Italy, only to discover that she is in the pay of his unofficial minder). Oh, and Barnabooth also aspires to be a writer.

So despite his repudiation of the burden of his property,

some of Barnabooth's desires are for kinds of identity that entail the maintenance or the making of roots and establishments. As such they figure as alternatives to more modern, discontinuous, urban forms of existence, but in a way they have themselves become modern in that they appear now as one of a range of lifestyle options. Roots, stability, continuity can be positively chosen or returned to, just like being a poet or a tourist or a café-goer. Yet at the same time there is a sense in which one identity, more than others, will be definitely decided for, settled on and settled in; the story ends, deliberately, at the point at which such a conclusion seems to have been made. There will be no more roaming, no more writing; or at least, a new and different way of life will be sought in the self-parodying form of the return as rich politico to the country of his birth. The friends Archie runs into have one by one reached their own peace of mind or place (these are equally far-fetched: in one case, conducting a massacre to restore order in a Russian province; in another, opting for chemistry among a selection of eccentric hobbies, when his work has been taken up seriously by university researchers).

Archie, who is all of twenty-three, has a strong sense of ageing as a process of growth and development: he is always comparing himself with how he was six years ago, or imagining how naive he must seem to his friends that many years older. But it is when he is back for a moment with a woman he came across several years before, Gertie Hansker, that he has a sudden fear of stasis, of *not* having changed:

> The same ancient hour was sounding in me in the middle of the same disillusioned sadness; all my readings, my travels, my conversations, the ideas exchanged and received, all that had left me the same. Despite everything that has traversed it, despite the holiday fairs, the village has remained the same, where the same poor old houses are situated miserably opposite one another, on the empty square. (p. 242)

Not changing – lack of development – is unequivocally negative here, and the comparison is with the village, the pre-
modern dwelling place par excellence. In its case continuity
is identified with monotony – 'despite the holiday fairs'.
There is a fear of not really becoming modern, of not really
leaving the village, which remains the underlying reality, in
spite of frantic efforts to do so. The next sentence switches
back from the life of the place to the life of the individual:

> And in fact I set about constructing a theory; I divided
> people into two classes: those who are capable of devel-
> opment and those who are incapable of it. I was in the
> first class and Gertie in the second. I saw her immobile
> and I thought I was advancing . . . (pp. 242–3)

Whereupon he slips away that night, in fear of the threatened
immobility.

The comparison with the monotonous village suggests that
this valorization of personal development, and corresponding
rejection of unchangingness, is meant as a consciously modern
way of thinking about the stages of a human life. In its parodied form here, the point is reinforced by the contrast with
what is imagined as the woman's opposite disposition. To remain the same, to stay put, is to be stuck, or fixed, or blocked,
or sad, or just boring.

In the Barnabooth diary, the absolute personal mobility epitomized by shopping sprees is represented as an extreme, fabulous condition. At this time, the capacity to move between
different identities was a mark of the freedom of the exceptional man or (occasionally) woman – dandy, artist, millionaire. Such mobility conflicted with the norm of a settled, given
self. Barnabooth's extreme form of infantile, hedonistic shopping aligns him with near-contemporary fictional characters
like Oscar Wilde's Dorian Gray – fictional men living in a
charmed world outside the constraints of normal existence and
defined by its being at the loose end of a continuum from duty
to dissolution.

Today, the choosing and moving of identities can be a settled and serious metaphor for the way that a life might or should be planned or experienced. For both sexes, such mobility is regarded as a good thing, a positive value in its own right; it is not in itself a form of rebellion. In principle, identities can be changed, claimed, affirmed, risked, juggled, all life long, with no horizon of eventual settlement, whether at twenty-three or sixty. This is not to say that it actually happens like this – any more than a real Barnabooth ever cruised about Europe – but that this is now a common way of imagining the desirable pattern of a life lived to the full. It is always possible to move forward; you always have a choice.

### From the department store to the supermarket

Shopping at the turn of the twentieth century did not suggest itself as a likely model for life-choices. In its everyday forms it was a matter of household duty, and in its exceptional forms – the trip into town, the seasonal sales – it was a diversion or a temporary aberration. And Barnabooth's outrageousness as the shopper *extraordinaire* is intensified by his sex. In the hundred and more years that shopping has been a notable topic of social commentary and psychological investigation, it has been far more often associated with women – both empirically, as something that they do rather than men, and more diffusely, through the idea that shopping is somehow peculiarly feminine. As such, though in many different forms, it has often bordered on the suggestion of excess and loss of control. The shopper, like the woman, wants too much, doesn't know what she wants, just *wants*.

In one scene from Theodore Dreiser's novel *Sister Carrie* (1900), the heroine receives 'the great awakening blow',[3] no less, when her walk down Broadway convinces her of her inadequate means, her inability to compete with other women in fashionable attire:

Such a crush of finery and folly she had never seen. It

clinched her convictions concerning her state. She had not lived, could not lay claim to having lived, until something of this had come into her own life. Women were spending money like water. She could see that in every elegant shop she passed. Flowers, candy, jewelry seemed the principal things in which the elegant dames were interested. And she, – she had scarcely enough pin money to indulge in such outings as this a few times a month.[4]

To have lived is to have spent. The mixed 'crush of finery and folly' is placed here as part of Carrie's desires, to be sadly reduced to the reality of available 'pin money'. Unstopped spending becomes the standard, defined by its lack of restraint and the gratuitousness of its objects – 'finery and folly', 'flowers, candy, jewelry'. Carrie's desires are also formed comparatively – 'And she, – she': where other women can have anything, she has 'scarcely enough' for 'a few times a month' of mere looking.

For Barnabooth, the constraint against which spending counts as freedom is not one of money but one of responsibility. Shopping represents his abandonment of the conventional obligations of manhood. He is letting go of rules and ties. When he shops, he behaves as if there were no tomorrow. His purchases have no connection with any self he may want to become, but they are also his way of taking himself back, as a millionaire has the means to do, into a childhood remembered for its high points of gifts and excitement. Shopping is playing at mobility; it is the parody of mobility as perpetual, happy, directionless to and fro.

Carrie's shopping desires are limitless, like Barnabooth's, and there is the same element of compulsion. But she wants the things themselves as well as the excitement of acquiring them. And endless spending for her does not have the meaning of transgression; it is an aspiration. For her the limitations and opportunities are progressive: the less you have, the less you can spend, and vice versa. There is a continuous line from poverty to infinite wealth, along which you sink or rise. Her ability to spend is her upward mobility, and it is the only desirable way to go.

Early in the novel, when she is looking for a job in Chicago, Carrie tries a department store. It is the first time she has gone into such a place, and she is diverted from the urgency of her work-seeking by the sight of all the things on show: 'She could not help feeling the claim of each trinket upon her personally, and yet she did not stop. There was nothing there which she could not have used – nothing which she did she did not long to own' (p. 22). Each item offers itself to Carrie 'personally', as though meant for her, postulating its special usefulness and desirability. The things actively make their 'claim', selling themselves to her; Carrie is passive to their effects – she 'could not help feeling'. There is no end to them: 'and yet she did not stop'.

The new department stores seemed to naturalize the limitlessness of female shopping desires: what other response could there be to the display of so many lovely things? 'What is shopping these days, but an unsuccessful struggle against overwhelming temptations?' asks a writer in the *Fortnightly Review* in 1895:

> We go to purchase something we want; but when we get
> to our shop, there are so many more things that we
> never thought of till they presented their obtrusive fasci-
> nations on every side. We look for a ribbon, a flower, a
> chiffon of some sort or other, and we find ourselves in a
> Paradise of ribbons, flowers, and chiffons, without
> which our life becomes impossible, and our gown
> unwearable.[5]

Once again, the negative comparison sets in, this time in relation to the customer's own life and dress, now rendered 'impossible' and 'unwearable' in relation to the new possibilities that have been glimpsed.

From one point of view, the shop that perpetually incites its customers to want ever more things can be seen as a form of psychological imprisonment: the *irresistible* object exerts a force as much as it elicits a longing. The metaphor of incarceration gains force from the circumstance that department stores did indeed form an enclosed, self-contained environment, with everything under one roof. But the idea of constraint and narrow horizons makes a different and more obvious kind of sense in relation to other, less glamorous kinds of compulsory shopping that have little to do with women's personal desires.

'What man would willingly agree to his whole life being taken up with spending?'[6] asked Evelyne Sullerot in 1965. She was referring not to Barnaboothian orgies of expenditure, but to the daily dullness of home economics: 'Spending small sums, little by little, in the agonies of choice: so many things, so many needs prompted, exacerbated, so many embarrassed and envious comparisons, so many examples, and such a small budget.'[7] As much as it might represent excess, affluence, leisure and self-absorption, spending also has its routine side for the housewife, as a regular task in the service of others.

In 1900 the buying of food for household consumption was not likely to figure imaginatively in women's consumerly desires, except for the wealthy or for special occasions. Food was seen primarily as a necessity, whereas clothes – necessary as they are – were the pre-eminent objects of fashion. This distinction made one of the fundamental contrasts in image between the grand department stores of the late nineteenth century, associated with luxury goods, and the supermarkets of the twentieth, associated with the basic necessities and principally with the sale of food; but at the same time, supermarkets were also taking food into the category of fashion.

In *Sister Carrie*, it is only an atmosphere of luxury that excites a buyer's longings. The day-to-day buying of food is of little interest, except when at one point it becomes a sign of the loss of status and manhood for Carrie's lover Hurstwood. He first has to take on the role of economical housewife, counting the cost of each purchase, and his decline is most cruelly marked by his ultimate resort to the midnight handouts at Fleishmann's bakery, where free loaves are offered to men on the streets.

Restaurant meals, on the other hand, take food into a setting of luxurious consumption. Several such occasions are

copiously described in Dreiser's novel, usually with a pleasurable accompaniment of minute details of the diners'
enjoyment. They recall Dreiser's depictions of comparable
sumptuous public spaces: hotel lobbies, department stores,
Pullman carriages, bars. Yet the most expensive meal is given
a very different kind of commentary: 'Once seated, there
began that exhibition of showy, wasteful and unwholesome
gastronomy as practised by wealthy Americans which is the
wonder and astonishment of true culture and dignity the
world over. The large bill-o'-fare held an array of dishes sufficient to feed an army, sidelined with prices which made
reasonable expenditure a ridiculous impossibility' (p. 332).
Food is the cause of this unique narrative outburst: there is
something obscene about that, of all commodities, being con-
sumed without regard to justice and proportion: too much
service, too much choice, too high a price and too much in
quantity for the needs of the few people round the table.

Because food is seen as the fundamental human necessity,
luxury food more than other luxury commodities seems to
prompt passionate criticism of the social inequalities of consumption. In *Sister Carrie*, this is not the dominant element to
emerge in the context of Carrie's hunger at the start of the
novel, or her companion Hurstwood's towards the end. But
other novels dramatize the contrast between the food of the
rich and the starvation of the poor to powerful effect.

Elizabeth Gaskell's *Mary Barton* (1848) was written in part to
show middle-class readers how families in a northern city
based on Manchester suffered from the injustices and insecuri-
ties of the current conditions of industrial labour. Here, John
Barton's son is dangerously ill; he has to get food but he has no
money because Hunter, his boss, has just gone bankrupt:

> Hungry himself, almost to an animal pitch of ravenous-
> ness, but with the bodily pain swallowed up in anxiety
> for his little sinking lad, he stood at one of the shop win-
> dows where all edible luxuries are displayed; haunches
> of venison, Stilton cheeses, moulds of jelly – all appetizing

sights to the common passer by. And out of this shop
came Mrs Hunter! She crossed to her carriage, followed
by the shopman loaded with purchases for a party. The
door was quickly slammed to, and she drove away; and
Barton returned home with a bitter spirit of wrath in his
heart, to see his only boy a corpse![8]

As in the *Sister Carrie* passage, excessively extravagant food sig-
nifies the ultimate abandonment of social justice. Here, rhetorically, one person's over-consumption is another's death. But
what renders 'edible luxuries' an indictment here – for the narrator as well as for Barton – is the exacerbation of class differences in the situations of the two people, neither of whom is in
the place of 'the common passer by' casually enjoying the window's 'appetizing sights'. Even after the bankruptcy that has
laid off the workforce, Hunter's wife does not appear to have to
live moderately. John Barton is hungry to the point of inhuman,
'animal' pain, itself overlaid by 'anxiety' for his son.

A century later, the supermarkets would be transforming
everyday food into a source of endless consumerly desires for
the ordinary passer-by, routinely confronted by shelf after
shelf of goods making their 'claim' upon her, insisting upon
their possible uses and pleasures. As she 'passed along the
busy aisles' of the department store (p. 22) in the novel of 1900,
Dreiser's Carrie was taking in a common dream of wealth and
leisure and luxury; she was also already moving into the twentieth century and the supermarket.

## 3  The Silent Salesman

'The purpose of this brush – in the salesman's hands – is to remove dust from furniture without marring the surface. Mere words [. . .] have not aroused prospect interest. But the convincing argument here is obviously the cleaning demonstration, and that argument evidently is a successful one.'

From *Salesmanship Simplified*, Opportunity Publishing Co., 1927.

> The alternative to the living salesman is the vending machine that gives chewing gum, postage stamps, shoe laces, confectionery, matches, or other goods in return for coins deposited in the slot . . . There is no mechanical device that can take the place of the real salesman.[1]

So said Paul Nystrom, in 1925, in an American book on retailing. He was right, and he was wrong. True, no mechanical device does what a real salesman does. If you take away the presence of the salesman from the process of buying, you change the nature of shopping out of all recognition because you remove the element of interaction between two people. Such a change did happen. But the alternative to the living salesman was not, in the end, the machine; it was self-service.

Self-service was the great retailing change of the twentieth century. The first big self-service food stores, quickly dubbed 'super markets', appeared in America in the 1930s; that story will be told in Chapter 7. Over the next decades, self-service would become the norm, and over-the-counter selling would take on the sense of a nostalgic throwback to an older way of shopping. The salesman would survive only as a sign of either exceptional attentiveness or unwanted intrusiveness. Shopping would be a relationship between the customer and the goods, with nothing and no one mediating between them.

Not even the question of payment. With the vending machine, the coins are an integral part of the purchasing process, for each item, one by one, coin by coin. In the supermarket, you can look at the things and touch and take and put back and take again, for as long as you like and with no obligation to pay. The physical separation of the aisles and the checkout marks a distance between shopping as choosing, and shopping as making a purchase. Self-service makes for a kind of dreaming, an endless 'perhaps'.

But looked at another way, the removal of the salesman increases shopping efficiency. The shopping is a job to be done as quickly as possible. The customer can pick up what she wants without wasting time, waiting her turn and then asking for each item and waiting again while it is fetched or weighed out or both. She is her own mistress, free to make up her mind between different products rather than be persuaded by some-one else. Prices and weights are clearly marked; there is no worry about inaccurate scales or short change.

Such positive ideas of self-service move between conve-nience and aesthetics, in terms of display; and between work and leisure, in terms of shoppers' sense of what they are doing. In ordinary language, it is the difference between, and perhaps the happy conflation of, 'doing the shopping' and 'going shop-ping'. Doing the shopping involves definite articles, a neces-sary task; going shopping is out of the way, open-ended, a diversion.

Both these ways of looking at self-service shopping can turn over into critical versions. Drifting up and down the shelves, picking up whatever catches her attention, the housewife is bound to take too much. Packets are designed to confuse her about what exactly is in them and how much of it. She may seek to be practical and rapid, but the supermarket is itself laid out as a 'giant shopping list', and 'even in the best arranged store, it is impossible for the human eye to see each of the more than 5,000 items in the average 20 to 25 minute shopping tour' (this is the American store of the late 1950s).[2] There is too much to choose from and everything is potentially something to have. The initiative is with the shelves, rather than with the shopper, whose limited 'human' capacities cannot match up to its vast numbers of products.

From this perspective, the absence of the salesman is less the removal of an interference than the loss of a human scale. Now the customer is all alone, with no one to talk to. Like the over-whelming number of items for sale, the big business of super-markets appears out of reach, beyond her view. It looks like a perpetually renewed plot to waylay the defenceless customer with more and more things – a different world from that of the humble store salesman suggesting a new product that madam might like to try.

And sometimes, the supermarkets put it like that themselves. This is from a report by the leading American trade journal in 1964:

> Despite the unpredictability of the shopper who may hem and haw, circumvent sections, backtrack and appear oblivious to the hullaballoo of soft sell and hard sell merchandising alike, the shopper can be conditioned.[3]

Here there is no need to invent the idea of a conspiracy to drive the customer mad – or rather to drive her sane, since she is to be conditioned into doing what the shopping environment requires.

But look again, and the picture changes once more. The supermarket offers cheap food and choice. It is egalitarian, its anonymity dropping individual distinctions of address. 'Self-service' puts all classes on the same shopping level, doing the work for themselves; the expression signals the end of an assumption that one class is there to 'serve' another. Everyone pushes a similar trolley, including the middle-class woman who now does the household shopping she used to have servants for.

Reading Paul Nystrom's book today, we can see in hindsight how the psychological space for self-service is already being sketched out even as he describes the situation in which the salesman played his most important part. In the large clothes store there are three classes of customer: those who know what they want; 'those who know their wants, but do not know exactly what will supply them'; and lastly, 'shoppers – those drawn in through curiosity, or who come in with friends, in neither case intending to purchase anything'. 'The third class', says Nystrom, 'require real salesmanship'.[4] Nystrom then gives an illustration of what this means:

> Suppose a lady enters your department (more than eighty

per cent of the customers in the retail trade are women)
and comes down the aisle slowly without any apparent
objective in mind. You approach her, and make inquiry as
to how you may be of service to her. She replies that she is
not interested particularly in anything, and that she is just
looking around, or that she came in with some friend, or
that she is waiting with some one. It has become a fixed
custom in this country to give people the privilege of
going about in a store without buying. This was something unheard of in England until recently. You are a skill-
ful, we shall say, a scientific salesman. You accept the
visitor's explanation, and extend the hearty invitation,
which is a policy of the store, to make herself at home. You
engage her in conversation upon some point that you are
sure will interest her, and artfully call her attention to
some article of new design.[5]

'Shoppers' are a new breed, 'just looking around', and legiti-
mately so. But here they must expect to have their looking
directed or interrupted by the salesman. Everything is thus in
place for the supermarket to appear to offer the last freedom for
'shoppers', now not only just looking, but able to go on looking
all day long (and later, all night long), without anyone asking
their business.

But when we look back on the old department store, its lights
dim for closing and its last shoppers gradually making their
way to the door, we may glimpse a mysteriously nebulous figure hovering in the background; it reappears in different
guises and at different points in the course of retailing developments leading up to the post-war supermarket. Neither a
person nor distinctly a commodity, but with elements of both,
this spectre, the 'silent salesman', is a prominent character in
the literature of advertising and salesmanship between the
wars. As we shall see, the silent salesman was a significant
transitional figure between the personal-service shopping that
happened everywhere from the big, luxurious department

store to the small, local food store, and the direct relationship between the customer and the merchandise in self-service, where a human salesman is no longer part of the scene.

What exactly is a silent salesman? Its identity is always more than a little ambiguous, as its forms are so varied. Most often, it is to be found in one of two particular embodiments: the shop window and the package, the subjects of the next two chapters. But it is also associated with other selling media – posters or print ads, for instance – that qualify for the name by virtue of their being something other than a flesh-and-blood, in-your-ear human being.

The silent salesman is implicitly seen but not heard. This has a number of possible consequences for its imagined character traits. First of all, the silent salesman, as noiseless, is differenti-ated from the overbearing type whom it is supposedly replac-ing. The silent salesman doesn't earhole you. It doesn't engage you in monologue or haranguing – whether one-on-one, like the domestic foot-in-the-door salesman or the assistant in the store, or one-on-many, like the street-market trader or the 'barker' outside the shop, calling attention to the goods for sale. Unlike these, the silent salesman is not vulgar and brash, not a shouting, outdoor character. It suggests instead a tasteful interior in which voices are never raised.

Silence may also be associated with cleanliness and order, as opposed to a link between noise, dirt and mess. An American manual of grocery window display from 1932 is particularly graphic in its contrast:

> An untidy, fly-specked window display, with soiled
> show cards, greasy price cards, clumsy and junky dis-
> plays, cries aloud to passing shoppers: 'Here is a poor
> merchant. His store is dirty. He is careless in handling
> food.'[6]

The mucky, messy window is identified with the outdoor noise of the street-market salesman who 'cries aloud' his negative message to passers-by.

With the silent salesman, thus, we enter a different selling world, polite and carpeted and away from the sounds of the street. Here, commerce and art seem to be naturally associated, not a contradiction in terms, when the silent salesman appears in the form of a pictorial advertisement or superbly designed package. Concealed in such associations is an implied history of marketing and advertising, in which both are regarded, in the early twentieth century, as having put behind them the chaotic, piecemeal or amateurish efforts epitomized by the shouting street-seller; and also as having classed themselves up, from the cheap market stall and the crudely printed advertisement, to a newly professional style. Like the barrow-boy, Victorian advertisements and Victorian selling in general are regarded as having had no subtlety; they simply blared their wares and hoped to get noticed by sheer force of volume or 'loudness' of colour and typeface. Carnival, street market, fair, circus – these are the images of noise and colour, mess and play, that return again and again to set the cluttered scene for a release into the calmer, aesthetic frames of modern selling methods.

First of all, then, the silence of the salesman is golden. But when this silence is thought of not as the absence of loudness but as keeping a low profile, it can have a more ominous side, an air of possibly hiding something. This is the second, more shifting feature of the silent salesman, in this respect simply a more devious form of the non-silent version.

Potential deceitfulness is, of course, a characteristic attributed to salesmen in general. For the live variety, it was often located in particular gestures and facial features, always open to contrary interpretations. In particular, the dubious 'commercial smile', or *sourire commercial*, was a slightly anxious point of minor debate between the wars, in relation to the virtues or otherwise of personal service in shopping. Either the smile was artificial, a simpering mask whose falseness was evident, and which therefore hindered what would otherwise be a more natural form of persuasion; or it was the sign of the genuine human warmth that marked the personal relations between sellers and customers, and which new 'scientific' selling methods were thought to be putting at risk.

But even if the silent salesman is not a conscious actor, it may still be seen as potentially two-faced, with an outward and an inner nature, not visible at first sight. The packaged article contains, presents, promotes something that it may in fact be concealing from view or at any rate disguising. Criticism of the package as an evil seducer making false promises reached its height in the decades following the Second World War when, as we shall see, packet and supermarket were linked together as micro- and mega-culprits in a great marketing conspiracy. But only the faintest of suspicions float around the inter-war package, which, in the main, bears a much more respectable character than its descendants – as emblem of modern hygiene and even, sometimes, of modernist beauty.

A further feature of the silent salesman is to *leave you alone*. The third party no longer present between the customer and the merchandise appears in light of the silent salesman as distracting or over-persuasive – rather than, for instance, as a source of assistance or information. In later forms of self-service, the 'impersonal' atmosphere of stores where 'nobody knows you' and nobody bothers you unless you ask can be represented in two ways, creating either a lonely shopper or an independent one. Whichever it is, the shopper with the silent salesman as opposed to the speaking variety is seen as being *on her own*.

## The written word

Instead of speaking, the silent salesman unchangingly is, shows, subtly presents and offers. But silence does not have to exclude the verbal. Often, for both windows and packages, as well as obviously enough in the case of printed advertisements, the written word contributes a sense of refinement. Special attention can be devoted to the choice of typeface or lettering for the window showcard, and especially for the package that will be reproduced many times.

At the same time, the provision of written information may signify quite simply that the prospective buyer is regarded as someone who can read. This gives rise later to one interpretation of supermarkets not as exploitative (of the vulnerable) but as informative (to the intelligent). The prevalence of packets with descriptions and instructions in self-service shopping was sometimes understood optimistically, as a sign of a literate, educated democracy. The printed word also carried more credibility; it wasn't trying to push a fast one. This idea suggested a transfer of initiative from salesman to buyer, as customers could contemplate the product and form a judgement 'in their own time', without being hurried by the talkative real-life salesman: 'The public today are being educated within the shops and stores to walk from department to department, to inspect and handle the goods, and to make up their own minds.'[7] In this British gloss from the mid-1950s, 'the public' is an able child being gently led into grown-up behaviour.

The superiority of the written word is linked as well to the suspicion of patter. 'We believe', says a writer in the *American Marketing Journal* in the 1930s, 'that the printed word of advertising is less subject to falsehoods than the salesman's facile tongue.'[8] Implicitly, writing is more reliable because it is more fixed than the glibly variable talk of the man.

### Personal and impersonal salesmanship

Whether or not the package or the window included words, they clearly and most obviously differed from other species of salesman by being something other than human beings. This lent itself to two quite different accounts of them, both of which have been replayed again and again, in numerous contexts, in the telling of the history of shopping. In the first, the personal is superseded by the impersonal. In the second, the amateur is superseded by the professional.

The first story goes like this. Once, there was a friendly relationship between salesman and buyer, clerk and customer, effortlessly blending business with human warmth. This happy model of the personal sale was attached to two types of transaction that were otherwise considered rather different: the routine purchase in the local store, and the exceptional purchase brought about through the efforts of the door-to-door salesman. In both cases, the sale rested – whether for a moment, or indefinitely, from week to week – on establishing a sense of trust, in which the salesman's personal interest in the customer was essential. Take an interest in her children! – this was the advice purveyed to the man who knocked on the American housewife's door with a vacuum cleaner to sell in the 1920s, and it did not differ from the advice to the grocery-store clerk who was seeking to secure the housewife's loyalty to his establishment over a longer term.

In comparison with this warm glow of personal salesmanship, the silent salesman appears as a cold sort of substitute. 'He' has become 'it'. There is no chat, no recognition; the customer looks at the shop window or picks up the packaged item but the human responses and reactions are all her own. She isn't known, she isn't at home; and even though the control is all on her side – she can take it or leave it, and no one is there to argue with her hesitations – she has lost what can now be thought of as one of the pleasures of the process of buying things.

This tale of the coming of impersonality became the standard story at the time of the post-war development of supermarkets, where the silent salesmen are not only the packages (supermarket windows were never used for display at all), but also the personnel, who don't talk to the customers any more than the cereal packets do. 'Self'-service, in this context, indicates that there's no one else to be nice to you but yourself.

In laments for the loss of the personal, it is usually the department store that provides the bygone image of a big shop that was nonetheless friendly, with its elaborately attentive services. But in the 1920s, and earlier, the department store actually occupied the other role, as the faceless city store that could never replace the virtues of small-scale, local shopping. There, according to a French book on food retailing, 'the buyer is just a unit, a fraction of a turnover'; instead, you should make your shop

> agreeable for the visitor, by giving him or her the
> impression of being at home, that it's a pleasure to have
> him. The buyer must think he is welcomed not for his
> spending capacity, but for himself.[9]

Although this is always presented as a relatively recent development, supermarkets have been trying for many decades to counter their reputation for impersonality by strategies of many kinds. They boast their involvement in community activities and charities, or they offer traditional counter service for particular product categories as an alternative to the ready-packaged items also available on the shelves. The imagined fall from the personal to the impersonal and the attempted recovery of the personal has happened many times over in many different shopping settings; it never ceases to be one of the principal frames through which shopping is understood.

The other story about the non-human salesman is the positive one, which more or less flips around the values associated with the first. No more patter, no more randomness, no more trial and error: modern salesmanship is planned, efficient, scientific. Here, what is human is messy – which can mean *unhygienic*, or can mean *wasteful*, of time and hence of money, according to the scientifically measurable criteria that are supposed to apply instead. The reiterated complaints serve as praise for new kinds of selling practice in the 1920s and 1930s, often moving from the would-be abstract to vivid evocations of the bad old days. Time and again we are offered a picture of the old-style grocery clerk laboriously weighing out the bacon or syrup or flour for each woman with his own hands, spilling a bit here or losing a bit there, taking his time and hers and that of the other waiting customers.

Silent salesmen also avoid the dubiousness of commercial smiles. No packet ever turned to the potential buyer with a smile of welcome, genuine or otherwise; but at the same time, nothing prevents a buyer from seeing a package as having a nice personality. And precisely because it is *not* really going to interact, the package, unlike the man or the woman, can get away with suggestions the salesman would not decently be able to make. 'Beware of the package that is beautiful but dumb,' says the American D. E. A. Charlton, in a book of the late 1930s.[10] An article of the same period in the journal edited by Charlton amplifies this enigmatic pronouncement, pointing out that all sorts of heterogeneous things are

> much enhanced when put up in this modern manner, telling their own story to the shopper in overtones and undertones of 'buy-me-now-and-take-me-right-home' that no salesperson could ever think of or imitate.[11]

The package can safely be cute and flirtatious; but the person can only be too personal, here in relation to a 1950s American survey on how women would like to buy stockings:

> More women voted for sealed envelopes, than voiced a preference for any other type of packaging. They like the protection of a package. They did not like salesclerks to run their hands through the hose to demonstrate shade, sheerness and quality.[12]

At the furthest extreme, violently negative feelings may be aroused simply by the salesman being a person demanding attention. From an American academic monograph of 1928:

> [Salesmanship] may quickly reach the point of saturation, even of nauseation, because the time and patience of every buyer have definite limits. The irritation and disgust of the prospect may prevent even an interview.[13]

### The cardboard salesman

The rotation of arguments about personal and impersonal modes of salesmanship masks another, more fundamental and disturbing issue, which is about the distinction between a human and a non-human salesman in the first place. It is often a reproach to real salesmen that they are artificial, with their put-on patter and their role-playing. In this regard, it may be preferable to be openly a fake or 'cardboard' mock-up of a person than to be a flesh-and-blood human being who appears to be other than genuine. The best illustration of this is an intriguing silent salesman called the 'Sell-Out', an American product marketed to the trade in Britain in the late 1930s.

The advertisement for the 'Sell-Out' shows a black-and-white photograph of a dark-haired woman in her thirties taking a blank white cardboard packet from a set of identical ones held out by a cardboard cut-out of a dark-haired woman in her thirties. The blurb says that 'Sell-Outs', which enable the customer to see before buying, 'are the most up-to-date method of shop salesmanship, a combination of the life-like and realistic "cut-out" and the actual goods'. It concludes: 'They make the passer-by *your* customer.'[14] Seeing is not believing in this case, since we have a customer warmly receiving into her arms a completely blank white packet, just as the saleswoman carries, as one of her cardboard prostheses, a label bearing the incomplete invitation 'Help Yourself To . . .' The name of the product, as with the packet, is presumably left out to enable the reader to imagine the pleasure of seeing his own brand name there; but as it stands, the pitch for a completely blank product is about as flat as the cardboard lady herself.

Of course, the customer doesn't anyway see 'the actual goods', if the actual goods are what is in the packet. But in a sense, they aren't. The package nowadays *is* the product, it is implied: so what better way of proving that the real thing doesn't have to be real than to have a saleswoman made of cardboard too? 'Actual size of this showcard 5'6",' says the text, in case we might need to be reminded – and very precisely, too – of what a human dimension is.

The black-and-white *vendeuse* is related to a long series of 'cardboard' figures who pop up as characters in accounts of modifications in the 'real' human interaction in modern buying and selling. There is a nice example in Richard Hoggart's *The Uses of Literacy* (1957). He is describing a new kind of furniture store, catering to the working classes, that has emerged in Britain since the war:

> At first glance these are surely the most hideously tasteless of all modern shops. Every known value in decoration has been discarded: there is no evident design or pattern; the colours fight with one another; anything new is thrown in simply because it is new. There is strip-lighting together with imitation chandelier lighting; plastics, wood and glass are all glued and stuck and blown together; notice after blazing notice winks, glows or blushes luminously. Hardly a homely setting. Nor do the superficially elegant men who stand inside the doorway, and alternately tuck their hankies up their cuffs or adjust their ties, appear to belong to 'Us'. They are not meant to. With their neat ready-made clothing, shiny though cheap shoes, well-creamed hair and ready smiles they are meant (like the equally harassed but flashier motor-car salesmen) to repre-sent an ethos. One buys the suggestion of education and elegance with the furniture.[15]

There is a parallel between the artificiality of the store and that of the dandified salesmen, all sham and veneer and ready-made like the furniture, even down to the smile. The combina-tion of imitation luxury products for the working classes and overpowering, slightly threatening lighting – 'notice after blaz-ing notice winks, glows or blushes luminously' – recalls the unreality of the windows that confronted Paul Morand in New York (see Chapter 1). 'Hardly a homely setting', however, keeps an ironic distance while giving the standard against which the artificiality is seen by the critic as such. And in fact Hoggart then goes on – past the 'first glance' – to restore the home in what is described as the surprisingly 'individual and domestic approach' of the salesmen. Here talk refamiliarizes what would otherwise be intimidating for the customers in the 'superficially elegant' personae.

When self-service came to the furniture store, the ultimately friendly cardboard salesman was replaced by a cardboard package that was neither alluring nor homely. The IKEA flat-pack levels all things to a single form, taking the package back to its pre-selling days as just a protective container for goods in transit, not an object of interest in itself. The customer takes it home and assembles the parts to reconstruct something like the thing that was on show in the store or the catalogue. Where the colours and differences of packaging are fundamental to marketing in other types of self-service store, the flatpack is the anti-package par excellence. It also extends self-service to a new extreme, beyond distribution right back to making the thing yourself. The customer not only seeks out, picks up and carries the product home, but actually puts it together.

## The ubiquitous advertisement

With the silent salesman, selling is both everywhere and nowhere. Now you see it (but you never hear it), now you don't. The silent salesman is most successful, perhaps, when not seen as such, when you don't even notice that the thing is selling to you at all. One of the more peculiar effects of the advent of packaging was to turn the home – or at least the bathroom and kitchen parts of it – into a multiple advertise-ment, decorated with more or less harmonious displays of branded bottles and cartons. Cans and packets and sundry containers of every kind made twentieth-century domestic spaces into idiosyncratic testimonials to the commodities that their occupants had chosen to buy. Carrier bags, meanwhile, cast customers as silent or unwitting salesmen, walking adver-tisements bearing the name of the store from which they had bought.

The ubiquitousness of salesmanship, the silent and the

unsilent, leads to different theories of how best to ensure that your own product will be noticed. One view is that you should make sure your package or message is designed in such a way as to blend in with its likely surroundings. In the store, cans mustn't clash with cans, jars mustn't jar with each other. But this view of how best to sell contrasts uneasily with another, in which what is recommended is that your product should stand out from its competitors, or your advertisement should be as different as possible in order to make its mark against all the thousands of others that surround it.

It's an issue that arises not only in relation to the visual presentation of windows, advertisements or packages, but also in relation to language. Standard advertising phrases, the clichés of the trade or the culture, are recommended as safe – people will recognize and accept what you are talking about – but they are also deplored for the very same reason: your product won't be distinctive. Without the contradiction being acknowledged, most writers on the subject of how to sell actually propose some kind of compromise between the two imperatives: be different (or you fail); be like all the rest (or you fail).

Before moving on to the shop window and the package in detail, let us for contrast briefly look at – or listen to – two noisy counterparts to the silent salesman: radio advertising and telephone selling.

### The radio

Between the wars, the wireless became a standard domestic object. Commercial radio offered an advertising medium that was all sound and no picture or person. Here was the sales talk, right in your home, but without the body of the salesman. Radio advertising in the United States began in 1925, before sound cinema. Like packages taking their place as permanent advertisements around the home, radio set the tone for a world of omnipresent background advertising. If you leave the radio on in the house, then advertising follows you, whether you notice it or not, into every room; it is not just something out on the streets or visible at certain predictable moments, such as when you open a magazine or newspaper. As Pierre Herbin pointed out in 1938, there is something scandalous about radio advertising: 'Forcing an entry into the most sealed-off houses, getting in through the window when you have shut the door on it, coming to find its victim at moments of intimacy, relaxation, recreation, how is it going to be welcomed?'[16] Just fine, in fact, Herbin goes on to say, to judge from the results so far in France. For A. S. J. Baster, a British economist writing in 1935, the domestic situation is precisely what gives radio its unobtrusive power against the more obvious aggressions of other forms of advertising: 'The family is in an intimate and receptive mood; the mental defences which each member has doubtless thrown up under the incessant bombardment of outdoor advertising are now relaxed.'[17]

Radio advertising in Britain was slow to develop, as it was confined to offshore commercial stations. When the journal *Shelf Appeal* ran a special feature on the subject in 1935,[18] it talked about the expense of the Sunday slots, for which no less than nine-tenths of all radio advertising was sold. It seems that on that day anyone with a wireless would be tuning in to the dance music on Radio Luxembourg in order to get away from the tedious religious offerings of the BBC. Ironically, Sunday was the most commercial day for no other reason than that it was officially not one at all.

*The telephone*

The other type of the quintessentially unsilent salesman is the one who phones. Like the classical foot-in-the-door man, he addresses his prospect one-on-one, in her own home. Like the radio, he is all talk. But there is no putting him in the background: he demands and unavoidably takes attention. Unlike the man in person, he cannot be identified before the conversation has already begun: no telephonic equivalent to the twitch of the net curtain will give a hint that this is not a friend calling. For this reason, phone selling is an invasion of privacy in a way that other forms of advertising are not. It is not recognizable as such; it comes right into the home; it necessarily interrupts.

This built-in intrusiveness makes it particularly ironic – or inevitable – that many commodities nowadays sold through the telephone play upon a sense of personal vulnerability to the outside world. Insurance has always been a staple; in Britain the commonest of all is double glazing for windows. Yet this item, which is for keeping out the noise and the world in general, barricading homes in their 'sealed units', is sold by the one method that proves in fact that the product can't do what it promises. You may shut up the windows but the phone will still penetrate your four walls as if they didn't make any difference.

## The window and the package

Those magnificent inter-war silent salesmen, the window display and the package, were destined to be the forerunners of and the prerequisites for the development of self-service and supermarkets and the customer orientations that accompanied them. But that is clear only in retrospect. To see how they did pave the way for the supermarket aisles, but also had features that might have pointed in quite different directions, the next two chapters look at each of these two silent salesmen in more detail.

Both the window and the package were taken at this time as examples of a new commercial aesthetic. This was strongly linked to the visual as opposed to the aural, overtly excluded by the 'silent' motif; though smell and touch, as well as sight, were occasionally associated with packaging. Both a window and a package gave their own shape, form, *image*, independent of the product or products involved; a window, and sometimes a package too, solicited contemplation, much as you might admire a picture or a sculpture, and such aesthetic considerations often appeared to take precedence over pragmatically economic concerns – in other words, getting the person to buy the thing.

Writers about both windows and packages are keen to make clear what they see as their far remove from the untaught crudeness of nineteenth-century advertising efforts. But the package is more complicated in this regard. In connection with food, there is often a wish to get rid of all the unhygienic associations of odour or handling that the package resolutely covers over and seals out of existence. A 'pure' modernist aesthetic implies not just doing away with messy old-fashioned designs, but also signifying the freshness of the product. Yet there is also something like a counter-lavishing of voluptuous attention on the tactile and other pleasures of newly invented packaging materials themselves; and we shall come back to this in relation to the sumptuous trade journals that promoted the new arts of packaging in the 1930s.

## 4 The Passer-by and the Shop Window

'A dummy shop display has been built within the window itself, with a "passer-by" standing in the foreground, already looking at the displayed merchandise. It is a stunt theme, but a very interesting one.'

From *Display for the Man's Shop, Style for Men*, The National Trade Press, 1938.

In the middle of a car journey through London in the mid-1930s, towards the end of Virginia Woolf's novel *The Years* (1937), a shop window is seen, as shop windows almost always are, in passing. Eleanor and her doctor niece, Peggy, are together:

> They were driving along a bright crowded street; here stained ruby with the light from picture palaces; here yellow from shop windows gay with summer dresses, for the shops, though shut, were still lit up, and people were still looking at dresses, at flights of hats on little rods, at jewels.[1]

It is first of all a historical point that is being made. The shops are *still* lit up, with an electricity they wouldn't have been lit up by, at all, or this late, in the past. The shop windows get allied with the cinemas as the lighted signs of the contemporary city. The shop window provides a modern illumination, at once darkening the past and making artificial, or strange, the present in which people are 'still looking' long after nightfall.

Woolf's shop window is shown as being at several removes. A shop window is always, to begin with, a mediating object. It enables you to see, but it is also an artificial framing device and a barrier that *only* lets you see, not touch or take or smell. That is the first remove. But Peggy and Eleanor don't just see the window in passing: they see those who are looking at it as well. And then at a further remove the narrator points out to readers Peggy and Eleanor looking, in passing, at the lookers. What curiosities does the window evoke, at any of these removes? What is its fascination?

The times and types of the shop window vary day by day, and with the moods of every passer-by. They also vary over the years: the shop window, like so many other city features, is a marker of changing sights and changing norms and possibilities of perception; it reveals or suggests the shifting forms of day-dreaming urban subjectivity. Peggy and Eleanor, in the car, anticipate what was to be a major preoccupation of post-war marketing psychologists, as we shall see: how to deal with the altered situation and speed of the potential customer, no longer strolling or even striding past the shop, but looking from a moving vehicle. Seen from the travelling car, the rows of shops appear like a moving picture – no wonder the picture palace is put next to the illuminated window in the literary encapsulation.

The window can be variously a source of pleasure, surprise, dreaming absorption, curiosity, desire, disturbance, and more, in all sorts of combinations. It elicits the attention and the inattention, the passions and the boredoms, of single strollers and gathered crowds and distant onlookers. The window can appear quintessentially new, now: here today (and not yesterday). It can also, as with Paul Morand's experience in Manhattan (see Chapter 1) seem strange and unnatural, even ghostly: artificial lighting, whether gas or electricity, is the classic scene for this. But most often, the shop window is simply an ordinary sight of the street. It is what passers-by pass by all the time, and only the exceptional window gets them to stop and stay and look.

## The passer-by

The passer-by is a ubiquitous figure in the street, and yet seems rarely to be singled out for observation or analysis or anything else. He or she is quite simply *unremarkable*, almost defined – not that anyone really bothers to stop and define him – by lack of significance. A marginal presence in every period or place but in none especially, he has tended to pass by, as by nature he must, unobtrusively, without arousing much interest (though the hero of Balzac's *Lost Illusions* [1843] writes a snappy sketch on *Les passants de Paris*). Somehow, the passer-by has none of the glamour of the *flâneur*, the idling walker in the street who became a theme in writing about nineteenth-century Paris, both at the time and afterwards. Yet the two are often one and the same: you cannot be a *flâneur* without being, from another perspective, a passer-by. In French – and certainly in the middle of an English sentence, if not of an English street – the *passante*, the female passer-by, may have a certain something that is lacking in her neutral or male counterpart, the ordinary *passant*. In Baudelaire and Proust, the *passante* appears romantically as the momentary object of a longing look. She is the woman who *would have been* the perfect one, but she is no sooner seen than she has passed on.[2]

In the neutral language of English, the passer-by is rarely – and certainly not by nature – an object of fantasy or suspicion or even curiosity. The passer-by is devoid of interest. There is a link here with the distinctive nineteenth- and early-twentieth-century American sense of 'passing' in relation to racial identity. Passing by is a form of not standing out, being seen only insofar as you merge in as 'anybody'.

But noticed or not, the passer-by has been around in the street for some considerable time. He is cited, if not sighted, in the *Oxford English Dictionary* as having put in an appearance as long ago as the fourteenth and fifteenth centuries. In the nineteenth century his role was shared with that of a figure who has since definitively boarded a bus or a train and left him standing there: the 'passenger'. 'Passengers' in Dickens's novels are often not travellers on trains or coaches, but those whom he also calls by the fuller expression 'foot passengers'. They are pedestrians on the way somewhere through the city streets. There is usually a sense that they are not in their immediate neighbourhoods but crossing from one place to another, with a definite destination in mind: they are not just out for a walk, not *flâneurs*, nor are they simply going up the street for a local walk or errand. Today, now that the 'passenger' is one who takes almost any form of transport *except* his own two feet, there is no surviving word to indicate the street-walker bound on a definite journey, as distinct from the one who is strolling around (the 'pedestrian' can be either).

When the passer-by moves away from the city he does show up differently, his urban nature revealed. In a poem by Coleridge of 1796 the contrast between the commercial and the pastoral worlds is marked in the form of a Bristol businessman out on a Sunday ramble, who passes by the poet's cottage:

Once I saw
(Hallowing his Sabbath-day by quietness)
A wealthy son of Commerce saunter by,
Bristowa's citizen: methought, it calm'd
His thirst of idle gold, and made him muse
With wiser feelings: for he paus'd, and look'd
With a pleas'd sadness, and gaz'd all around,
Then eyed our Cottage, and said, it was a Blessed Place.
And we *were* bless'd.[3]

The speaker imagines the passer-by being distracted from urban and commercial concerns and gaining sustenance from the sight of the pastoral idyll; and the sight of the passer-by serves the same function for him, confirming that 'we *were* bless'd'.

In Woolf's novel *The Waves* (1931), a future urban passer-by similarly takes strength from an image of the country, removing himself into a higher form of passer-byness almost out of this world. Louis, who has just left school, is looking out of the train window, thinking about the difference between the privileged destinations of his peers and his own future in city commerce. His resentment dissolves as he goes past scenes of rural life:

But now disembodied, passing over fields without lodgement – (there is a river; a man fishes; there is a spire, there is the village street with its bow-windowed inn) – all is dreamlike and dim to me. These hard thoughts, this envy, this bitterness, make no lodgement in me. I am the ghost of Louis, an ephemeral passer-by, in whose mind dreams have power, and garden sounds when in the early morning petals float on fathomless depths and the birds sing.[4]

As his own ghost, in two places at once, Louis is able to do what the passer-by normally doesn't: to see himself as a passer-by. Free from the pressures of 'hard' emotions, he is 'disembodied', at ease with ancient and natural things. The indifference of the world to the passer-by becomes the passer-by's own indifference to the world. But the passage also shows up a kind of ghostliness that always hovers close to the figure of the passer-by, who is by nature a visitor, a transient, an indistinct figure, never fully present, never at rest.

There is normally no sense that the passer-by might have any special perspective or mode of being, like the *flâneur*. He is seen in relation to the place or person he passes, rather than the path that he is following himself. This seems to lead to the hint of an association between passing and passivity, as though the passer-by had no independent existence apart from the moment and place of being seen to pass.

Back in his urban milieu, the passer-by is generally not regarded as an agent in his own right. He or she does not appear to have any moral responsibility for what else comes to pass; in this respect he is in a similar position to that other street figure on the sidelines, the 'innocent bystander'. But in the parable of the Good Samaritan there is a suggestion that passing by might amount to a positive act of omission: *antiparerchesthai*, to 'pass by on the other side' a dying man.[5] And in Nietzsche's *Thus Spake Zarathustra*, passing by becomes a deliberate expression of contempt, directed against the city itself. Returning to his wild habitation, Zarathustra is detained at the gates of the big city by a character who talks in mock-Zarathustran tones and rails against the place. Zarathustra dismisses both him and it at a stroke: 'I offer you in farewell this precept, you fool: Where one can no longer love, one should – *pass by* [*vorübergehen*]!' Which he promptly does himself: 'Thus spoke Zarathustra and passed by the fool and the great city.'[6]

The passer-by has something in common with a related nonentity, 'the man in the street'. But the man in the street is marked by a generality that often makes him indistinguishable from the statistical identity of the 'average' man, a figure of speech and number far removed from the particularity of any concrete pavement or sidewalk. This passage, from the early 1950s, nicely brings out the difference:

> Advertising, in general, is mainly directed at that anony-
> mous and ubiquitous creature known as the 'man in the
> street'. His likes and dislikes, his opinions and predilec-
> tions have excused a multitude of solecisms in the adver-
> tising world. In the world of window display, however,
> the man in the street is not a mythical agglomeration of
> all human virtues and frailties, but a real person with two
> legs, two eyes, personal needs of body and spirit and, it is
> fervently hoped, with money in his pocket.[7]

As we are about to see, it is at this one point – where the otherwise abstract man in the street takes on a body – that the
passer-by, too, gets a starring role. For the passer-by did, in
fact, have a moment of glory; though, being who he was, that
moment was of its essence, and necessarily, a passing one. It
happened between the wars, and the cause is quite clear to see:
it was the passion at that time for the art of window display.

## The shop window

Perhaps it was appropriate that it should be the shop window
that brought the passer-by into temporary prominence – for
the window, like the passer-by, is as though invisible, there
but unnoticed. This was a feature stressed by writers on the
subject. The glass panel helped in the showing of the display,
which was both completely visible, with nothing in the way
of the sight, and kept at a well-designed distance. You could
see it but not immediately touch or have it, so you were
bound to see it as a 'sight to behold', set apart from where you
were by the transparent partition. New glass technology in
the nineteenth century had increased the size as well as the
transparency of panes; but it had taken until now, or so the

proud innovators of the 1930s said, for the aesthetic potential of this new medium to be recognized.

*Parade*, a French monthly founded in 1927, was devoted to every aspect of the art that its subtitle called 'street decoration', *'le décor de la rue'*. Each issue had diagrams of designs for readers to copy; there were book reviews, features on the cultural importance of display, items of local and international design news. Like other design journals of the time, *Parade* saw 'propaganda' and education in the new display aesthetics – for practitioners and for the general public – as being an important part of its project. When the Salon des Artistes Décorateurs featured a mock-up street, with shops and window displays, the journal rejoiced:

> In short, this is the definitive acknowledgement that the presentation of goods for sale is gaining a more and more important place. The cause is increasingly being won . . . We are very happy to see that finally, that which is the passer-by's visual recreation is gaining a place which it should always have had.[8]

Writers of textbooks and handbooks for retailers enthused about the newfound possibilities of the window, treating it as the 'silent salesman' whose visual qualities would take the place of, or prepare the way for, the verbal qualities of the personnel within. In the marketing theory of the period, as we shall see further in Chapter 9, the role and technique of the salesman was a fine art, itself elaborated in numerous books addressed to practitioners of all kinds; the window presented special conditions for selling.

Salesmanship essentially involved four stages in a two-person relationship between seller and buyer. With some minor variations of terminology from book to book, they were as follows: 'attracting attention'; then 'interest'; then 'desire'; then 'sale'. They date from the late 1890s, when salesmanship began to appear as a subject for semi-formal learning from textbooks. It became an article of salesmanship faith that psychology, represented as an exciting new field of thought, was indispensable. To know how to sell you had to know something about the minds of buyers. Conversely, the continuing study of the mind and its workings was itself considered crucial to the perfection of selling techniques. Connections between the disciplines of marketing and psychology are evident at every level, from the academic monograph on psychology in advertising, through to the modest teach-yourself salesmanship manual, always with a separate chapter on the importance of psychology.

Buyers, in these discussions, could take many forms and shapes – from the generic, universal 'mind of the buyer' to specification by sex or class or age, or any number of other variables. Categories might be situational, referring to the mood or type of customer in particular kinds of shop; such divisions typically take the form of little sketches followed by sage advice for dealing with figures like the 'mother accompanied by her daughter' (avoid stirring up tensions) or the 'last-minute shopper' who comes in just when you are on the point of closing up for the day. But when selling through the window was the focus, the potential buyer was never anyone but the one and only passer-by.

A book called *Window Display Above All*, by Herbert N. Casson, a prolific British writer of manuals on selling and business and much else, devotes a whole chapter to the subject of passers-by. He is proud to announce it as unique: 'I have never seen in any book on window display a chapter on "The Psychology of Passers-By".'[9] We can willingly grant Casson the 'first' he claims for himself. But, like the passer-by in person, the passer-by in print is ubiquitous when the subject is window display; the potential spectator of the window is never anyone else. She it is who must be stopped in her tracks, brought to a standstill before the appeal of this particular window; it is her attention that must be 'arrested', just as her feet are halted on the spot.

Applied to the window and the passer-by, the elements of

control and liberty implicit, on both sides, in the standard four-stage salesmanship scenario acquire a distinctive form. The passer-by is imagined as drifting, free-floating in his attention, which must be given a definite interest and direction by being drawn and attached to the window. The wandering of the passer-by is indeterminately that of the mind or the feet. The passer-by, unlike the *flâneur*, may well have a set destination – going to or from work, for instance – but that does not preclude his thoughts being aimless or open; indeed the regularity of a routine journey that requires no concentration, the 'automatic pilot' of the streets, may well be just as conducive to mental drift as the mood of the strolling walker, consciously looking about him. Mind or legs are on the move; they are to be stopped, or at least interrupted, by the appeal of the window.

Paul Nystrom describes the process from the point of view of the one outside:

> There are very few people who can say that they have
> not been stopped by window displays. All have had the
> experience of being arrested for several moments, even if
> they were in a hurry. Many of these persons were after-
> wards drawn by interest into the store to see the goods,
> and to purchase.[10]

Nystrom carefully alludes to each of the four selling stages: arrested attention; the arousal of interest; inspection leading to desire; purchase. Here is Casson's summary, from the other side:

> The truth is that most people walk like automata. If they
> are thinking at all, they are thinking of their destination or
> of their own private affairs. Very few go out for the sole
> purpose of looking at windows. It is only the window
> with a PULL that can be sure to attract their attention.[11]

The window is supposed to 'attract' attention – as with advertisements, to 'turn the mind', *animam advertere*, of the one who encounters it. Whatever may preoccupy it is pushed out of the way.

How does the window do this? In many accounts, it is to be regarded primarily as a striking work of art: 'The actual display as it appears before the public is the creation of the window dresser's mind, and embodies the principles of art, blended with a certain amount of commercial feeling.'[12] The widespread 'selling' of the window as a work of art is partly intended to establish its credentials in relation to other forms of store advertising, through newspapers or posters: put crudely, to get a bigger budget for display, or just any budget (or time) at all. At this time, doing the window was often regarded as requiring no special skills or training, something that anyone could turn their hands to in a spare moment.

In making the case for the window's aesthetic superiority, it is possible to point to its affinities with many different art forms. The window is like a painting: it is clearly framed, set off behind its exhibiting glass, and draws spectators to it as something designed to be looked at. Its three-dimensional space, on the other hand, can additionally or alternatively make it appear as a stage. Special lighting effects are crucial here, and – as in Morand's New York description – the window, like the theatre, comes into its own at night, when the street is dark and it stands out as an image in a completely different world from its surroundings.

But in the particular kind of play that the shop window puts on, it is important for the characters to be likeable. The British writer Cyril Freer issues a ghastly warning:

> The ordinary window dummy figure is a lifeless and
> uninteresting personage. He fixes you with his glassy
> eye, makes you feel how small and mean you are, and
> gives you the impression that if he did come to life he
> would be the perpetually cigarette-smoking villain in a
> particularly lurid and blood-curdling melodrama.[13]

What is the alternative to this sinister figure? It is, of course, French and feminine: 'The tailor should take a leaf from the French *costumier*, whose charming dummy ladies are a delight to the eye.' Freer goes on, without the sequence of thought being entirely obvious: 'A row of trouser-lengths are about as tempting to the passer-by as would be a row of brooms.' Yet even the aesthetics of the broom, as we shall see further on, are worth pondering; broom beauty, like any other kind, is in the eye of the beholder and the art of the window dresser.

Insofar as the window provides a 'show', it is frequently compared not only to the theatre, but to that relatively new form of night-time entertainment, the cinema. The window, it is suggested, has to work harder than the cinema because its audience is not expectantly seated there but has to be drawn in one by one. But the window can learn from the cinema the advantages of 'moving' images, 'motion' pictures; the attraction of movement is presented as an established psychological fact.

It is in this connection, where aesthetics and psychology cross, that the literature of shop windows reveals some of its most intriguing ambiguities. On the one hand, display is proudly vaunted as an art form, meaning something illusional and composed: *made up*, in both senses. On the other hand, its psychological appeal is derived from the fact that it shows *the thing itself*. In the case of shop windows, it is said, seeing and believing are naturally united. The implied comparison here with other forms of advertising refers not only to the contrast between image and reality, but also to the difference between images and *words*. What you see is what you believe in, whereas words are treated as open to doubt, as either true or false. *Ergo*, the visible presence of the real thing must be the most convincing advertisement of all: 'To see the thing itself – that is more likely to create desire in people's minds. People sometimes say – "Oh, that is only an advertisement," but they never say – "Oh, that is only a window display".'[14]

The effectiveness of the visual is compounded by a further form of immediacy. Again unlike advertisements, which are seen or read at a distance, the window is right there at the point of purchase, and the customer has only to cross the threshold into the shop.

The window display is thus presented at two extremes. It is a setting for stylish modern art; and it simply shows the object itself. It is framed, aesthetic, for looking at; and it is just the things as they are, making a direct appeal to the potential purchaser. It is for contemplation and it is for action. You can admire it at a distance, and you can go in and get it right now.

Occasionally, there seems to be an acknowledgement of a separation between the gut appeal of the thing and the aesthetic appeal of its presentation. The gap shows up when the thing itself is regarded as intrinsically not an object of desire:

> There is always some way of making any kind of goods worth looking act. Mr. Austin Reed once said in one of his public addresses – 'I never imagined that an attractive window show could be made from household utensils, like pots and pans, until one day walking down a street in Clacton I was pulled up short by a shop window in which these very goods were so cleverly assembled that I had to stand for minutes admiring the ingenuity and skill which had brought about such a result.'

We seem to be dealing here with a fellow practitioner admiring the skill with which even those dull things, 'household utensils' – the ultimate routine function, housework as anti-art – could be given a veneer of aesthetic polish. But the 'result' breeds another, as Reed continues: 'The result was that I persuaded my wife to buy a number of articles which she insisted we did not want, whilst I had an interesting talk with the man responsible for the display.'[15] Were the articles ever used in the Reed residence, we wonder, or were they artistically arranged – or perhaps resentfully binned?

A writer on the value of seasonal window displays in *The Modern Grocer and Provision Dealer* is more tactful, if more wishful, in his advice:

> In March, towards the month's end, goods suitable for house-cleaning, such as brooms and brushes, leathers, house-flannel, polishing pastes, soap and cleansing materials

should have attention. It is then the thoughts of the house-wife turn to spring cleaning, and the grocer who is wise will aid her by suggesting that he provide the materials which will make the process a pleasure and a joy, rather than a hard and unpleasant task.[16]

'It is then that thoughts of the house-wife turn to . . .': the categorical clean sweep from the 'hard and unpleasant task' to the 'pleasure and a joy' even manages to suggest that doing the chores is equivalent to spring-time falling in love.

The display is itself aesthetically 'created', but is also meant – the phrase is used over and over again – to 'create' an impression in the mind of the possible buyer. In Casson's formulation: 'A good selling window is one that compels most passers-by to look at the GOODS, and creates the thought in their minds that the goods are desirable and worth the price.'[17] This neatly shows the combination, in the window's 'attraction', of force and pleasure, the compelling and the desirable. Creation passes from an aesthetic to a persuasive, even irresistible mode. Its attraction is because it is beautiful; or its attraction is that of a magnet, pulling mechanically. And if a good window 'compels' the pause that makes for new desires, so bad art is a bad impression. As a writer on grocery display in the early 1930s put it: 'If the displays . . . are more or less slip-shod and the windows shabby, a distinctly unfavourable impression is created in the minds of all who pass by.'[18]

If the passer-by is already, intentionally, looking at shop windows, whether in pausing or in passing, then well and good: it remains only to emphasize and reinforce an interest that is present from the start. But when this is not so, then there is typically supposed to be a waywardness in the mental (and, it is sometimes assumed, the physical) movements of the passer-by, whose state is characterized as one of distraction. He is there and not there, walking down the street but in another sense absent from the scene – whence the opportunity for the window to pull him in its definite direction, to *at*tract against his own absent-minded *dis*traction; or (put another way) to distract him either from his own thoughts or from the other objects of his attention. Discussions of how to get the passer-by to stop or at least look at your window allude to different kinds of competing mental occupation from which he will need to be drawn away.

If the passer-by's concentration is elsewhere, the elsewhere may be either inside or outside: either the pavement and the road, or his own private internal thoughts. In the second category, the personal world may be a pleasant or an unhappy one, or else one that has no particular emotional colour or weight, but is enough to *preoccupy* his mind so that it will need something quite striking or novel to take over from it. Whichever it is, the point is to pull him from one space to another, to move him mentally and stop him physically.

Herbert Casson adumbrates a theory of urban walking as a form of therapy or diversion:

> It may be taken for granted, I think, that most passers-by are walking the streets with a sense, more or less, of pleasure . . . Many shut-in women, lonely in their homes, walk past the windows with a slight sense of freedom and adventure . . .
>
> A small percentage of the passers-by may be depressed. They may have suffered a loss or a bereavement. They may be worrying. But it may be taken for granted that almost all passers-by are lighter hearted when they are on the street than they are when at home or at work. It is a habit of quite a few people, when they have fits of depression, to go out on the street and 'walk it off'.[19]

Depression is mentioned as an extreme case, but most people's lives are habitually loaded down, to be made 'lighter' by the differences of the street. The language of confinement versus openness here extends across several areas. The 'shut-in' place of women's lives, and then more generally of 'home and work', presumably for men as well, is contrasted with release or freedom in the street, associated with its windows and with the activity of walking. Passers-by are *out of themselves* by nature, already open to pleasure and solicitation.

In the first category, external competition for the passer-by's attention, the alternatives are divided between other windows and completely different phenomena, such as traffic noise. In the case of other windows, the solution is to be aesthetically superior so that your window gets as much notice as or more than the others; in the case of other sights, it is the capacities of window display *per se*, as something that can turn heads, that is stressed.

In some descriptions, both internal and external objects of interest are regarded as simultaneous rivals. The passer-by is both inside himself *and* looking about in all directions. The following passage is from a French book of the late 1940s, still dwelling on the street at a time when most commentators are more concerned with what is to become of the passer-by in the middle of the cars and shopping centres that are running him out of town (in reality in America, as an imminent possibility in Britain and France):

> But the passer-by marching down the street has so many worries in his head, his eye is attracted by such a variety of spectacles, that the interest he gives his surroundings quickly fades, and he can walk past plenty of things without them making an impression, I don't say on his memory, but even on his retina. Indifference is the No. 1 enemy of display.[20]

There may be no impression at all, but there is also a difference, to which we shall return, between long- and short-term impressions, the retained and the merely sighted.

It is fascinating, too, that *other* passers-by are never considered as sources of interest, almost as though the commercial preoccupations of the writers had blocked out the possibility of imagining that objects of desire or curiosity might be anything other than purchasable. One writer, however, does give a warning about mirrors: 'Mirrors on the back wall are not desirable. Human nature being what it is, passers will stop to admire themselves in the mirror instead of looking at the merchandise.'[21] The dangerous counter-attraction of this one person thought to interest the passer-by must be prevented. Yet 'people-watching' is often mentioned as a worthwhile activity for the window-dresser or salesman to engage in, so as to gain an understanding of the psychology of the buyer:

> Every now and then, a Display Manager should stand where he can see the faces of the people who pass one of his windows. The more that he can know about their thoughts and feelings, the more skill he will have in designing efficient displays.[22]

But far from having any wish to look at their own *semblables*, passers-by themselves may be deliberately avoiding them:

> [W]e must not forget that the eyes of passers-by are dull to a certain extent because they are meeting other people on the street. As it is bad manners to stare, they are likely to walk along with set faces.[23]

Such a lack of human interest adds to the sense of the *isolation* of the passer-by – not so much as lonely, but as absolutely on his own, unaccompanied and uncommunicating. Passers-by are separate units, each to be individually solicited – and this makes them, together, add up to a very different version of the urban crowd or mass from the kinds appearing at this time in books on the distinctive, often menacing characteristics of 'crowd psychology'.[24]

Passers-by are no threat. They never join forces in violence or come under the collective influence of a compelling leader; they are never far removed (though they may be a little removed) from their 'usual' selves, customary for them personally and nothing out of the ordinary on the street. They are not transformed into creatures of instinct, out of control, wild and abnormally emotional; instead, they are harmlessly *vacant*, not concentrating on anything in particular. Only in one situation, when they all congregate in front of the same window, does their behaviour slightly resemble that of the crowd; and when one commentator mentions this, he switches from the observed passer-by to the subjective first person, as though half-conscious that he is moving into a different psychological frame: 'If I see others looking into a shop window I too am inclined to stop and look.'[25] Here, it is the imitation of others' attraction, not the attraction of the window itself, that causes the halt.

The tranquil, peaceable stream of passers-by has remained hidden in the byways of minor commercial psychology. It has none of the dramatic, none of the fearful or politically contentious qualities of the more visible street crowd. Passers-by are not seen to cast off the trappings or the protections of a 'civilized' behaviour conceived of as overlaid upon one that is 'primitive': emotional, infantile, possibly violent. Yet like crowds, passers-by are regarded as being anything but focused or directed in their behaviour. Like crowds, they are not especially rational, but this is not to say that they are *ir*rational: the alternatives simply do not apply to their particular intermediate state. They are literally neither here nor there. Like crowds, passers-by are not quite their 'normal' selves, but they are not 'alienated' either into an identity that their usual selves might detest or refuse. In the common as well as the technical phrase, they are 'open to suggestion'.

It is this indeterminacy that seems to make the passer-by the perfect candidate for the catching and latching of attention that the window is meant to secure. The passer-by's lack of a firm identity, a firm footing in one place rather than another, makes him ready to receive the 'impression' of the window. And although it is rarely said explicitly, there are two different ways in which the mind may be impressed; they correspond to the distinction in the quotation above (p. 64) between the retina and the memory.

In the first case, the one most often implied, the effect is instantaneous; it involves a collapse of time to the point where impression and desire come together at once – immediately and at the same time – to push the passer-by into the store on 'the spur of the moment', the absolute automatic insistence of having to have it and *now*. From a manual of 1937: '[T]he person who sees the display should experience an irresistible desire to go in and make a purchase, and this, of course, is the ultimate object of every successful display.'[26] Or, quite irresistibly put, in a book on starting a sweet shop: 'A window display . . . in plain words . . . should tempt the window-gazer so that he knows no peace until he gets what the window has made him want.'[27] In these instances, first and last impressions merge into one another: the impression is compelling but disappears without trace with the relieving purchase of 'what the window has made him want'.

But there is also a second category, that of the *lasting* impression. This is invoked with regard to goods which, it is recognized, are too expensive or too specialized, or both, to lend themselves to the sort of immediate result that can be procured by the momentary impressions and desires of the first type:

> A series of interesting and inviting windows may have the
> effect of creating such a favourable impression of the shop
> in the mind of a person that he or she will be unconsciously
> attracted to it when in need of the service it offers.[28]

Corresponding to a division between moment and memory is this division of the mind into conscious and unconscious aspects, with 'unconsciously' reinforcing the time-lag. There are two different times, that of the initial impression and that of its subsequent effect in response to a specific new situation; the first impression, put away in the mind's own store, makes a second impression, this time from within, when the appropriate occasion draws it out.

Wedding dresses are a ready example of the 'ultimate' rather than 'immediate' effect:

> Every good class drapery house reckons to have one
> bride window each year. Obviously few girls require a

bridal gown and trousseau at the time it appears, but firms have noticed that a good bridal display lasts in the memory of prospective brides, who return to the shop where they were impressed by a display made months or years before.[29]

Here, a past that has not yet been and a future that has already happened are joined together: the fond 'memory' of an ideal wedding and the 'prospective' bride's anticipation of its reconstruction. The image of the past returns not as ghost but as promise. In this second type of window impression, it is the present that disappears to make way for the relationship between past and future; in the first, time is collapsed into the 'immediate' urge of the present moment and the experience leaves no trace for another time.

We have already encountered one example of a bad window, the one containing the sinister 'glassy-eyed' dummies. But there is a type of window whose only purpose in guides is to serve as a kind of admonitory figure, the obverse of the normal persuasive window. This is the 'dead' window, to be avoided at all costs, just as passers-by will inevitably avoid it. The 'dead' window is the window that has nothing new or distinctive to differentiate it from others, or that has gone stale, become so familiar to its passers-by that it no longer makes an impression: 'The same display cannot subsist for long at the risk of losing its attractiveness, of not playing its role, of soon being dead.'[30] This is from a French annual handbook of 1936 on salesmanship and advertising. The section on window display is considerably expanded from earlier editions, signalling its growing importance for the small shopkeeper. Even in a shorter version, though, the bad effect of the bad window is underlined almost more forcefully than the positive advantages of the one that is well designed: 'A lack of *savoir faire* on the part of the sales staff or the manager, makeshift display artists, produces the most deplorable and unattractive results.'[31]

Writers typically treat the artistic refinement of shop windows as a recent phenomenon. The benighted nineteenth-century past is condemned for its lack of imagination; department-store show windows are passed over as if they had never been. Yet in Zola's *Au Bonheur des Dames*, the 'dead windows', *'vitrines mortes'*, of the traditional small shops are already condemned in comparison with the exciting displays in the department-store windows that face them.[32]

There is, however, one type of store where dead windows might seem appropriate. Shops selling mourning clothes did a vast business in the nineteenth century, though one that died out apparently of natural causes, and relatively unmourned, in the early part of the twentieth.[33] In the shopping section of the 1892 edition of a fashionable guide to London we find the dead window par excellence held up as a burst of glorious spring life. A description of Jay's as the place to obtain 'deep-mourning, half-mourning, quarter-mourning' and more, begins: 'For "Mourning" (a depressing topic to touch upon, in this generally lively and careless work), there is no better authority in London than Jay of Regent Street – Jay's, whose unmournful *façade* sometimes shows so brilliantly in the rare sunlight of a May morning at the Oxford Circus end of the leading thoroughfare.'[34]

The criticism of unattractive or old-fashioned windows serves as a foil for exalting the virtues of contemporary window aesthetics. As a writer in *Parade* puts it in 1927: 'But in the middle of these beautiful little shops, what an unpleasant surprise to find oneself suddenly in front of disorderly displays, clearance loads of goods, piles of articles of all sorts where you see a bit of everything and where you don't see anything.'[35] In Britain, the key word in this development is 'stocky'. 'Stocky' is what old windows suffered from being and too many present ones still do. 'Stocky' often occurs in splendid semantic isolation, with no reinforcing adjectives, as though it says it all, which is confusing since in this usage the word seems to have disappeared along with whatever it designated. It appears that what we are meant to see is an image of *too much stuff* all piled up, looking like something out of the stockroom rather than something meant to be admired.

The passage from the stocky to the artistic is presented as both inevitable and desirable; nature, progress and aesthetics all happily coincide. Frequently, there is a latent Darwinian story, with approval for the survival of the best fitted windows, applause for the deserved and overdue extinction of the stocky species, and dark hints at the possibility of reversion to type in some quarters if effort is not maintained.

While there is ostensibly one clear line of historical and natural development, it sometimes appears that it is not so universal after all. The superior type may be found to apply only to distinct categories. In this instance, the subject is the display of men's clothes: 'There is a very real reason why the old, stocky, crowded type of window is outmoded to-day. It showed the merchandise, certainly, but it did not make it look *attractive* enough. Nor was it psychologically suited to the masculine mind. Therefore, it could not last – and the type is fast becoming extinct.'[36]

Windows evolve to suit masculine minds, while masculine minds remain forever themselves. And the writer goes on both to assert and to speculate in a most intriguing way by offering a definition of masculinity which makes it every bit as elusive and enigmatic as the most eternal feminine:

> And, further, remember that men do respond to what might be called masculinity in a window. What is it? It is difficult to say, exactly. Not necessarily severe, but certainly not fussy. And never obviously insincere in the message it hopes to put over. There should be nothing tawdry about it, nor flimsy.[37]

Masculinity is one quality that turns out, unexpectedly perhaps, to be associated with all the positive aesthetic characteristics that belong to the superior window display. The other quality, more predictably, is high class. Richard Harman has three severely differentiated cases:

a A shop in a working-class neighbourhood must show a good selection along fairly stocky yet clear lines.

b A business catering for the popular trade should have less stocky windows, but of a good selling type with frequent attractions.

c A high-class concern must aim at creating an atmosphere of exclusiveness in its windows, but not lose sight of selling values.[38]

Clearly, the stocky and the creative are inversely related, 'stocky' appearing in the first two categories and 'creating' only in the third, as an index of both social and aesthetic exclusiveness. As if to drive the point home, Harman goes on to relate a somewhat implausible moral tale:

Never make the mistake of attempting to produce a type of window unsuited for the business.

As an actual example, a store in Regent Street, London, doing a high-class business, decided to alter its window to a stocky type, thinking it would improve business. The very opposite happened; business fell right off, and the store quickly reverted to the type which obviously appealed to its class of customers.

Tastes differ: what pleases the person working in a factory repels the bank director's wife.[39]

Interestingly, 'reversion to type' in this instance is taken as an appropriate mark of civilized rather than primitive qualities: the shop had simply denied what must be seen as its natural superiority.

Class is also mapped on to regional differences – here with a striking north/south explicitness: 'The display man should always have in mind the class of business which his firm is catering for . . . This is where discretion comes in, for the style of window which appears in Bond Street, London, would not answer in Wigan, and vice versa.'[40]

This is the only appearance of Wigan windows that I have

come across, but Bond Street figures all the time in the literature of display, in such truisms as: 'A Bond Street window
would be a failure in the Old Kent Road'.[41] Its role is not only,
as here, to suggest the most classy sort of establishment, the
height of both good taste and expense, but also, sometimes, to
indicate the one place where a knowledge of window display
may not be necessary. To the extent that the window is an
advertisement, it is eschewed by the shop that can disregard –
and distance itself from – commercial considerations, acquiring a kind of counter-prestige from the very fact of being seen
not to participate in them:

> The West End tailor whose window contains nothing but
> a dusty curtain; the hatter who carefully preserves the
> eighteenth-century façade of his shop, and who displays
> in the window not the latest models but battered speci-
> mens of the headgear of a bygone age, is each, in his own
> way, 'window-dressing'. It might be said that he is
> advertising to the haters of advertising.[42]

As we move into the post-war period, stocky windows survive only as the debris of a long-gone time. In Richard Hoggart's *The Uses of Literacy* (1957), a book that is consciously
ambivalent about its perspective on the forms of change affect-
ing English working-class life, the stocky window is treated as
a sign of anachronism as well as of class:

> In the working-class area itself, in those uneven cobbled
> streets to which until recently motor-cars seldom pene-
> trated, the world is still that of fifty years ago. It is an
> untidy, messy, baroque, but on the whole drably baroque,
> world. The shop windows are an indiscriminate tangle of
> odds-and-bobs at coppers each; the counter and every
> spare stretch of upper space is festooned with cards full of
> proprietary medicines. The outer walls are a mass of
> small advertisements, in all colours. There are hundreds
> of them, in all stages of wear-and-tear, some piled a quar-
> ter of an inch thick on the bodies of their predecessors.[43]

The sense here is of a conflation of mess and mass, the words for each proliferating just like what they are evoking: 'untidy, messy', 'indiscriminate tangle', 'odds-and-bobs', 'a mass', 'hundreds of them'. There is, assuredly, no discrimination, no *choice* to be had here; the window is not a clean aesthetic space for making it new, as in modern display, but a grotesque counterversion of this, moving from the harmless dullness of the 'drably' baroque to the profanely heaped pile-up of small-ad corpses. Even the arrival of the motor-car, in other connections an intrusion upon the peace and permanence of traditional towns, can figure here as a modern relief from this stuffy claustrophobia of a bygone age, its very *modus vivendi* one of tatty decay.

A different emphasis appears in a post-war American book by the architect Morris Ketchum, where the passers-by themselves appear to have speeded up to match the cars:

> In choosing a location, the potential customer traffic must be measured not only in terms of quantity but also in terms of quality. A crowded street corner might be ideal for a drug store or a 'pick up' convenience shop, worthless to a high grade jewelry store. Dense pedestrian traffic in theatrical and financial districts and near transportation terminals is high speed foot traffic. People are hurrying to their destinations and have no time for either window shopping or leisurely buying. By contrast, sidewalk traffic in a neighborhood shopping district has the time to look and buy. Too much sidewalk traffic of the wrong kind is worthless to stores that sell high quality merchandise. They are better off if the traffic that does pass their doors is the type that has both the time and the money to buy their wares.[44]

Here there is an implicit association between the packed streets and the packed timetables of the 'traffic'. Just as there is no space between them on the street, so there is no space in their densely filled schedules for window-shopping. The association then broadens to a class distinction in which unoccupied time is equivalent to unoccupied space on the sidewalk, while a surplus of money equals a surplus of leisure. It is significant too that the people are represented abstractly as 'traffic', while the 'minds' of the passers-by, which featured so prominently in inter-war discussions, have disappeared to give way to a quasi-arithmetical calculation of a relation between time and money.

This move away from the individuality of passers-by, now classed as 'high speed foot traffic', is partly precipitated by the relative decline in the importance of pedestrians as opposed to cars. As early as 1927 Jean Fouquet, a writer in *Parade*, was describing leisurely walking as a thing of the past and making the same links as Ketchum between the speed of the pedestrian and the pace of life:

> In the old days, the city-dweller would enjoy strolling along streets and boulevards. He went for a walk. He stopped in front of every shop front, scrutinizing the window, examining in detail the goods on display.
>
> On the road, one or two placid horses would be pulling their vehicles along.
>
> Nowadays the street is restless. Impatient cars are driven past along the road or else pile up in a traffic jam.
>
> The pavement is no longer for a walk. The pedestrian walks fast: he is in a hurry. Often with his mind on other things, on the way, he thinks about his work. And it is only when something interests him strongly that he stops, eliminating what doesn't seem to him utterly worthy of interest.
>
> Whether we like it or not, we live fast. Our activity pushes us into relishing straightforward images that are rapidly readable.[45]

It is not only that cars have spoiled the peace of the stroll; it is that life itself has speeded up. Cars then become emblematic in a world where walking is no longer about looking around, but about getting somewhere quickly. Even the aesthetic has to be fast: images compete for the exceptional show of interest, and when they do succeed in attracting it, they have to be instantly comprehensible.

In Europe, the decline of walking and window-gazing, and the increasing dominance of the car, are often regarded as a process of 'Americanization'. Writing in the late 1940s, Sartre remarks on the absence of walking in most American cities, where the pedestrian hardly even has a footpath to walk on. New York is a partial exception:

> New York is half-way between the city for pedestrians and the city for cars. You don't go for a walk in New York: you pass by in it [*on y passe*], it is a city in motion. If I walk rapidly, I am relaxed; if I stop, I get flustered and wonder: 'Why am I in this street rather than one of the hundreds of others like it? Why in front of this drugstore, in front of this branch of Schrafft's or Woolworth's rather than in front of any other branch, any other one of these millions of drugstores, all the same?'[46]

Not much appeal in the windows here. As for Paul Morand, the New York experience is one of disorientation; yet it occurs not from the shock of the unexpected, but because there are no differences. The walker has no place to go because all shops and all streets are identical.

The comparison between pedestrian and automobile traffic means that now the possibilities of attracting the passer-by are evaluated in the quantifiable terms of time. 'Passing' trade passes faster in a moving vehicle than on its own two feet. Morris Ketchum again:

> The first impression created by any store may come from a fleeting glimpse as one drives by in an automobile, while riding in a street car or bus, or else from a closer view while walking along the sidewalk. It has been estimated that a typical pedestrian takes less than 7 seconds to pass an average show window and that fast moving motor traffic takes only 3 seconds.[47]

Differences in the types of attention that the passer-by may be giving to the shopfronts have ceased to be specified.

Yet the passer-by was to return to the literature of shopping – changed utterly, and in some ways scarcely recognizable as the same character who strolled or strode on the city streets of the 1930s. What brought him, her (and their children) back was the shopping centre or mall, that indoor street to which people came – in their cars – expressly to walk from shop to shop. They were not going anywhere else. And this new passer-by is for that very reason less sharply defined than his or her fore-runner or forewalker, either against a background of other possible influences, or in relation to a shop window whose special task it would be to bring him to a halt and draw him in.

If the essence of the passer-by is that he or she is first of all passing, without intending to stop, then the shopper of the shopping centre does not qualify for the title: shopping is what she can be assumed to be there to do, whether it is a matter of particular purchases or more casual looking around. Her mind is already a buyer's mind and does not have to be pulled in that direction.

The second, complementary difference is in the environment. There is no clear demarcation between shop and non-shop. The street has no other function than to act as a path from one shop to another; it is almost an extension of the shops. This means that the windows and doors no longer mark boundaries between the shop and its outside. In many interior malls, indeed, the controlled temperature means that the shops can do without doors at all, with customers wandering in without that implying any particular intention or interest.

In this context, the role of the window is much diminished. It can still beckon, surprise and 'create desire', in the time-honoured way; but it no longer represents a mid-point between two differentiated areas, the street and the store interior. Like the stores themselves, the shopping centre is locked up for the night; the windows have no independent life of being lit up and open to view when the shop is closed. Nor do the window's aesthetic effects, in particular its distinctive lighting, stand out in an environment that has neither rain nor sunset, neither stone walls nor kerbs and roads – none of the 'grey', metaphorical or climatic, attributed to the ordinary city street. The 'windows' of internet shopping take this one stage further: no need now even to move your feet; just stay in one place, cruise through a virtual street, and click.

Yet in one respect the advent of the shopping centre constitutes a return to one of the very first forms of shopping environment. The early nineteenth-century arcades of London and Paris predate the great department stores by several decades, and malls by more than a century; they are the first point of reference in histories from every period of the development of shopping as a specialized leisure activity, and for Walter Benjamin their ambivalent presence as relics of past shopping dreams in the Paris of the 1930s provided the inspiration for his own distinctive *Passagen-Werk* of urban cultural history.[48] The arcade, like the mall, presents an interior street, removed from the real one. It differs from the mall in that its passers-by may be using it not to shop or window-gaze, but simply as a quiet route – *passage* being the French term for arcade – from one street to another. The shop window thus has more of the actively soliciting part to play that it loses in the modern mall.

As far back as 1937 a British architectural book on glass advocated the conversion of department stores into a new form of the arcade, in which the inside would be like a series of streets and the building would consist principally of glass walls rather than the present 'imperial façades':

> [T]he entire building will be as natural a promenade as the street, will therefore relieve the congestion of the street and will benefit accordingly. That this will entail a different attitude in the minds of both the public and the shopkeeper goes without saying, but a change of attitude is usually undergone quite unconsciously under the encouragement of a *fait accompli*.[49]

What is interesting here is not just the prescience – it is virtually a description of the late-twentieth-century indoor mall – but the remark, almost in passing, that changes in shopping require changes in shoppers, which normally come about 'quite unconsciously'. Earlier shopping mind-sets, earlier shoppers on two feet, are left behind and forgotten.

It is some of these lost shoppers that this book is seeking to recover and get to know, in the curiosity of both their difference from and their resemblance to our present shopping natures. This chapter has considered the conjunction of the passer-by and the shop window as producing or creating one such figure in the history of how the potential shopper has been imagined. By this time, the urban environment has come to be conceptualized as a mass of appeals competing for the attention of a subject thought of as a passer-by: someone whose mind is *elsewhere*, whether focused or not. As such, it has to be pulled towards this particular object of interest, this particular window display, against the counter-attraction of other possibilities, be they his or her own thoughts or other windows or just the other sights or sounds on the street. From the point of view of Louis Aragon's *passant rêveur*, daydreaming passer-by, in *Paris Peasant* (1926), it is now going to be '*la lumière moderne de l'insolite*', 'the modern light of the unusual', that will hold the attention, stop him in his tracks.[50]

But just as the collectivity of passers-by is not seen as a threat, so all the appeals and attractions that seek the passer-by's notice are not normally conceived of, as they would be by the 1950s and 1960s, in the form of an assault, or a bombardment of conflicting messages. Something of Aragon's surprising modern light may perhaps strike us now, revisiting or stumbling upon these ghostly delineations of shoppers past and passed.

# 5  The Package

Frontispiece to Richard Franken and Carroll Larrabee,
*Packages that Sell*, Harper & Brothers, 1928.

There's a classic 'before and after' story about how progress in packaging went together with changes in foodstores. Here is a British version from 1927:

> Tea, cocoa, and oatmeal, for instance, are no longer shovelled out of dusty bins, weighed in insanitary scales, poured into bags blown open by the breath of the shopkeeper, the last crumbs being swept in with scrupulous honesty, if doubtful cleanliness, from off a littered counter: they are packaged in hygienic, air-tight containers, as fresh and clean and wholesome as when they left the factory.[1]

After the dirty, dawdling build-up, the long sentence moves with relief into the clean succinctness of properly packaged modernity.

Richard Franken and Carroll Larrabee's *Packages that Sell*, an influential American book published in 1928, is illustrated with two glossy frontispiece photographs (see p. 79) designed to show unmistakably the differences between bad old and good modern grocery stores. The captions read as follows:

> Interior of typical old-fashioned grocery store before the era of modern packaging. Crackers and sugar in unsanitary barrels, tea and spices in bins – and only a few canned goods to mark the beginning of a new merchandising era.

> A modern grocery store interior. Everything is packaged in sanitary containers which are designed not only to convey but also to sell the products they contain. A merchandising revolution has taken place.[2]

The rhetoric of revolution and a new era presents the 'few canned goods' of the first picture as a kind of advance battalion of the occupying forces, as 'sanitary' relentlessly drives out 'unsanitary' with the noble and irresistible power of modern, scientific hygiene. Crackers, tea, spices, barrels and bins are scattered around in the first description. Amid the mess, it's surprising that the writers miss the chance to point out the sawdust on the floor, one of the standard markers of differences between new and old types of store.

In the second description, no individual fixtures or foods are mentioned at all; instead, we have only generic 'products' and 'containers'. This makes everything alike in one way, at the same time as things are also being made different in a new way, suggested by the appearance on the wall of an advertisement for Uneeda Biscuits. There is also a swift inclusion of the capsule twofold packaging philosophy, of which more in a moment: *convey*, but also *sell*.

The captions don't mention the people in the photographs. In the first, there is a large customer in a baggy, striped skirt. She is carrying a big basket from which purchases protrude, evidently contributing, like herself, to the clutter. There is a stool by the counter, suggesting that loitering may be positively encouraged. The second picture has no customer at all, but shows the man behind the counter wearing a starched white coat, as though he is working in a sterilized environment. Cans are neatly arranged behind a glass front underneath the counter, as well as on shelves behind him.

The opening to the main text of the book elaborates on the silent revolution the pictures are supposed to have demonstrated:

> Slowly, quietly, unobtrusively, the package has revolutionized modern merchandising. It has changed the buying habits of a nation.
>
> The American of day before yesterday asked for a pound of crackers. Today his grandson demands a box of Uneeda. Grandmother took the familiar stone jug to the grocery and had the grocer fill it up with vinegar. Granddaughter consults her shopping lists and asks for a quart bottle of Heinz's vinegar . . .

The package has changed the appearance of stores. It has revolutionized window display. It has brought about surprising economies for both the manufacturer and the consumer, and it has given to the consumer great gifts in the way of convenience.[3]

The elision of the parental generation is characteristic. Here it may be partly because the 'Mom and Pop' store is one version of the crude type that is in the process of being superseded. It is also, I think, because shopping histories need the grandparental distance in order to signify just how old (and therefore outdated, in need of change) these particular practices are. Age can also shade into nostalgia more readily than would a more recent past. In the progressive story, where modernization is welcomed, Grandmother is clearly an ancient survival, the last shopper just waiting to die out and usher the new age in; at the same time, she and Grandfather can be looked back on with affectionate distance, as though seen in a fading sepia print. They are more like children, innocently asking for their pound of crackers or presenting the 'familiar' stone jug, whereas the granddaughter, consulting her efficient lists, is an adult professional.

Some of the things that are cited as examples of the grandchildren's modern purchases have gone off a little in the meantime:

Memory takes us back to the days when we used to cut bacon from a slab, and what a tussle it was to cut a few even slices. Today we buy it in a glass jar and fish out the greasy slices with a fork as we need them.[4]

To the granddaughter's granddaughter, these fished-out greasy slices probably sound not so much modern as revolting. Faced with the choice, she would no doubt go back with a sigh of relief to the slicing method; and this, of course, is precisely what many supermarkets and delicatessens now offer her, as one of the wheels of the twentieth-century food retailing revolution comes full circle and returns to its starting-point.

In this connection, a final point of interest in the passage is the revolutionary alliance of package and window display. It seems natural here, but it soon came to an end when the supermarket offered the package another starring role but did away with the window as a mode of selling altogether.

Yet it is not clear that the package has suffered less. The window no longer occupies such a prominent place in the shopping world, but its aesthetic credentials remain unchallenged. The package, like the shop window, was the object of intense imaginative interest between the wars. The pre-war package stood proud on the shelf and in the pages of glossy trade journals, the bearer of a new commercial aesthetic. But there was a dramatic fall; and now it is difficult to believe that the package's artistic future once looked bright. After the war, distinction was transformed into vilification when the package became the symbol of corrupt mass-marketing practices. That will be one subject of Chapter 9. But before that, let us restore to the disgraced package some of the promise of its youth.

Packaging was the new thing in marketing between the wars, and a wonderfully multifarious thing it was. In two words, the package had to *convey* and *sell*. It had to be functional, getting the thing to its destinations; and it had to be appealing: food merchandising was becoming a field for fashion and design.

In practical terms, the package had to be roadworthy, capable of carrying the product from source to shop to home, and it had to be packable and stackable along with its peers. Packages made honest commodities of products of all kinds, boxing them up, measuring them out, assuring the world they were clean and came from a decent, ascertainable source. At the same time, packaging offered the possibility of an attractive exterior that might be quite unrelated to what was inside, or that might show it in a better light, through a transparent wrapper. As an economist put it in 1928: 'The fancy package, together with the advertising of it, stimulates the senses, arouses the imagination, and therefore creates a fictitious value.'[5]

The impact of packaging was greatest in food and pharmaceuticals, areas in which virtually every product could seem to be only awaiting its ideal package, to beautify it and to guarantee its cleanliness. But quite apart from considerations within retailing and manufacturing, the conjunction of practical and aesthetic criteria made packaging a natural field for experiment at a time when the topic was of widespread interest to artists and designers.

Like most innovations in twentieth-century marketing, packaging first became news in the United States, and old-world countries to some extent saw their role in the 1930s as trying to 'catch up'. The American journal *Modern Packaging* was started in 1927, the British *Shelf Appeal* in 1933. *Shelf Appeal* regularly reported on the winning items from the national 'best packages of the year' contest run by its American opposite number, and put them on display to its own manufacturing and designing public as inspiring examples – in an annual exhibition, as well as within the magazine. In 1950 Harry Jones described the backward state of British packaging in the early 1930s: 'this vast industry, trading in visual appearance, was untouched by design'.[6] For Jones, *Shelf Appeal*'s arrival changed it all.

*Shelf Appeal* certainly gets the prize for the witty name ('sex appeal' was a phrase that had only recently crossed the Atlantic along with its Hollywood images). But at the time, *Modern Packaging* was by no means as dull a verbal combination as it may now seem. The connotation that has been lost from the American title is the excitement associated not only with the modern but with packaging, a word now more likely to suggest cardboard, or a wasteful use of natural resources. 'Packaging' was a new word, meant to give a sense of package design as a distinctive art. Indeed, if you believe *Shelf Appeal*, the term entered Britain in or about the month that *Shelf Appeal* was born, in July 1933. In 1936 an editorial explains:

'Packaging' is actually a coined word and was not used

in this country until about three years ago. (Incidentally the original name for this journal was PACKAGING, but various difficulties prevented this, so that the more comprehensive title of SHELF APPEAL was finally adopted.) Packaging is really packing plus something else . . . The something else is selling ability, thus giving the package a double function – that of containing and protecting and then of publicising and 'selling'.[7]

*Shelf Appeal* regularly uses the delightful adjective 'package-conscious', to refer to the state of enlightenment that can be attributed to manufacturers who have profited from their reading of *Shelf Appeal*. The first *Package Omnibus* in 1936, a *Shelf Appeal* compendium providing information of the where and what and how-to-obtain of everything to do with contemporary packaging, included an article entitled 'The Packaging Age'.

Packages at this time did provide an exciting new focus for designers eager to make everyday objects that were 'modernistic' or 'modern' in their abstract simplicity and their 'streamlined' merging of form and function. Both magazines are themselves gorgeous objects, practising what they teach through the quality of their paper, typography, colours and page layout, and often including in their advertisements feelable samples as well as visible illustrations of possible packaging materials.

Against the norm of trade journals, *Shelf Appeal's* covers were resolutely kept free as an experimental rather than an advertising space. One cover, in November 1935, was a design by Moholy-Nagy, shortly after his arrival in England. Another, in a somewhat different vein, was proudly announced as being probably the first ever magazine cover made of aluminium. Over sixty years later it remains a fabulous object, still demonstrating that aluminium can be made into an attractive 'sheet' for print.

Given that packaging is something for manufacturers to adopt or modify as part of a coordinated sales campaign, it is remarkable how little reference there is in either journal to profitability as an issue (there's more in *Modern Packaging* than in *Shelf Appeal*, but still very little). 'Economy' is a major criterion for the appropriateness of a package, but the monetary sense of the term becomes overlaid by the aesthetic sense, meaning an avoidance of superfluous ornament. In packaging, as in every other field of contemporary design, modernism can be negatively defined by its repudiation of the fussy ornateness associated with Victorian style.

'Elimination' is a significant word in this crossover between the economic and the aesthetic. Here it is about thinning out a crowded image. Elsewhere, as we shall see in Chapter 7, it may relate to the removal of personnel for the sake of a staffless self-service simplicity; and in wartime Britain, there is no need to make the artistic argument at all, since elimination has become a practical obligation. Firms are advised to use advertising to explain the reasons for lower quality, reduced supplies, reduced packaging and 'the elimination of unnecessary sizes and packs'.[8] Where economizing on materials is morally and practically obligatory, it is not clear what will count as a 'good' package: 'It's odd', says *Shelf Appeal* in 1940, 'that no one has thought of making a propaganda virtue of this necessity, and of urging patriotic purchasers to buy the product *because* it is flimsily packed.'[9]

*Shelf Appeal* made a point of its commitment to aesthetic education, both as part of its own project and as something to be generally advocated. There were numerous articles and book reviews about contemporary international and British designers and artistic movements, in relation to debates about the use and value of good design. The journal also thought that the general public should be better educated in these matters. A pamphlet produced by the government's Council on Art and Industry in 1935, called *Education for the Consumer*, provided the statistics for an editorial to say that if the six hundred thousand children in each secondary school year all had classes in design, then ten years from now there would be six million tasteful buyers.[10]

Though less aesthetically disinterested, *Modern Packaging* too is proud of its educational uses. The textural and visual pleasures of the thing are so marked a feature that at one point the magazine features an advertisement for itself, where the pitch is that all the small sons of present-day subscribers will be following in Dad's professional footsteps because of their pleasurable early experiences with *Modern Packaging*. Potential advertisers, meanwhile, should be aware of the importance of young readers. 'Frank Fairbanks, Jr. reads MODERN PACKAGING', runs the caption; underneath a circular photograph of a boy in a shirt and tie engrossed in his reading, the blurb begins:

> Frank, Jr. is eight years old – and a reader of MODERN PACKAGING. And there are thousands of Frank, Jrs. and maybe a few Frances's who would raise merry Ned each month if dad did not bring home that beautiful copy of MODERN PACKAGING that has gotten to be a habit around the house.
>
> Maybe it's the elaborate inserts – maybe it's the beautiful tipons, or maybe even the superb photography that fires little Frank's twentieth century imagination – what difference!
>
> [ . . . ] He is too young to appreciate the deeper significance and the powerful aid that MODERN PACKAGING is to dad in the office. But, in a few quick-silver years, Frank, Jr. – all the Frank, Jrs. will be sitting in dad's executive chair and then it is going to be your job to sell little Frank. But, it is going to be a much easier job because quite unconsciously, all these years, Frank has been absorbing your messages.[11]

The future is effortlessly aesthetic, and effortlessly successful too, as Frank, Jr. slips into Dad's place (Frances seems to have been dropped from the story by this time). But in its own idiom, the text echoes *Shelf Appeal*'s faith in the power of packaging to fire something as grand as a 'twentieth century imagination', and its conviction that children's art education matters.

*

In getting their ideas practically adopted, advocates of the new packaging faced a difficulty that does not apply to other forms of advertising: the package's relative longevity. The reasons given for this are both economic and psychological. Newspaper advertisements or window displays or posters can be changed quite quickly if they are found not to work. But when packages are wrong – and they can be wrong either functionally or aesthetically – they take far more time and money to change. The package may fall apart in transit or let the air in and damage the goods: the thing can no longer be sold. Or the package's appearance may put buyers off: the thing is all right but doesn't sell. To change a package takes long-term planning and investment – not just to redesign it, but to coordinate the different aspects of its production in relation to the contents and *their* production and the efficient dispatch of both to the points of sale.

The second reason given for packages being slower in their mutations than other species of advertisement is wholly psychological and follows from the first. If packages stay the same over a long period, then much of their appeal, if they do appeal, is in their familiarity. Packages should be recognizable – even before self-service, it is considered an advantage if the customer can identify the brand on the shelf behind the counter, and then ask for it by name. And they are supposed to guarantee reliability and continuity: if the packet doesn't change, then neither, it can be supposed, does the quality of what's in it. This is the positive aspect of the package's association with the movement towards standardization, a crucial term in American debates of the 1920s and 1930s about mass production and mass consumption.

Given these constraints on change, it is more difficult for packages to be modernized or 'made new' with the kind of experimental spontaneity that is possible for the shop window or other advertisements. 'Change for change's sake' is not recommended for established products. But when there are reasons for a change, it should be done in one of two ways: either dramatically, at one fell swoop, with lots of accompanying advertising to explain; or else very gradually, with the package undergoing minor alterations over several years, and never losing its familiarity in the process.

And change there must be, says the designer Norbert Dutton, if your package has anything remotely reminiscent of a nineteenth-century feel to it:

> Off with antiquated patterns and floral borders, decorations, panels, ovals, garlands and the whole tawdry bazaar of Victorian 'art'. Off with the bird's eye view of the works taken in 1911, off with the Chairman's signature ( – none genuine without – ), off with the short history of the firm and the forty-seven gold medals. Prestige to-day depends on a constantly tested standard, not on a grand prix at Boulogne-sur-mer in the middle of last century . . .
>
> Look at aeroplanes, motor cars, liners. They are products of the twentieth century. They are designed to work. You will find in them no pleasant fancies, no frills, no garlands wreathed round the working parts.

Here is packaging's modernist aesthetic of form, function and standard ('constantly tested'), epitomized by smooth, speedy, modern transport and contrasted with a caricature of old-fashioned mess and muddle. A black-and-white photograph of a Victorian gentleman with long whiskers occasions this terse comment: 'You wouldn't let your salesmen go out dressed like this. Yet countless products on sale to-day are just as inappropriately dressed.'[12]

*Shelf Appeal* ran a regular column called 'The Package Jury', to which manufacturers sent in their samples for criticism. A serial over several months satirized the typical difficulties encountered in a firm's attempt to get its package redesigned. In these and other articles, a constant theme is the reluctance to give up stock features that connote, to the designer's eye, a cluttered Victorianism. In the passage above, it is the chairman's endorsement or the little picture of 'the works' tucked away in a corner. Another such feature, staple motif of the much-discussed chocolate box, is the Pretty Girl.

## The Pretty Girl

Pretty Girls are generally regarded as good for selling products (though why this should be so is in fact a matter open for discussion, as we shall shortly see). They come in all shapes and sizes, appearing on all kinds of products, and whatever else they do, they seem to personify the problem of the package's *longue durée*. If you are changing your package radically, it might seem a good idea to go for the ultra-modern image; but since the girl is a figure of fashion, the package will look woefully out of date within a few years, and you will be back to the drawing board while having gained nothing in terms of the lasting familiarity of your package. A *Shelf Appeal* writer calling himself 'Newtimer' makes a more personalized attack on the problem:

> He [the hypothetical salesman] knows that a realistically reproduced pretty girl is an asset to every package. But he does not realise that there are many interpretations to 'pretty'. *A man's idea of prettiness usually boils down to what his wife looked like when he proposed to her.* That is why most 'pretty girls' on packs are old-fashioned. They are chosen by salesmen of a certain age.[13]

If you *must* have a pretty girl, the only solution (not a satisfactory one, it is universally agreed), is to go for the *really* old-fashioned girl, one so ancient as to be out of the fashionable world altogether. That means some kind of mythological or legendary female, such as a nymph.

But why go for pretty girls in the first place? A designer called J. de Holden Stone, writing in the same issue of *Shelf Appeal*, in 1934, denies the Pretty Girl even the dignity of the moment of betrothal; she is now just a figment of male adolescent daydreaming:

Ah, those pretty girls, instinct with everything which
becomes unattractive when a boy leaves his prep.
school. In the first flush of youth they are bad enough,
but when they are dished up again the Christmas after
in their clothes a year out of date it becomes suddenly
obvious how repulsive they are. If the rapidity with
which dress fashions change nowadays does nothing
else, it at least makes an uneconomic proposition of this
craze for sticking every type of female form – shooting,
swimming, dancing, or just existing – on to boxes containing the cheaper type of luxury product, investing it
with a hall-mark of its cheapness perceptible to any
housemaid now that she has seen 'exclusive' looking
things at the same price. The only girls with shelf
appeal are the really smart girls dressed in the very latest clothes, and these young women have to be
redrawn and reprinted far too often for the manufacturer's liking.

Stone then moves on to a rather different tack. Having asserted
the fundamentally 'repulsive' nature of the Pretty Girl, he turns
to the oddity of her role in advertising a commodity presumably
meant to appeal to women:

Women eat most of the chocolates. Yet surely nobody
sets out to entice the normal woman to buy chocolates by
showing her a picture of a girl. We can take it therefore
that these would-be pretty girls are displayed either for
the express purpose of attracting the man who has
decided to buy chocolates either for himself or for a
woman, or for the purpose of suggesting that he should
do so. I submit in all humility that it won't work. Seeing a
pretty girl doesn't make me hungry for *food*. And the
argument that the pretty girl will remind me of my own
pretty girl, if any, to whom it would be a nice gesture to
present some chocolates, is typical of the false reasoning
which must be responsible for so much of the wasted
publicity we see. I give a girl chocolates to please her

rather than to feed her. Primarily it is essential that the box shall flatter her by my appraisement of her good taste . . . I don't care a rap whether these chocolates nourish her, selfish beast that I am, but it is of world-shaking importance that they shall make her say 'Oh, *Jimmy*!'[14]

The critique mixes together a deliciously varied assortment of hypothetical factors in the psychology of the chocolates-buyer. What does he really want? Probably not chocolates. A woman, perhaps, who may want chocolates or may want her taste flattered and therefore favour the giver. But a woman – at least, 'the normal woman' – does not want a pretty girl. *Ergo*, since pretty-girl boxes are mostly meant for giving to pretty girls, they must be a marketing mistake.

The assumed lack of symmetry in the responses of the two sexes to this particular image goes together with the consideration that the relations between the sexes are, as Stone says, the principal *raison d'être* for boxes of chocolates: they are for presenting as gifts that are meant to reflect well on both givers and recipients. Following Stone's own lines of reasoning, the Pretty Girl might be thought of as making the Real-Life Girl think (he thinks) *she*'s Pretty. Or: if the gift is intended to arouse grateful desire in 'the normal woman', it might be more logical to put a Pretty Boy – or at least a Normal Man – on it instead. This is in fact the assumption of a British book published the following year, in which 'the haunting face of the chocolate box girl, whose help is now enlisted to push the sales of cigarettes, soap, electric lamps and motor cars' is perfectly matched by 'the over-idealised type of advertised male humanity'.[15]

Stone concludes from his own selective syllogisms that pretty girls are out. But apart from the analysis of the sexual transaction involved, his opening paragraph had already damned them on quite different grounds: first, the fashion argument (you have to change her every year); and second, more surprisingly, and less prominently, the class and taste argument: *even a housemaid* would know these are just cheap chocolates. This paves the way for a further layer to the discussion.

It might be assumed, says Stone, that these pictorial boxes are only aimed at 'the lower class markets'. Not so, he maintains, for distinctions of class in matters of taste are rapidly giving way to homogeneity. This 'mass' taste for mass-produced objects is seen not as a levelling down but as an improvement all round: 'the taste of the suburbs and slums is fast becoming amalgamated with "West-End" taste into one coherent public which will show its taste for aesthetically pure things in no uncertain manner'. 'Aesthetically pure' in this context means both free of the interference of class *and* free of the clutter of an untidy, pictorial design; the phrase makes a striking connection between the new art and classlessness. Instead of the Pretty Girl, there should be 'one abstract and entirely unclass-conscious pack which would have some chance of sweeping the country by means of the fact that it was inspirationally well designed in the first place'.

'Aesthetically pure' might be expected to suggest the autonomy of a realm of art uninvolved with daily life or practicalities. But that would be a mistake: 'Surely the aesthetic status of a work of art lies in the degree to which it can affect or influence people?' From this it is a short step to the assertion that 'In the final analysis aesthetics is salesmanship as far as packaging is concerned.' The aesthetically pure, as in the abstract design, appeals to tastes or pleasures in form or colour that are universal, not a matter of class-based or other distinctions. At some level, everyone's responses to an image are the same, and if you want to be assured of a similar response you must avoid all the features in a design that will appeal to some kinds of people but not to others.

Rowntree's Black Magic box is to be understood here as the obvious example of this solution. With its simple black background and minimal lettering, without even the manufacturer's name appearing on the box, it is repeatedly referred to in the pages of *Shelf Appeal* – it was launched in 1933, like the journal – as an indication of the style of chocolate boxes to come. Today, it is true, there isn't a pretty girl or a dog or a pastel village scene to be found as an invitation to chocolate-buying. And already in 1937 *Shelf Appeal* could boast of its avant-garde prescience, remarking that its very first issue had had a story 'on Rowntree's *Black Magic* chocolates which were, at the time, the joke of the confectionery industry (though the laugh has subsequently proved to be Rowntree's)'.[16] In fact, the new brand was not so evidently eccentric: it was based on market research involving interviews and chocolate samplings with seven thousand consumers and two thousand retailers. The twelve soft centres proved as resilient as the box design, remaining unchanged for decades apart from when *Shelf Appeal* announced 'a war-time casualty among the star brand-names . . . *Black Magic* chocolate has gone to honourable retirement.'[17] There was a substitute brand, unromantically named Cranton.

Stone loses sight of the argument about chocolates and courtship when he makes his conclusion about the breakdown of aesthetic hierarchies; it would be going too far, perhaps, to suggest that the 'aesthetically pure' abstract design indicates something about changes in sexual as well as in class relations. But the argument about class and aesthetics is a significant one, all the more in light of post-war assumptions that mass production and mass consumption tend towards a lowering or a vulgarization of taste.

Such arguments were already widespread in *Shelf Appeal*'s time. The literary critic F. R. Leavis and his followers, for instance, made it their mission to counter what they regarded as the deleterious effects of mass culture, arguing for the importance of literary education at every stage of the school system. Here, the American influence is a negative one, the bad shape of commercialized things to come; but the critique of American culture is itself derived from America. Leavis's *Mass Civilisation and Minority Culture* (1930), and the pedagogical *Culture and Environment* (1933), written with Denys Thompson, draw on *Middletown* (1929), Robert and Helen Merrell Lynd's study of recent social changes in a middle-sized American midwestern city. Here, the 'standardization' of both goods and cultural activities is unequivocally taken to be a levelling down, which does away with differences of value and individuality, reducing everything – people and products – to a homogeneous 'type'. The argument is the other way round from the *Shelf Appeal* postulation of an alliance between modernist aesthetics and classlessness.

In Britain and the United States it was the coupling of mass production with blandness rather than aesthetic potential which won out, both ideologically and in practice: if packaging was an American import, it came to be seen far more as a dull or even insidious one than as an object of interest or appeal. In the 1950s and 1960s no one expected to find or to argue for artistic innovation on a packet of washing powder or cornflakes; or even on a box of chocolates.

## The bar of soap

The case of the chocolate box is such a special one that in some ways it may obscure the more general force of the move towards modern, if not modernist packaging. Boxes of chocolates are most often bought to be given; it is already in their chocolate-box nature to show that they are packaged and presented in wrappings that have little to do with utility and much to do with beauty, lavishness, gratuitous excess. Even down to the name, the 'box' of chocolates makes the packaging an integral part of the product. So it might seem natural to talk of a chocolate box in aesthetic terms in a way that for most other products it wouldn't.

Take, for instance, soap.

Here is R. Haughton James, writing in *Shelf Appeal* about the uses of photography in package design:

> A tablet of soap sitting unwrapped in a chemist's shop
> holds no more glamour than it can claim while waiting
> beside the bath. Surround it with a repeated design of
> engagement rings – a fatuous suggestion enough, yet alive
> – and there's some part of the general population will buy

it. Why? Because you've stimulated into activity something bigger than a desire for a clean neck.

Somehow the soap itself, 'sitting' and then 'waiting' patiently,
has taken the place of the dreaming girl whose longings it is
meant to set in motion. At any rate, this anticipatory piece of
soap is preceded by a kind of hymn to the power of the package
which does indeed suggest that it, or she, has incomparable
powers of seduction:

> The package has a bigger job to do than any advertise-
> ment. It is the manufacturer's final effort for attention;
> and where his advertising has passed unnoticed – sales
> stand or fall by the impression the package makes. A
> good package can make great friends; it can charm the
> retailer into giving it prominent display; it can beguile
> the reluctant coin from the pocket of a purchaser totally
> confounded by the competing array of mediocrity. It can
> suggest new uses for an old product, it can awaken
> desires long repressed in the name of economy.[18]

James's example from his own work is rather peculiar in the
light of this build-up. It is a packet for a formula called 'Milka',
which, he is proud to announce, shows a black-and-white photograph of a miserable baby 'about to lift its voice and cry for
sustenance'. This, thinks James, will win favour with mothers
because: 'It is *her* child; it is the child of every mother who cannot feed her baby herself. The smug, fat faces of other people's
babies, bursting with undeserved health, only revolt her.'[19]
This seems a far cry from the awakening of new or repressed
desires; by the same logic, the engagement rings ought to dis-
gust the unbetrothed maiden and it would be better to show
her a picture of a resentful bridesmaid or let her stick with her
plain desire for a clean neck.

However, it so happens that the bar of soap does provide the
occasion for a far more plausible promotion of the power, not
so much of the package, but of advertising in general. Walter
Dill Scott's *The Psychology of Advertising* appeared in 1908. This

was the first book to make a systematic argument for the importance of psychology to advertising, in the context of a case for the power of advertising in general. Scott, a psychologist at Northwestern University (of which, in the 1920s, he became President), was quickly taken up as the authority on what did indeed come to be seen as a stimulating new area for research, in Europe as well as in the United States. Here is Scott on soap:

> The questions which naturally arise in the mind of the advertiser are, Can I create such a sentiment in favor of my commodity that it will be seen enshrined in sentiment? Has a glamour ever been created for an article of merchandise by advertising? This last question must certainly be answered in the affirmative. If the advertisements of Ivory Soap have accomplished anything, it is this very thing. All of these advertisements have been of one class for a quarter of a century. They all bring out the one point of spotless elegance. These advertisements have created an atmosphere, and when I think of Ivory Soap a halo of spotless elegance envelops it, and I do not think of it merely as a prosaic chunk of fat and alkali. I have had this idea of spotless elegance so thoroughly associated with Ivory Soap by means of these many advertisements that I actually enjoy using Ivory Soap more than I would if the soap had not been thus advertised. The advertising of this soap not only induces me to buy it, but it influences me in my judgment of the soap after I have bought it.[20]

Scott gives a number of quite disparate reasons for the success of the soap advertisements. First is familiarity, which was to become such a point of insistence in discussions of packaging: these advertisements have been 'of one class for a quarter of a century'. But what have they done? They have 'created a sentiment', 'created an atmosphere', such that the soap is seen differently from how it otherwise would be; it is 'enshrined in sentiment' and 'a halo of spotless elegance envelops it'. In other words, it is packaged. It has an outer layer which *becomes* it, beautifies it and makes it what it is so that it cannot be seen apart from it. Its 'sentiment' is an attachment or connotation; but it is inseparable from the thing itself, which cannot be seen as such. The 'prosaic chunk of fat and alkali' is simply a fiction of how the soap *would* appear if it wasn't already accompanied by its poetic wrapping.

'Enshrined' and 'halo' suggest a religious effect, a matter at once of mystery and belief. The soap is surrounded by an aura. Walter Benjamin's use of that term twenty-five years later makes Scott seem almost sacrilegious. For Benjamin, 'aura' belongs to the work of art itself as distinct from copies of it. The work of art, religious in origin, is tied to a fixed place, because it is a unique object; whereas the mechanically reproduced photograph of a painting, recording of a concerto, or can of Campbell's soup, is everywhere and therefore nowhere in particular.[21]

Scott's Ivory Soap is an object of veneration; his analysis might be applied to a religious or aesthetic transformation of an otherwise ordinary article of consumption or contemplation. Bread and wine, for instance, through long-term propagation of the message over the course of two millennia, have been experienced, in certain circumstances, as something both more than and quite different from the 'prosaic' dietary elements they constitute at other times. And indeed Scott insists, anticipating all the critics to come of advertising as a creator of false values, that he really does enjoy Ivory Soap in a way that he wouldn't if advertising had not given it the sense of 'spotless elegance' for him. The 'atmosphere' remains beyond the context of looking at an advertisement or seeing the soap displayed in the store; it comes home with the purchaser and imbues his every soaping experience with the very same sentiment.

There seems to be no worry here about being manipulated or fooled by something that is not what it purports to be. Later, a different kind of distinction between surface and depth would be affirmed with force in critiques of advertising in all its forms, including packaging. In this version, advertising is an immoral form of persuasion against a better judgement or better nature of the person being persuaded, and against a better or simpler nature of possible objects for purchase. Just as there is, or should be, a clear distinction between the article and its packaging, so there is, or there should be, a clear distinction between the real thing and its added values, or between the genuine and the fake experience. Peel away the layers of falseness and fabrication, and you might uncover or recover real experiences and real things.

Scott mocks at the idea of the primary content or primary experience, by describing his pre-atmospheric soap as a 'chunk of fat and alkali' – not so much 'prosaic', perhaps, as disgusting. Yet this is what gets you clean, and if the choice is between rubbing yourself with what you think of as a lump of fat and rubbing yourself with what you think of as spotless elegance, then it is not obvious that the dupe would be the one who opted for the second.

This raises another issue, too, about the status of what is taken to be the thing-in-itself prior to adornment or advocacy. The soap could equally well have been described in its elementary form as, for instance, a solid white substance, measuring two by three by one inches and weighing four ounces. Or, the 'fat and alkali' line could have been put more scientifically, giving the formula for the chemical composition of the soap. And there might be any number of other possible kinds of definition. Thus the 'basic' alternative to the 'atmospheric' description is a kind of retrospective fiction, as variable as the enveloping 'halo'. Even the hypothetical division in types of primary description, into the object as perceived and the object as actual substance, is itself only another version of the two-level division between object and atmosphere or substance and wrapping.

For their critics, advertising and packaging raise a worry that what we are buying or eating or enjoying is *not what it seems*; or, in a slightly different version, that since what we buy is being presented in a false light (its packaging, its image, all the ways it is advertised), then it is bound to lead to disappointment when its true – prosaic, or worse – nature is revealed. Such criticisms may also themselves operate in the very way that they describe occurring in the case of advertising: in other words, we are persuaded by the argument against the advertising just as we might be persuaded by the advertising itself, and henceforth experience precisely the disappointment in relation to the commodity that the critique has led us to expect.

Scott's uncompromising analysis of the power of advertising to make a halo and, by extension, the indispensability of the halo or envelope to the perception of the object itself, took on a very particular application with the development, beginning before the First World War, of *transparent* packaging.

### Transpapers

It could be the name of a 1990s on-line journal of post-colonial literary theory; but 'transpapers' was in fact the word proudly coined by *Shelf Appeal* to get over the problem of a trademark. In 1935, the manufacturers of 'Cellophane' complained in the journal's letters column that their name was being taken in vain: it was being used without its capital letter or its quotation marks, and thus losing its individual identity among the many competing products. *Shelf Appeal* agreed to take a stand on the side of 'Cellophane'. Instead of saying cellophane, they would say transpapers.[22] And transpapers it was, in *Shelf Appeal*, from then on; though ironically, cellophane has outlasted both 'Cellophane' and transpapers, surviving still as a familiar word, if not such a frequently encountered substance.

There was certainly a crowd of transpapers to be negotiated. The previous year, *Shelf Appeal* had run a technical piece on 'transparent viscose wrappings', comparing the qualities of Cellophane, Diophane, Sida, Viscarelle and Durex Cellulose Tape (of which more to come).[23] These were not the only ones; a few months later, for instance, there was a big advertisement for something called 'Rayophane', a 'Transparent wrapping paper, Guaranteed Odourless, Hygienic, Dust-proof, Oil-proof, Grease-proof, Germ-Proof' – which seems to cover just about every possibility.[24]

Possibilities, indeed, may be the main thing that the trans-papers *are* covering. Their supposed utility, as this glorious display of defensive adjectives suggests, is in protecting either product or consumer from ever more fantastical forms of puta-tive contamination, whether it's the smell that might emanate from the thing inside, or the many mucky elements that might get at it from the outside. Their form of protection is far removed from the more solid stabilizing services rendered by the cardboard box which, however pretty it may also be in 'this packaging age', has the real job of preventing the article from being bashed about as it travels from factory to store to home. If packaging is neatly divided into functional and aesthetic aspects, the functions it is supposed to fulfil can be multiplied ad infinitum, the more categories you invent for potential dam-age to product or user.

Transpapers also came to symbolize the new importance of wrapping merchandise attractively: in other words, how pack-aging had taken over from mere packing. In *Packages that Sell*, it is stated that cellophane (no quotation marks) has 'increased the sale of dress shields, powder-puffs, bath salts, towels, candy, and bacon';[25] among this incongruous collection, we can at least be relieved that the bacon has been moved from its greasy glass jar into something a little more palatable to the later twentieth-century sense of packaging decorum.

*Packages that Sell* includes an illustration of packaging's lack of discrimination about what it packages: 'The average con-sumer never used to think of a wrench as a gift for a man, but with the introduction of a special holiday wrap Walworth Still-son Wrenches were put in the gift class.'[26] This example clearly struck a chord with marketing men (and women), since it is cited repeatedly in subsequent British and French literature. The triumph of non-functional packaging is complete when even a thing that is regarded as purely functional gets given a fancy wrapper and 'put in the gift class'. When you've done it with a wrench, you can do it with anything. Commentators never tire of providing instances of ever more extraordinary candidates for the transpaper treatment, from the humblest to the grandest of commodities. 'Woolworth's have found that even mothballs and elastic sell more rapidly if wrapped in transparent cellulose!' exclaims one *Shelf Appeal* writer.[27] Another time, a correspondent feels moved to write in about remarkable American uses for cellophane [*sic*], including the wrapping of grand pianos in shop windows, with the 'parcel' pulled together at the top with a giant bow like a chocolate box. (*Shelf Appeal* responds curtly with an italicized reminder about the importance of saying transpaper instead of cellophane.)[28] But if your trade happens to be manufacturing wrenches, then your fate is really sealed, as J. de Holden Stone, he of the Pretty Girl chocolate boxes, points out in a hypothetical case: 'A small tool-maker puts out a new type of wrench, which he insists on packing, having read "Shelf Appeal".'[29]

If transparent wrappings are only dimly functional, their main quality, of course, is in their power of enhancing an image of the actual product. What you see is indeed what you get, but it is given a gloss and a shine (and also, though this is not said, a crackly or smooth appeal to two other senses as well). Transpapers show the product, as though through its own private window; in the words of one advertisement, '"Cellophane" puts your product in a showcase of its own.'[30] In the late 1930s, *Modern Packaging* has numerous advertisements for different brands of sliced bread (well established in the United States by the 1930s, and just beginning to be marketed in Britain) where the parallel between the wrapper and a shop window is made in witty ways. The word APPEAL rises up in large free-standing letters reflected on a shiny surface, in front of a 'glass' section on the printed transparent wrapper for a Bohack's loaf; a cardboard house with doors and windows contains a loaf of Home Pride. This is the visible, or invisible, incarnation of Walter Scott's enveloping 'halo', signifying a kind of transubstantiation for the humble loaf of bread or bar of soap.

As well as their visual appeal, transpapers also make it possible for customers to touch the goods; and the idea that they might naturally expect to do both with food was new. Street markets for fresh produce had always let the customer see, but not handle, and so did butchers and bakers; but the goods in grocery stores – those legendary barrels of flour or cookies – were not regarded by either customers or shopkeepers as meant to be looked at or otherwise experienced before the routine purchase. Now, though, 'Adults with an itch to squeeze a package, do so,' says *Modern Packaging* in 1937, slightly nervously. This is a first foray into the topic of 'The Packager and the "Super Market"'; twenty years later, the journal would have practically no other.[31] Similar sentiments were being voiced in Britain too, like this caption to a photograph of a traditional grocery store: 'The typical grocer's shop puts a barrier between public and goods. Sometimes they can see the goods: often goods are hidden away in drawers. And to be able to feel and handle without asking and then waiting is a rarity.'[32] The counter and the unspecified human being are both reclassified as barriers. The assumption is that customers both want and have a right to get at the goods; if they can't, the goods count as 'hidden away'.

In this new purchasing situation, transpapers neatly fulfil a double function. On the one hand, they let the goods be seen and felt, and aestheticize them with an artificial sparkle. And on the other, they guard against the problem that handling (especially squeezing) would otherwise make, since they provide a hygienic shield. In retrospect, it is clear that transpapers were one of the preconditions for the development of the cling-film culture of the modern supermarket. To Georges Blond, a French visitor to the United States in the mid-1950s, cellophane could appear as the most visible, and virtually suffocating, feature of the supermarket: 'Cellophane is an obsession; after a moment you wonder if you aren't yourself shut up in a transparent case.'[33]

*Transtapes*

Transpapers in the 1930s had not yet attained the self-sufficiency that their descendants, like cling-film, would eventually enjoy. In these early days of their evolution, they usually needed the help of companions called 'transtapes', which survive today in numerous species of the genus now known as Sellotape. Sellotape's sphere of sticking is now more or less confined to small-scale 'office and domestic' uses: it has been made redundant in packaging by transpapers acquiring the sophisticated capacity to stick to themselves. If *Shelf Appeal* were itself alive and well today, the casual use of the brand name 'Sellotape' would doubtless be censured with appropriate severity. Even at the time, transtapes – though they did bother to coin the word – attracted the journal's attention much less than the far more exciting, centre-stage transpapers that they were meant to assist as unobtrusively as possible.

One transtape that does interest *Shelf Appeal* is a product called 'Durex' Cellulose Tape, made by a Birmingham company called Durex Abrasives, which came up before the Package Jury in 1935. Like any transtape, 'Durex' was in fact a product for sticking papers and packages. But the problem with 'Durex', the jury decided, was that it was hard for the customer to grasp its purpose from outward appearances. The product was generally sold from counter display trays, but what was it? 'The Jury were amazed to find that the only directions, apart from the package inserts, were printed on the *bottom* of the front display tray, so that it is necessary for the retailer to sell 16 packets of *Durex* before the public can see what it is to be used for.'[34] Durex's regular advertisements for the trade, which appear in the pages of *Shelf Appeal*, attempt to be more explicit:

> Sealed in a moment with "DUREX" Cellulose Tape, pressure-sensitive and proof against the wildest vagaries

of climatic conditions. Applied without heat or moisture, comes off as easily as it goes on, yet never comes off at the wrong moment. Why not go into your closure problems with us?[35]

Perhaps as a response to the comments of the Package Jury, subsequent advertisements offer further enlightenment: '"DUREX" Cellulose Tape is not very expensive, and is available in a wide variety of colours and widths.'[36]

## Sanitary goods

"Durex" was not yet Durex, even if the words of the advertisement seem to be practising for the future identity. *Shelf Appeal* did in fact give attention to contraceptives and other sexually sensitive categories of product. Since these generally elicited either silence or coyness in many much later publications, both trade journals and consumer testing magazines, *Shelf Appeal*'s openness in the 1930s is all the more striking. In 1934 there is an approving piece on the packaging of 'Ortho-Gynol', a new product from Johnson and Johnson, with the comment: 'Hitherto, attractive packages have not been a feature of contraceptives. In these days, however, there is no reason why an attractive pack should not help sales for such products.'[37]

*Shelf Appeal* more than once considers new packets for Lilia sanitary products, awarding them one of the prizes at its First International Exhibition of Modern Packaging in 1937.[38] On another occasion it looks at the particular problem posed by the packaging for such items, the special case of a kind of anti-package. It has to be unobtrusive, fulfilling the double condition of being both identifiable before purchase and, as far as possible, unidentifiable after.[39] Lilia's solution is a two-colour carton designed 'to give as much display value in a quiet way as possible'; from this the salesman draws out an anonymous plain package to hand to the customer.[40]

Later on, in the context of self-service, the problem becomes how to combine this absence of vaunted packaging with ease of recognition for the customer, who does not want to linger over this particular purchase. One American manufacturer takes out an advertising feature several pages long in a mid-1960s issue of one of the supermarket trade journals, fronted by a profile shot of a woman's head and shoulder in shadow. Never in the history of retailing literature has a woman looked so enigmatic, so mysterious. Her eye is completely dark, her mouth is open, as if to speak. If it weren't for the bouffant blonde blow-wave effect, still visible in the darkness, she would look as if she had just walked in from a different film set entirely, away from the usual fluorescent brightness of supermarket lighting and supermarket advertising. 'Who is she?' reads the caption. 'She spends 70c of every household dollar. Her loyalty is the way to increased profits. She knows what she wants . . . but she won't ask.'[41]

The manufacturer's argument rests on a larger issue of 'loyalty': the handling of sanitary goods is 'one of the key yardsticks women use in "making up their minds" about a store'. The text is strewn with self-conscious ellipses: 'When it comes to sanitary protection, however, she won't ask . . . she won't say anything . . . she won't even spend undue time searching the shelves.' Unlike the earlier concern about anonymity, there is no suggestion here, for a self-service environment, that the packet should be in disguise; instead, it must announce itself as clearly as possible, so that the customer can pick it up and be quickly on her way. Sanitary protection becomes a special kind of silent shopping, where doing without spoken words is a saving of embarrassment.

## Books

With a book too there may be reasons for a discreet brown-paper wrapping; but there are other considerations that make it a special packaging example. The book is in fact an ancient precursor of the modern package, a product that comes with its 'outer cover' built into it as part and parcel of the whole. Like the package, the book's cover serves the double function of protection and presentation. It keeps the pages from damage and also provides written information about the contents. During the period when packages in general were moving from functional to aesthetic roles, the dust that the dust jacket might keep off was coming to matter less than the design it might attractively bear. Dust jackets were ceasing to be something to be removed and discarded – as they still are in most libraries – once the book had been bought.

Not only the book as proto-package but also its mode of sale looks like an anticipation of late twentieth-century norms. Here was a product that you could look at and handle before you bought it, and that was available on the shelves for you to pick up yourself, without the intervention of either a counter or a clerk.

In an article of 1934 called 'The Packaging of Books', Beatrice L. Warde – a rare female contributor to *Shelf Appeal* – notes a trend towards more lettering and less image in cover design; the example is the 'talkative' wrappers produced by the publisher Victor Gollancz.[42] She also mentions a new book for children called *The World of To-morrow*. This book was much discussed, in *Shelf Appeal* and elsewhere, but nowhere more than on its own jacket blurb, which is not so much an advertisement for what's in it as an advertisement for what it's made of, packaging and all. Two-thirds of this text describes the book itself as an object, only a third its semantic 'contents'; among its other innovations, *The World of To-morrow* has a special new kind of typeface.

The book boasts a whole catalogue of new packaging materials. There is 'Diophane' paper for illustrations, which, according to the blurb, 'gives a luminosity which is almost stereoscopic'. The cover is 'made of translucent "Rhodoid", on which the design is printed'. There is a 'Yapp' fore-edge to protect the book from wear, and the whole cover is 'stainless and washable'.[43] *The World of To-morrow* was reviewed by Nicholas Cain in *Shelf Appeal* as a rare example of a publisher attempting to experiment in the design of the book. But Cain is not especially impressed by the various efforts (or indeed by the inside text, which he does consider as well: it is for instance 'appallingly casual in its statements of offensive weapons in future warfare').[44] The illustrations, which are supposed to show through the 'Diophane' onto blank sheets beneath, don't; while the 'Rhodoid' is itself covered by a further layer of Cellophane – unnecessarily, says Cain.

The Cellophane has gone now from the copy in the Bodleian Library in Oxford, but apart from that, the rest of the book is holding together better than Cain said his was in 1933 – perhaps because, like a package from an earlier age, it has been more stored than stared at in the intervening years.

*Package psychology*

In the first glitter and rustle of transpaper excitement, it is the pleasures of the package as a surface and outer envelope, enhancing the enjoyment of what it covers, that are uppermost. The package establishes an identity for a product that is pure display, pure surface; it may resemble what is inside, but it also may not, or its resemblance may partially shift the way that the contents themselves are then seen or experienced. But insofar as it is the outward sign of an identity, the package also treats that identity as changeable. Like a hat, it can be put on or off at will; it is not fixed once and for all.

Much is made in the literature of the connection between packages and the idea of mobility. On the one hand, small packs are designed to be easily moved about, and to move about a lot is what modern people are assumed to be wanting to do. Fixed-price stores – especially Woolworth's in the United States and Britain, Monoprix and Prix-Unique in France – lead to the manufacture of small packs to fit ready-given tiny prices. Small packs are also thought to be suited to households that are themselves decreasing in size: apartments rather than houses; fewer children, fewer or no servants for the middle and upper classes, the emphasis varying depending on the country. The package makes it possible to treat the local 'store' as just that, where previously – in grandmother's time, of course – the much larger house with its cellar and larder would have fulfilled the role. Daily life is lived on a smaller scale and at a faster rate. As much as possible has to be 'packed into' both the space and the time: 'We live in a compact age, in our baby flats which we may leave at a moment's notice for a week-end of motoring or a trip abroad. We stand poised on one foot, ready to go here, there, anywhere, and can no more tolerate ugly, clumsy goods than we could settle down comfortably amidst red plush, heavy furniture.'[45] Life is decidedly un-Victorian: light chairs, easy going. For that weekend excursion you can even buy a special 'motoring' box of chocolates.

The package's mobility is parallel to that of its users; and so are the mobile identities of both. The new package embodies the sense of identity as something that can be chosen or enhanced, put on and off without being fixed once and for all. This was the period in which the idea of 'multiple selves' of this kind became popular in modernist literary and artistic milieux. Valéry Larbaud, as we saw in Chapter 2, had invented a particular version of this, truly the last word in mobile consumerly identities. Another example is Virginia Woolf's Orlando, hero and heroine of the novel published in 1928, who in her twentieth-century incarnation rejoices in some two thousand selves. She can call on any of them at will, and takes particular pleasure in their availability when she is shopping in London department stores.[46] Multiple selves in this fantasy offer imaginary escape from the fixity of being in one identity; they suggest an expansion of possibilities to suit different moods or situations.

The analogy between the package and the person also looks towards another prospect, but one that is as restricted as the mobile, mutable package appears to be open. The mass-produced packaged product goes with mass consumption. Mass-produced packages are, by definition, all identical; they are compared to superior goods that are not mechanically made but individual, crafted by hand. The 'masses' of mass consumption, meanwhile, are similarly represented as other than human, indistinguishable from one another: here 'mass' acquires a long series of negative connotations: vast; mechanical; stupid; homogeneous.

People packed into public transport 'like sardines' in cans suggest another image that also hovers around notions of mass consumption: that of confinement. Mass consumers modge together without individuality; they have no thoughts of their own and they are absolutely fixed. The negative associations of the package probably find their purest product of all in the notion of the 'package tour' – an expression that first made its appearance in the late 1950s. The 'package' here is implicitly the all-in-one holiday, all wrapped up in one metaphorical parcel without the need to find and buy each separate element – travel, accommodation, meals, insurance, excursions, and so on. But it also, just as much, suggests the homogenization that flattens out in advance all differences between places, all experiences of them, all the travellers who go to them. Package tourists are then the quintessential mass consumers. They are all in the same boat, or the same plane; they really are locked in like sardines, because they cannot get out while they are in transit: their mobility appears as the opposite.

When supermarkets became dominant after the war, it was the bad package of mass consumption that came to the fore, not the package associated with mobility, modernity and aesthetic experiment. But in the 1930s, such bleak associations had yet to engulf the new shopping environment for the package that was beginning to be known as self-service. It is this that we turn to next, after a brief exploration of some of the characters who set the scene for the entrance of the supermarket shopper.

2 lb. GIPSY CHOCOLATES 2 Layers
Selling Price: **9d.** per ¼ lb.

Rowntree's Gipsy Chocolates, *c.* 1930. Photo reproduced courtesy of York Castle Museum.

*Good taste*

What became of the Pretty Girl after she was summarily re-moved from the chocolate box? Perhaps she crept off into chocolate heaven, there to consume in confectional bliss that divine substance from which several layers of luxurious paper had tantalizingly separated her before. Perhaps she lies un-seen, unbranded and long decayed, amid the rubbish-heaps of packaging history. At any rate, it is clear that in this chocolate-buying world, she is now no more.

But what of the Pretty Girl *off* the chocolate box? Did she too disappear, now deemed identical in her tastes to every other kind of consumer? According to the high hopes of *Shelf Appeal*'s 1930s aesthetic philosophy, modernist design had a universal appeal that would raise the taste of everyone, not draw all down to a lowest common denominator. Give everyone the same simple, stylish packages and you will show that everyone has fundamentally the same simple, stylish preferences.

Here something like the Rowntree's Black Magic box (see chapter 5) could appear to promise a new style of sophistica-tion in packaging art. Take away the pictures, the fussiness, all the despised ornateness associated with Victorian art, and you are left with the cool design – black background, plain gold lettering – that has survived for Black Magic with little modification ever since (there's a suggestion of red now, and Nestlé, who took over Rowntree's, have put their brand name in the top left corner). Meanwhile the picture has gone from practically every other chocolate box too; if there is an image, it is likely to show the chocolates themselves, either dis-played through a transparent cover or illustrated on an opaque one.

Elsewhere than on chocolate boxes Pretty Girls, like other consumerly categories, have faded in and out of advertising visibility, whether as consumers or as images, depending on the products and the times. Far from a modernist universalism winning out, advertisers and manufacturers and critics of both of them have continued, as they were doing in the 1930s, to put together knowledge and imagination and preconceptions of every kind in the attempt to figure out whether everyone everywhere wants, fundamentally, in the same way, and what they might or should be encouraged to want that they don't already. And if they want in different ways, or if some want and others don't, the question is always whether the differences are fixed or whether they are open to modification – by advertisers and social critics, among others.

Whether explicitly named or not, the four categories of sex, class, age and race have retained their position as the primary advertising differentials throughout the twentieth century. As well as offering the possibility of infinite detailed variations and combinations, each of them lends itself to dualistic, hierarchical schemes – man/woman, higher/lower, older/younger, white/black (or western/colonial, indigenous/immigrant, and so on). It often happens that the subordinate categories get lumped together as likely to share some particularly unsophisticated (which may also mean exploitable) predilections. So women and children are often (though not always) found in the same imaginary shop, as are children and 'natives' or (earlier) 'savages', the putative beneficiaries of an enterprise known in the first part of the century as 'colonial marketing'; but there is no consistency in the affiliations or indeed in the categories. Quite contrary assumptions are made in different contexts about natives (or indeed about the validity of that one classification), as they are about the female sex (or its subdivisions into types such as pretty girls or housewives), and about all the other possible categories and subdivisions: in many contexts, for instance, it is obviously youth, not age, that is the preferable attribute. In this chapter, we will be looking at some of the imagined consumers who form the background to the invention of various kinds of supermarket shopper.

## Colonial marketing

Discussions of colonial marketing are usually brief – it's a side-line, something to be used for illustrative or didactic purposes but clearly not a central concern. For instance, 'savages' provide a comparative frame of reference for discussions about whether there are universal types of response to given shapes and colours. An American book of 1916 confidently states that it was 'found that the colors were preferred in the following order by savages':

1 Red          4 Blue
2 Yellow       5 Green.
3 Orange

The list conveys a wonderful certainty in both the rankings and the demarcation of the colours themselves. Adding to the impression of a kind of fabulous fact-making, it is said to have been reliably gleaned from 'questions put to returned missionaries' – which must certainly have saved on fieldwork expenses.[1]

Later on, the savage develops some complexity and variation, being described in terms that are both more diffuse anthropologically and more pragmatic economically. Those intending to sell their products to the African or Indian markets should be aware that the associations of some colours and shapes may differ from one culture or religion to another. The picture is no longer one of identical savages, and the differences are not thought to be given by nature.

But there are further difficulties to overcome. One is called illiteracy, another naïvety. Not only can the buyers not read information that manufacturers might think of supplying, but strangely enough, they are apt to suppose that the picture on the tin has something to do with what's in it. Images of lions – and what else would you put on a jungle-bound can but those everyday colonial creatures? – are thus not to be recommended, for fear of the contents being misconstrued.

As in many contexts apart from marketing at this time, the 'savage' or 'native' is presented in some of the same terms as another special category of consumer, the child, to whom we shall return later on. Both are barely literate and naïve. Both are also thought to want to keep the package once it has served its first purpose; many commodities, like the Mickey Mouse box of sweets that becomes a toy shop, are designed with this 're-use value' for children's play in mind, just as colonial tins are expected to take on a second role as domestic containers.

There were, however, specialized advertising agencies based in colonial countries whose pictures of their target markets were as complex as those that western agencies had of theirs. In both cases, market research supplied sociological data that was available in no other form. In India, the principal agencies such as Keymer's, founded in 1844, and Stronachs, which also had branches in South Africa and Egypt, translated advertisements into numerous languages and varied the advertising according to the local culture. 'Cases in which general advertisements serve in India are the exception and not the rule,' said a *Shelf Appeal* piece in 1941.[2]

Particularly in wartime, it was also possible to see a political role for advertising in maintaining or changing ideas of nationhood and culture. In 1940 one advertising professional responded to another agency's suggestion of how to use advertising as propaganda. That agency had produced an advertisement with the slogan 'Advertise our Freedom!', the freedom concerned permitting cricket on the village green and comparable pursuits. Instead, advertising should be a force for social change:

> Before the practical advertising man can assume the job
> of explaining the British tradition to the British people, it
> would be just as well if we recognised the fact that the
> world requires us to reconsider, in the interests of
> humanity, a tradition which has been, so far, peculiarly
> advantageous to some of us, but not so beneficial to, say,
> British miners, agricultural labourers and unemployed
> people, Kaffirs, Blackfellows, Indians, Polynesians and
> others on whom trousers, bibles, industry and other parts
> of the British tradition have been conferred.

All this is not to say that we haven't a much better case than the Nazis, and can offer humanity a better world order than can Hitler. But we have got to think it out. Last century's model won't sell.[3]

### Men, women and 'that perfect duck of a hat'

In *Shelf Appeal* and *Modern Packaging*, the significance of sex in thinking about the relationship between the consumer and the package is usually assumed rather than debated. The piece on the Pretty Girl chocolate box is a rare exception, all the more interesting because it also brings in the possibility that mass-marketed products may be diminishing consumerly differences in another area, that of class. *Shelf Appeal* assumes pragmatically that men are what you give wrenches to and women are what you give chocolates to. Given existing distinctions of labour and leisure, consumers of both sexes are taken to be susceptible in their own spheres to the same kinds of mixed appeal to the functional and the beautiful. Both sexes are also assumed to have an interest in looking at things to buy, though perhaps not to the same degree or in the same way.

A 1936 issue of *Shelf Appeal* has a seven-page feature on men's clothing, prompted by Simpson's opening their new store in Piccadilly. The huge success of Daks, Simpson's brand of ready-made flannel trousers, is attributed confidently to 'Alex Simpson's knowledge of men's clothing psychology', clothing psychology evidently being a category that is applicable to both sexes but also different for each.[4] We saw in Chapter 4 how windows for men's clothes rather than women's were seen as the cutting edge of a modernist aesthetic of display in the 1930s.

At the time, there were no less than three British trade journals dealing with men's clothing. This industry is seen to have undergone rapid changes through the introduction of more upmarket ready-made goods, with a different experience of time for both consumer and maker:

There was much snobbery, fetish and ceremony about the whole thing, but 80 years ago men had more time to pick, discuss and wait for suits, whereas in this epoch this precious time cannot be afforded for what, after all, can be done much more effectively by organisation and machinery.[5]

The craftsmanship of tailoring is as much a misuse of valuable time as the buying rituals surrounding it; time has become a 'precious' resource to be carefully measured out.

Compare this masculine combination of casual fashion and time-saving with two passages about women's consumption that both come from the first issue of *Shelf Appeal* in 1933. The first, on cosmetics, is by Eileen Mayo, 'who writes both as a consumer and a designer':

A preparation, however good, that has offended the fastidious eye of its owner for weeks or months, stands less chance of renewal than one which has given a thrill of pleasure every time it has been used . . . Let beauty specialists set forth their wares in attractive modern dresses, trusting not alone in the hidden virtue of the preparations themselves. All may not be gold that glitters, but the glittering is an incentive to the final appreciation of real worth.[6]

This is like Walter Dill Scott's description of the bar of Ivory Soap that really is enjoyed more for being advertised in a certain way, because it emphasizes the glitter or atmosphere, the 'dress' as well as the 'hidden virtue' of the product. More than Scott, however, Mayo tacitly maintains a category of 'real worth' in the product. Some contents are superior to others, but without the 'glitter' the 'gold' may go unappreciated.

The second passage concerns that very new American thing, sliced bread:

We are all lazy buyers nowadays. Even the woman who used to pride herself on judging good flour by the feel of

it now shops for bread by 'phone. Often she saves time
for bridge or the movies – time that she would have to
spend picking out a particularly crusty loaf – by phoning
for So-and-So's ready-sliced, standard-baked bread,
which has no 'particular' variances within the bread.[7]

For the woman as household manager, time is a limited quantity to be saved or spent, as it is for the man who no longer has
'spare' time to go through the old-fashioned practices associated with ordering a new suit. But whereas the man now has
no leisure for time-taking 'fetish and ceremony', the woman
saves on her work time – picking out the best loaf – in order
precisely to earn leisure, 'time for bridge or the movies'. For
both sexes, the demands on time nowadays make it a valuable,
finite quantity to be spared and saved and carefully managed
so that it is not wasted; but the kind of activity for which time
should be ultimately reserved is different.

In the bread-buying passage, shopping is a matter of convenience; the 'standard-baked' description suits the commodity whose 'particularly crusty' variations are given up to
make possible other consumerly pleasures. The bread is
thereby shifted into a category of basic consumption, not
worth the attention of choosing. In the passage on cosmetics,
however, you shop for something that not only is attractive
when you buy it, but will even provide a 'thrill of pleasure'
every time it is used. This is consumption as consummation,
not just once but over and over again. It is in a different consumerly universe from sliced bread and indicates a division
between kinds of consumption that was itself becoming standardized at the time, both in marketing literature and more
widely. The functional and the aesthetic aspects of the package are thus replayed in the two ways that shopping and consumption are conceptualized: the matter of fact and the
special pleasure.

There is a succinct example of this in Stuart Chase and F. J.
Schlink's *Your Money's Worth* (1927). This American study was
instrumental in the formation of the Consumers Union, which

began to test and report on goods in its magazine *Consumer Reports* from the early 1930s:

> All the testing bureaus in the world will not stay one determined woman from buying that perfect duck of a hat. But they have stayed her from buying ketchup made of rotten tomatoes, and they may yet stay her from buying dubious vacuum cleaners – and a thousand other things.[8]

The purely gratuitous purchase is in a class of its own; it stands out as that one and only 'perfect duck of a hat', just as its buyer is 'one determined woman'. The exceptional, one-off category is left free for the feminine whim, but otherwise – for those 'thousand other things' – consumption should be a matter of rational, sensible planning. Hats are one thing, housekeeping is another. And like the two categories of product, the woman herself is a bit of both, the flighty and the functioning.

As we have seen, packaging literature at this time was assuming consumers' interest in both practicality and attractiveness. The critics, coming from another direction, accept the same division but with reluctance. How nice it would be, Chase and Schlink imply, if everything could be rational in consumer decisions; but alas, it is not so.

That perfect duck of a hat is the one that gets away in rational accounts of consumer choice; it is worth pursuing a little further. Naturally, it turns up in unlikely places, one of which is a Rupert Bear children's story about women, children and shopping.

### Rupert and the shopping women

Like all Rupert stories, 'Rupert and the Winter Sale' was first published, in 1960, as a serial in the *Daily Express*; like many, it was reprinted in a Christmas annual half a generation later, in 1975. In this story, Rupert is the involuntary subject of an initiation when he accompanies his mother to the opening day of the January sale at the local town's department store. Rupert buys nothing himself, nor does he have any desire to. For him, the day's experience is not an introduction to the pleasures of shopping, but a lesson in how men have to live with the waywardness of women's shopping. Shopping in the Rupert world is a female mystery, in which men's role is that of innocent bystanders or helpless victims.

The story begins and ends with sardonic bonding between father and son; in the meantime, Rupert has seen what a man has to see in matters of female shopping. At the start, he is being woken early for some as yet unknown purpose. Mummy is said to be in a hurry, while 'Daddy seems in no mood to explain' what is going on: 'Oh dear, she does this once a year and I do wish she wouldn't.'[9] Breakfast is eaten, with Mummy 'busy jotting down notes on a piece of paper and murmuring to herself' (p. 99). Jobs for husband and son are briskly distributed:

> 'Now then Daddy,' she says briskly. 'Mind you have the washing-up done when I get back. I've decided to take Rupert with me. He's good at carrying parcels.'[10]

As the others depart, Mr Bear 'chuckles', and suggests that Mrs Bear buy Rupert a suit of armour: 'He will need it!' (p. 99).

On the bus, which is full of 'all the ladies of the village', battle lines are drawn as Mrs Bear and Mrs Badger decide not to 'go together': 'We might fight over something we want!' (p. 100). When they arrive, Rupert's mother points out to him the principal object of her visit, a particular hat in the window.

The store opens and a 'flood' of females streams in. Rupert gets pushed about and crushed, but in the middle of it finds time to reflect on the situation:

> 'Whew, this is weird,' he puffs. 'I've never seen Mummy and Mrs. Sheep and Mrs. Badger as excited as this. There must be something very important here.' (p. 102)

Shortly afterwards, he loses Mummy altogether; then she reappears, upset because she has failed with the hat: 'Somebody else got there first.' (p. 102). In a moment of practical lucidity, she bestows a bus fare on her son so that he can take himself home if they get separated again. They go up an escalator, then:

> Mrs. Bear buys several things, and gives Rupert two parcels to hold as well as some smaller packages to go in the carrier. Then she takes him to join in the scramble at the glove counter, and pops another packet into the carrier. As she moves away as briskly as ever Rupert becomes anxious. (p. 103)

As well he might, poor Rupert! But fortunately our overloaded little bear has the resources of common-sense and planning to stay his quite reasonable anxiety: '"I can't carry much more through this crowd," he thinks, "but I must keep Mummy in sight. Thank goodness the pattern of her coat is easy to spot"' (p. 103).

Detective work on the coat pattern proves, however, to be his mistake. The next time Rupert loses Mummy, he carefully plants himself at the point where he thinks she is most likely to appear: 'To his delight, after a long wait he catches a glimpse of the familiar pattern on a coat moving as fast as ever, and he dashes between many people to keep close to it. Rupert has to work hard to keep up. "Whew, Mummy's going faster than ever!" he puffs. "She's not normally so excited"' (p. 105).

But actually, it isn't his Mummy at all – one coat, like one excited woman, can easily be confused with another. After a while, poor patient Rupert is picked up by 'one of the shop managers' (a man), and taken off to 'an office for lost children' – despite his protestations that it is not he who is lost but his mother.

Now while he was looking for his mother, Rupert had noticed what he thought was the fall of 'a small reddish object', which disappeared underneath a counter. Right on cue, while he is in the internal office, a lady in a fur coat turns up lamenting the loss of her purse. Rupert is able to go to the spot and retrieve the object, to everyone's amazement and admiration.

Rupert is asked whether there is anything he would like as a reward. He says no, but he would like to get a present for his Mummy, who didn't get the hat she wanted, which he describes with professional exactness. There follow some murmurings between the lady and the manager, during which the 'smiling motherly nurse', who clearly identifies with the interests of the store, thanks Rupert. She also provides him with a useful gloss on consumer psychology: 'I'm glad you helped that lady . . . She's a good customer and although she's very rich she enjoys coming to the sales just like everybody else' (p. 110). Pleasure in hunting for bargains, even where money is 'no object', is the great social leveller.

After a while, a hat is produced that appears to be the very one Mummy didn't get, and now for the first time Rupert too gets emotional: 'The shopman grins at Rupert's excitement. "This isn't really the hat your Mummy saw," he laughs. "It looks like it, but this is a better one from our new stock. This kind lady has decided to buy it for you because you have done her a good turn. Won't your Mummy be surprised!"' (p. 111).

The rich lady then gives Rupert a lift home in her chauffeur-driven car. Mummy is not back yet, so he 'has a lot of explaining to do' to Daddy: 'When he has finished Mr. Bear gives a sigh. "Well, I'm not surprised that things went wrong," he murmurs. "I've always thought that Winter Sales ought to be forbidden by law!"' (p. 113).

Ever loyal, however, Rupert then rushes off – despite the fact that it is now snowing heavily – to meet the next bus, from which, sure enough, Mrs Bear descends. Mr Bear puts the kettle on, Mrs Bear cheers up on being 'teased about her outing' by Mr Bear, and then 'sets about her housework': order is restored (p. 114). It is only at this point that she notices the parcels, including the extra one, whose contents she 'tries on in delight' after hearing that it is 'a present from the rich stranger' (p. 114).

In the 1975 annual, Rupert stories appear in two versions: pictures with two-line verse captions on the upper half of the page, and a more extended prose description below. Here, the caption to the picture version has a proud father: '"You battled for it like a knight!"/ Laughs Mr. Bear, in great delight.' The close of the prose version underneath tells a slightly different story: '"Well, I'm glad it's over," laughs Rupert. "Next year *you* must go to the Sales, Daddy, and see if you have an adventure as good as mine." Mr. Bear pretends to shudder. "Oh, what terrible, *terrible* things you say," he grins. "I'd be *much* too scared of all those ladies!"' (p. 114).

The men are defeated by the ladies; the men conquer on behalf of the ladies. The men laugh about the ladies' peculiarities, and so do the ladies. Rupert takes on a spoof manly role as knight in shining armour to two different ladies in one day. Only the men (and the boys) stay sane amid the crush and chaos of the ladies' world. This is a midwinter madness, a moment of lunatic excess when Mummy and other ladies are in the grip of an enthusiasm that affects them at no other time. They act against their normal natures – ignoring the needs of anyone else, competitive with their female friends, enlisting the men and boys as lackeys for the day. They have but one object in view, some particular thing, which takes the place of all other attachments, small sons included.

In the course of the day, Rupert becomes practised in the paternal habit of withdrawal from the scene, and also becomes an expert clue-spotter. He notices items of female apparel in meticulous detail, yet his coat-watching and hat-watching are both related to his mother: in the coat's case because he doesn't want to lose her, in the hat's because he is interested in what she wants.

The coat confusion reveals that the same coat does not the same mummy make; but the case of the identical hat reveals that one hat can indeed be as good as another. One of the morals that Rupert's experience seems designed to teach is that hats and coats – at least until they are worn and made your own – are interchangeable goods; while mummies aren't. This might seem a fairly standard part of bear education. But there is a further complication, one all the more important for being a kind of exception to the main point. Mummies may be unique in a way that their hats are not. But mummies too become interchangeable in the heat of the sales day, when something 'weird' happens and they all become different in the same unfamiliar way – 'I've never seen Mummy and Mrs. Sheep and Mrs. Badger as excited as this.'

Rupert has learned some vital lessons about the separate longings and separate lives of the sexes. Women go periodically mad, and men stay sane. Daddies, in this situation, are better off staying at home and doing the washing-up, while mummies go off and battle each other in the wide shopping world before returning home to rest their feet (and get back to the housework) at night. In this odd grown-up world, Rupert has begun to see himself as a romantic man, chivalrous in his solicitous aid and tenderly tolerant of the women's temporary redirection of their interests from menfolk to things in sales.

His packed day has initiated Rupert into another peculiar feature of adult life. He may be a knight for a day, but the world is also shaped by the difference between the bus and the chauffeur-driven car, or between the identically patterned coats of Mummy and the other ladies, and the fur coat of the grand lady who is such a 'very good customer'.

Now this isn't, of course, a story much given to verisimilitude, when ordinary country folk are bears and badgers while the majority of the shop's customers, and all its staff, appear to be human beings. But the polarization of the class contrast fits with the other fairy-tale elements grafted on to a relatively modern scene of department-store shopping. The lady can be a Lady Bountiful, who gives her munificent gift in a symbolic gesture that emphasizes the store's aristocratic image, apart from the cheap equalities of the sales. Mrs Bear ends up with a *better* hat than the one she was after: it may *look* identical, it may even *be* identical, but it is superior because it is surrounded by various haloes of quality. It is 'from our new stock', it costs more, and it doesn't have to be fought for.

For Rupert, shopping is not a matter of his own desires, frustrated or fulfilled by hindering or helpful parents; its value is that it provides a means of being nice to Mummy. Another Rupert story, from 1954, starts off once again with an incident of erratic maternal behaviour. Mummy smashes a much-loved piece of china – 'Quite suddenly I felt giddy and I think I dropped a plate' – and off goes Rupert to find a replacement at a shop in a nearby village.[11] He ends up buying one that just happens to contain a small fortune in diamonds belonging to an old European family; *noblesse oblige*, its louche-looking representatives turning up to recover the missing plate, willingly give Rupert a vast sum in gratitude. Poor Mummy can then be taken off to get well again in 'the South', just as the doctor ordered.

Yet another message may lie behind all this. Long-suffering men and boys endure the women's *faiblesses*, their quirky fancies and strange afflictions; they even cater to them. Daddy is at home doing the washing-up, but even more important, the store managers have thoughtfully laid on just the business that will give Mummy what she wants. In this regard, the real-life supermarket spokesman of the 1950s was taking over from his department-store predecessors a well-established presentation of himself as woman's wonderful benefactor, giving her everything she desired and more. She was the queen, the boss, the eternally favoured Mrs Consumer:

> To give her all the benefits of this freedom of choice, he has introduced many features . . . He eased her shopping and preparation by prepackaging perishables . . . To further her shopping comfort, he gave her air conditioning. He provided a large parking lot where she could park, safely and conveniently, to do her shopping leisurely . . . He put home economists in his stores, so that Mrs. Consumer could consult with an expert on the preparation of her meals . . .
>
> With all these extra conveniences, by virtue of his tremendous sales volume and huge traffic, he could still decrease the cost of his food to the lowest in the history of retail food distribution.

So much for his service to the consumer.[12]

And how could she ever thank him enough?

## Children's commercial world

The Rupert stories offer parables of the difference of the sexes in a mythical time when shopping was shopping and mummies in deadly pursuit of 'that perfect duck of a hat' could be allowed their temporary aberrations. But behind them lies another tale of the place of children in shopping, which starts like this:

> At the foot of the women's page in the issue of Monday, 8 November 1920, there appeared a single panel drawing of a small bear with a shopping basket under his arm being sent by his long-skirted mother on a shopping errand, while in the doorway of their humble cottage the nonchalant father bear lolled with a hand in his pocket.[13]

*Plus ça change . . .* Such were the modest beginnings of Rupert Bear in the *Daily Express*, where he still appears every day. He was born into a thoroughly commercial environment, on a page that also included a feature called 'In and Out of the Shops' and an illustrated advertisement for an 'Economy Week' at Dickins and Jones's department store. In this first story, 'The Little Lost Bear', a simple shopping expedition leads Rupert into danger:

> Two jolly bears once lived in a wood;
>> Their little son lived there too.
> One day his mother sent him off
>> The marketing to do.
>
> She wanted honey, fruit, and eggs,
>> And told him not to stray,
> For many things might happen to
>> Small bears who lost the way.

And sure enough, Rupert does get lost and has some strange encounters, before being happily reunited with his parents after thirty-six episodes, a few days before Christmas.

Children's comic strips in daily newspapers began in the First World War, when weekly comics, which dated from the 1890s, had to cease publication. One way of filling the resulting gap was to provide a substitute – and a spur to sales from the influence of young consumers – in the parental newspaper. Lord Northcliffe's *Daily Mail* started the trend in 1915 with Teddy Tail, who was followed by the *Daily Mirror*'s 'Pip, Squeak and Wilfred'. Pip was a dog and Squeak a penguin; in 1919 they adopted Wilfred, a baby rabbit. Rupert, in 1920, was a late entrant on to the scene.

From the first, these characters were big business, their regular newspaper appearances backed by related toys and books: at their peak, the Rupert annuals sold a million and a half copies. Wilfred had his own fan club, which raised vast amounts for charity; a rally held at the Royal Albert Hall in 1928 was attended by a crowd of nearly ninety thousand. Such figures still seem remarkable, but the comic-strip heroes were soon to cede the limelight to international movie cartoon stars, above all Mickey Mouse. Mickey's visibility in the 1930s, as he bestowed his image on every possible commodity in a child's daily life, from toothbrushes to sweets to bedspreads, makes even something like the Teletubbies' rapid colonization of the world in the late 1990s appear as no more than a minor episode in an often repeated tale of children and consumption.

Rupert's fan club started in 1932. Its members were enjoined 'to respect their elders, assist the aged and the crippled, and be especially caring of very young children, while always maintaining a cheerful disposition'. In a post-Hollywood, post-television world, such charming manners – Rupert's own, of course – would acquire the additional virtue of being old-fashioned and quaint. It did not seem to matter if the stories in the annuals were reprinted from serials that had run in the newspaper years ago: even at the time of their first appearance, they evoked an imaginary world of 'the olden days'.

This is especially the case with shopping, always – from the very first day of Rupert's newspaper existence – a prominent theme. But Rupert's altruistic lack of any shopping desires of his own is completely at odds with the hectic world of children's consumption in which the stories were read, and in which Rupert, as a commodity if not as a consumer, played his significant part.

### Sweet shoppers

Children are the objects of special attention in salesmanship literature between the wars: sometimes as a way to the maternal heart (if you tolerate or take an interest in her children, she will like you better); sometimes through products meant to appeal to the 'parental instinct' as being necessary for the child's well-being; and increasingly, as consumers themselves. From one point of view, children can even be pointed out as the most important consumers of all, since they are both present and future buyers. And they are most discriminating, as a British 1939 manual on running a sweet shop describes:

> We have found that in most shops children's trade is a thing that can be cultivated considerably, and that it helps rather than hurts general trade, as the parents come in and buy also. But, you must be prepared to take the trouble to give them exactly what they want. There are few better shoppers than children, who are always on the look-out for something new, and want good value for money.[14]

The writer then goes on to recommend putting on special displays for 'children's rush times', such as the moment when they come out of the Saturday matinée at the cinema; there is also advice about keeping up with 'new "monster" lines'.

In contrast to what happened in subsequent decades, when stores became larger and fewer, there was an increase in the number of shops in Britain between the wars, including many

small ones. Returning soldiers wanted to start their own businesses; new suburbs were being built, with their own little
'parades' of shops. The number of sweet shops rose more than
for any other category. Little investment was needed to start
them, and in the 1930s new kinds of sweet and chocolate bar
were appearing on the market all the time. *Shelf Appeal* attrib-
utes this to 'the inevitability of packaging and the meteoric rise
of the Mars Bar', launched in 1933:

> This year, American influence is more pronounced than
> ever. British confectionery houses are straining their
> vocabularies to outstrip their rivals in finding queer
> names for their bar lines. Here is an assortment. Angel
> food, Three Deckers, Bumpers, Hu-Ha, Jakko, Punch,
> Scrum, Foozely Boo, Rip, Nutzipan, Chumps, Eccos,
> Choccos, King, Happy Day, Nutz and Humpty![15]

Sweet shops are the places for those local, frequent, small-
scale purchases that take on the colour of a long-lost past in
the light of adulthood. That was the time when shopping was
a daily pleasure and when things cost nothing. But for British
children of the 1930s, this natural myth of the shopping past
had a particular historical reality. If their parents had the
twopences to give them (which many, in the Depression
years, did not), they really did grow up in a little sweet-shop
paradise, to be abruptly brought to an end by wartime
rationing.

At this time, shopping for pleasure tends to be considered a
natural inclination for both women and children in a way that
it isn't for men. Whether they are after the latest cosmetics or
the latest monster, both groups are happy to be fashion-
conscious and package-conscious as a matter of course. Girl
shoppers and boy shoppers are never distinguished in the
period before the war; 'children' in general are regarded as
keen consumers. This leaves a small enigma surrounding the
passage from childhood to adulthood. Though it is obvious
how girls who shop become women who shop, the development

from boys who shop to men who don't – or not much – is never mentioned and remains a mystery.

## Responsible women shoppers

Women's enjoyment of shopping can be seen as feminine whim or harmless madness. There is also women's obligation to shop, given their role in the family as housekeepers. When it is being considered as more a duty than a desire of the sex, women's shopping gives rise to other kinds of judgement. It may not be done madly, but it can be done badly.

In 1948, John Newsom published a little book called *The Education of Girls*, prefaced by the architect of the 1944 Education Act, R. A. Butler. One chapter is addressed to an issue entitled 'Women as Purchasers'. In view of past and future arguments and assumptions about women, consumption and national identities, it is a fascinating text:

> The position of woman as purchaser is of great importance. By her standards, or lack of them, will be decided the type and quality of goods produced – goods which will adorn the homes and bodies of millions of English people, provide satisfaction or irritation to those who live with them and affect the value of our export trade. She it is, in fact, who determines our standard of living. It is too much to expect the average manufacturer to design two quite distinctive articles for home and foreign consumption, and however poor our domestic criteria there is a strong probability that foreigners will be expected to like and buy the same products. Unfortunately, foreign buyers are no longer restricted to the purchase of British manufactured goods and if they disapprove of our quality and design they will go elsewhere. It is of national importance, therefore, that the home market should be critical of ugliness and inefficient commodities, not only because they will desecrate our own homes and countryside, but because they will react on our trade balance.[16]

Newsom begins by making an empirical fact – women do most of the shopping – into a moral condition – 'woman as purchaser'. He then moves to a somewhat doubtful inference that it is therefore 'woman' – not, for instance, manufacturers – who will determine the quality and nature of goods produced in the future. Further assertions follow. There are absolute aesthetic standards, and if women are not up to them, then not only the domestic environment but also the national economy will suffer. If the colonies can't be made to buy our rubbish any more, it is women's fault that we are making it. And colonial consumers, by implication, naturally have the good taste that the English women lack: they know shoddy goods when they see them.

There are wild swings in the writing: from the lyrical to the mundane – 'She it is . . . who determines our standard of living' – or from the apocalyptic to the bathetic – 'they will desecrate our own homes . . . they will react upon our trade balance'. Quite literally, this passage is poised halfway, or rather at both extremes, between poetry and economics. There is a lurking inversion of Alexander Pope's poem *The Rape of the Lock* (1714), in which the woman is satirized for her narcissistic adornments, all the exotic creams, perfumes and jewels of colonial trade, 'the various offerings of the world'.[17] Here, instead, she is criticized for her failure to perform as a competent export agent or to provide an aesthetic environment for the masses in the form of 'goods which will adorn the homes and bodies of millions of English people'.

From another point of view, this could be seen as a twentieth-century rewriting of John Ruskin's lecture, 'Of Queens' Gardens' (1865). There, the woman is responsible for the 'sweet ordering' of domestic life, and also, in a negative sense, responsible for all social ills, including war, because only she can prevent what might otherwise be outbursts of masculine aggression.[18] In Newsom's version, both aesthetic and moral duties find a new place in the sphere of consumption. The woman has a responsibility for the success of her country's economy – it is her fault too if it fails – and also for the beauty of the domestic milieu.

*Changing consumers*

Newsom's discussion is one kind of sequel to 1930s ideas about the importance of aesthetic education for future consumers (see chapter 5). In this post-war text, both the education and the consumption fall as a burden of responsibility upon girls and women alone; they are not a source of pleasure or interest. And before long, women's 'position' as consumers was to change again. They would be seen not as blameworthy, but as the pitiable dupes of a malevolent environment called 'consumer society'.

In the consumerist arguments of the 1960s, women and children were linked together as shoppers not so much in their putative enthusiasm or irresponsibility, but as vulnerable groups. Women and children were the targets of intensive marketing which, for different reasons, was regarded as illegitimate. Two kinds of solution were mooted: control the marketing or educate the consumer.

With very small children, the argument is always about restrictions, voluntary and legal, for the simple reason that they can't be educated about a problem they can't yet see. For instance, a Federal Trade Commission report in 1973 said that it is only around the age of six that children start to be able to tell advertisements from non-advertisements on television.[19] But older children could be educated – whether positively, in good taste, or critically, in the analysis of advertisements. Generations of teachers trained in the Leavis school passed on to post-war pupils not only the values of the literary tradition but its accompanying critique of advertising and mass culture. In 1937, *Shelf Appeal* had excitedly reported on how Eton's drawing master, Robin Darwin, was putting the journal's educational ideas into practice by getting his pupils to design packages. He also set up a Chamber of Horrors display of 'the most horrid specimens [of packaging] Mr Darwin could find' in local grocers.[20]

For women and other grown consumers, there were efforts on the part of magazines and dedicated consumerist journals –

the American *Consumer Reports* was followed by *Which?* in Britain in 1957 and by *Que choisir?* and others in France. There were also numerous books at this time exposing confusing selling practices, especially in supermarkets, and encouraging housewives to fight back. As we shall see in Chapter 9, what was perceived as vulnerability was logically corrected by arming the potential victim.

In the 1980s a striking new political rhetoric gave the consumer a new place a long way from the sales or the supermarket. No longer a silly shopper, he or she acquired a grand new exemplary stature as the very type of rational modern citizenship. This consumer-citizen was an individual of no particular sex, with interests and rights and choices. Yet in the light of this character, personally seeking the best deal for himself or herself in every department of life, some other features of the Newsom consumer ideal are revealed. It involves ideas of collective responsibility (as well as feminine culpability), and includes a concern for social welfare (as well as national interests).

But the consumer-citizen did return to the store and in doing so acquired once more some moral responsibilities. Green consumers and ethical consumers are now marked off as separate categories of shopper, making their choices on factors which go beyond their personal interest in getting a good deal or a good product. For them – and for the supermarket chains now seeking to present themselves as responsive to social and environmental concerns – the supermarket has become a place of ethical behaviour more than a place of either convenience or temptation. It is the very reverse of the jolly, carnivalesque associations of the first supermarkets, beginning, as we shall see in the next chapter, with a bear of somewhat different species from Rupert.

Advertisement for Big Bear, 1937.

*Big Bear and friends*

> In December, 1932, the food world was startled to read
> that a huge circus-like retail store had opened up under
> the name of Big Bear in the abandoned plant of the
> Durant Motor Car Company in Elizabeth, N.J. People by
> the thousands flocked from a radius of forty and fifty
> miles away . . . [1]

The first supermarkets came hastily into the world, with little
planning, an impulse sell prompted by the circumstances of
the Depression. Big Bear was the brainchild of two businessmen, Robert Otis and Roy Dawson, who had visions of what
could be done with an empty manufacturing plant, and joined
forces with a local wholesale company to try them out.

It was not only 'the food world' that took an interest in the new
arrival. The event was reported in national newspapers under
melodramatic headlines like 'Big Bear Crashes into New Jersey'.
Writing a few years later, M. M. Zimmerman, an inveterate commentator on and promoter of new retailing trends in America, is
recalling the birth of Big Bear as a media event, with news stories
'flashed around the country'. What interested them was this:

> [T]he barny structure with its crude interiors, fixtures
> made of rough pine lumber and its huge displays of mer-
> chandise as the center of attraction, with thousands of
> people who were swarming around them with baskets on
> their arms, content to wait on themselves.[2]

It would not be many years before this matching of 'huge'
displays and 'thousands' of people would become the banal
symmetry of 'mass' display and 'mass' consumption. For
now, the emphasis is on the novelty of both kinds of size,

even though the word 'mass' is already being used for both the things and the takers. Zimmerman stresses the necessity for 'huge mass displays' so that a number of customers can serve themselves at the same time, and he describes how Otis and Dawson went to the wholesaler 'with a plan for attracting the masses from a much wider area than was customary for people to travel for food and other necessities'.[3]

There is also the novelty of people 'content to wait on themselves'. That they should be doing it at all is one thing; that they should be *content* to be doing it is something else again. The word implies that they are already at ease with the transformation, not just putting up with it but positively enjoying it: 'As people entered, they received a market basket and were left to themselves to walk about, helping themselves to whatever attracted them.'[4] Instead of being a matter of getting through a mental or actual list of requirements, each one requested individually across the counter, household shopping became an occasion for taking anything you liked the look of, 'whatever attracted'. 'Left to themselves' dismisses the clerk as an interference.

There is a childish element in this. No limits are placed on customers' desires; they can pick up anything they see, and stay for as long as they like. The 'circus-like' scene and the name itself tend to a kind of happy infantilization for everyone. From the start, going to Big Bear was a family outing. It would involve a trip in the 'Model T' Ford, by this time a standard possession for even quite modest households; a free parking lot had been leased across the road to accommodate them. But from an economic point of view, as with the surprise that people would willingly 'wait on themselves', this was very odd behaviour. People were doing their own distribution, coming a long way (some over fifty miles) to take the goods on the last stage of their journey to the point of consumption.

So peculiar was the Big Bear phenomenon that it was dismissed by many as 'a depression set-up' that would dismantle itself when better times returned – a suggestion of transience that was reinforced by the physical provisionality of 'this crude outlet'.[5] There was this 'barny' building, with its 'rough' furniture; indeed, 'the entire layout of fixtures was of cheap construction, giving a temporary bazaar-like appearance'.[6] But five years on:

> Contrary to the prognostications of Big Bear's early demise, it not only survived but many other Big and Little Bears have appeared in many of the large Metropolitan cities throughout the country, under such fantastic names as Giant Tiger, Big Chief, King Kash, the Whale and what not. Today there are over two thousand of these Big and Little Bears operating in thirty-two states.[7]

Those big, cuddly creatures were not, alas, to remain so jolly. After the war the language of the Giant and his fellows remained, but now, whether they were personifying the supermarket itself or the GIANT size of the packet, they tended to be regarded not as harmless and funny, but as predatory.

Big Bear quickly became the stuff of legends of retailing history. Whether or not it was the first, and if so the first *what*, remains a question. The 'first supermarket' prize is sometimes disputed with the King Kullen Market in Long Island, opened in 1930 and dubbed 'The World's Greatest Price Wrecker' – whereby hangs another legend of origins. This involves, romantically, a brilliant letter ignored by the man it was sent to, and a poetic vindication.

Michael Cullen, then manager of a southern Illinois branch of Kroger's, the Cincinnati-based chain of grocery stores, had the bright idea in the 1920s of a type of store that had most of the elements of what was yet to be the supermarket: large size, low profit margins, self-service, parking lot, location away from the city centre to keep rental costs down. Being a keen and loyal employee as well as an enterprising one, he wrote it all down in a letter to the chairman of his corporation, William Albers, went in person to see him, and was turned away by his deputy. Cullen resigned on the spot and headed east to do the thing himself. He founded the King Kullen Market in 1930;

within a few years it had become a chain with fifteen branches. Cullen died in 1936. Albers, meanwhile, who had come east in late 1932, at the time of Big Bear, saw his mistake in not having taken up Cullen's offer. He too resigned from Kroger's and in 1933 founded Albers Super Markets, Inc., in Cincinnati. And despite the loss of both president and junior pioneer, the Kroger chain too was not far behind in going the supermarket way.

Ironically, it was Albers's chain that first used the expression 'super market' – two words rather than one in the American form, as it remained for many years. Zimmerman, who would know if anyone did, admits that the origin of the term is not clear; he presumes it has Hollywood associations, 'super' being a new word at the time coined by film promoters on the same lines as 'colossal' or 'stupendous'. When the supermarket was exported to Europe after the war, the word, on the whole, went too. The 'supermarket' in British English was never abbreviated, as it can be in American, to 'market'. It translated easily – in French to *supermarché*, for instance (sometimes the hyphenated *super-marché* to begin with), and in German to *Supermarkt*. Before the overweening and all-French *hypermarché* entered the arena in the 1960s, to be duly translated back and exported to America as the 'hypermarket', the *supermarché* had a sweet little sister in both France and America called the *superette*: this was the name for a small self-service convenience store.

René Uhrich, writing about France, stresses the way that the language and the practices are bound up together: 'New formulations are appearing, unfamiliar words are entering into everyday language. "*Libre-service*" [self-service] is spreading, and the "*supermarché*" is becoming the housewives' meeting place.'[8] (Curiously, '*self-service*' was adopted in French only as a name for the self-service restaurant, also known as a '*self*'.) The generational difference between the two sides of the Atlantic is also shown up in this, since Uhrich is writing thirty years after Big Bear, in 1962.

But if the words stay much the same in the transatlantic

crossing, the thing itself undergoes some important changes. Statistical definitions of the supermarket have in any case necessarily changed along with changes in the typical supermarket of the times: the 'large' store operating self-service and selling a wide range of food and other goods grows bigger and bigger with every decade. As we have seen, there is also a significant time-lag between American and European developments. But one consistent formal difference is that in America, the minimum size of a supermarket is defined primarily by turnover, whereas in Europe, where land is less readily available, it is defined by surface area.

King Kullen predates Big Bear by a couple of years, and there are other contenders for the 'first' prize, including a number of California stores that go back to the late 1920s; all tended to occupy disused factories and warehouses. But Big Bear's debatable honour of being the first can also be attributed to the national publicity that followed the launch, all those stories 'flashed around the country'.

Big Bear's wider notoriety was helped by the opposition of competing retailers in the area, who resented the low prices and managed to get it banned from advertising in the local press – as Zimmerman puts it, they brought pressure 'to bear'.[9] Supermarkets, like every retailing newcomer over the years, made allies of former enemies. Independents versus chains, or co-ops versus other chains and independents – they had all fought each other over local loyalties for years, but they could now band together against the latest upstart intruder. Big Bear responded by issuing a four-page broadsheet of its own called (what else?) *Bear Facts*.

Another reason for Big Bear's immediate newspaper fame is that one of the founders, Roy Dawson, had previously worked in advertising; and *that* fact may have something to do with the constant presence in the store of a 'performing bear', who walked about pretending to be a customer. Its photograph appeared on the front pages of the newspapers, and copy-cat Big Bears, all hiring a bear of their own, opened up rapidly as far afield as North Carolina and Ohio – in Michigan, for instance, Detroit had *eighty* supermarkets by 1936.

Ultimately, rather like the perennial question of which was the first real department store, the 'first supermarket' question fizzles out into problems of varying definition, language and perception. Not only are there competing candidates for the supermarket title, but self-service, the great supermarket innovation in retailing practice, has its own history, as we shall see in a minute, with stores that then subsequently look as if they were proto-supermarkets on a smaller scale.

In 1918 Joe Weingarten had opened something very like a supermarket in Houston, Texas; his claim to fame is that it was the first self-service store to have baskets on wheels. Actually, the term 'self-service' goes back as far as 1912, when it was already in use to describe the Alpha Beta stores in Los Angeles; the shortage of labour during the war then added to the advantages of the practice. These stores had three prescient slogans:

> Pile the goods high and sell them cheap.
> Let the buyer do the work.
> Maintain a market day atmosphere all the time.[10]

## Piggly Wiggly

There was also Piggly Wiggly, that first fantastical shopping invention of the redoubtable Clarence Saunders, born in Virginia in 1881. When the first Piggly Wiggly store opened in Memphis in 1916, roses were presented to all women with red hair. Piggly Wiggly had a self-service system whereby the shopper 'wiggled' round, up and down the short, narrow aisles; it sold only prepackaged goods that were 'pre-sold' by advertising. The customer, it was supposed, went in knowing what she wanted and was able to recognize it from the package; no clerk need intervene to make a suggestion or find an article.

At first, losses from pilfering were as much as 6 per cent, so stringent security measures were introduced of a kind that were later to become the norm in post-Big Bear supermarkets.

Unlike the conventional store arrangement, points of entry and exit were separated. There were turnstiles to get in and proto-checkouts in the form of separate tables for cashiers with room for only one person to pass through at a time. The effect of these changes was to reduce the rate of loss right down to 0.75 per cent. In the process was born the rigid difference between the inner aisles of a self-service store as a free space in which you can pick up whatever you like, and the point of exit as a 'control' where you have to pay to get out. Ironically, it's the customer who has bought nothing that is the one who appears to be in the wrong, passing the checkout furtively with nothing to declare.

By 1923 there were over two and a half thousand Piggly Wiggly stores; but that was the end. There was a fall in share prices because lots of little Piggly Wigglies had popped up that were not owned by Saunders (this species is still flourishing). Despite attempts to fight Wall Street speculators and a campaign in Memphis to persuade people to buy shares, Saunders was ousted when he refused to show his accounts. There was also criticism locally of the vast pink mansion he was building himself in the city.

But being in the red was not something to put off a man with a penchant for pink palaces and strawberry blondes. Saunders rose again with a set of stores called 'Clarence-Saunders-sole-owner-of-my-name' – until he once more went bust in 1930. After that there was Keedoozle, the first 'robotic' store, in 1945. Customers used a 'key' to unlock display cases and signal the goods they wanted. These were then dispatched along an automatic conveyor to the checkout, where they were identified by the key number. When Saunders died, in 1953, he was about to try yet another experimental venture, the 'Foodelectric' store.

Clarence Saunders's Piggly Wiggly stores were small, and in that sense they do not appear as anticipations of later supermarket forms. But in another respect they can be seen, in their very minimalism, as a sort of Platonic idea of the supermarket that never was to be. The whole apparatus of entrance, exit, shelved aisles and basket is there; and unlike the supermarkets that survived, Piggly Wiggly sold only those products – advertised packaged goods – that exactly suited the new self-service form, as though they were made for it.

'Packaged goods formalised the store because they simply *asked* to be stood in rows on shelves,' said an article in *Shelf Appeal* in 1934.[11] But the store selling only packets and cans had no future: the point of the comment is that 'the store lost its rather crude vitality and became static'. Crudeness, as we have seen, was one of the characteristics attributed to Big Bear; and throughout the following decades battles between the crude and the formal, the vital and the static, would be fought out in many different forms. Of these, the most prominent was the often class-laden opposition of 'pile it high' versus 'quality and convenience'.

Apart from their size and their restriction to packaged goods, one other feature of Piggly Wiggly that makes it stand out from later supermarkets, though in this case less obviously, is its concentration on food. Here too, Piggly Wiggly suggests an ideal blueprint form of the supermarket, from which later empirical manifestations departed. For in fact only 30 per cent of Big Bear's selling space was dedicated to food; the rest, in a large circle round the main selling area, was leased out in concessions, as regularly happens in department stores. At Big Bear you could get, for instance, automobile accessories, paints, electrical supplies, radios and hardware. You could also eat or drink at the luncheonette or soda fountain. In terms of the goods and services offered, the distinction between this and a department store hangs by a very fine thread: Big Bear did not sell clothing, whereas department stores sold clothing first of all, but everything else as well, including in many cases food.

Following the language of Zimmerman's descriptions, it could be said that Big Bear and his pals inaugurated a kind of 'rough' supermarket tradition. The principal selling point is the low price; there is no display and there are no elaborate shop fittings; self-service means, among other things, doing a job of work yourself; and there may be a 'loud', disorganized atmosphere recalling the street market or country fair. This tradition can be summarized in the 'Pile it high and sell it cheap' slogan that, even though it goes back to before the First World War, has been repeatedly reinvented or reasserted, as stores make their stand on their sense of what the 'basic' supermarket should be. In Britain, Tesco's made it their own in the 1960s when they were fighting legal restrictions on price-cutting; in the 1990s, when Tesco's had gone upmarket, the discount store Kwik-Save ran a poster campaign that claimed it for themselves, implicitly accusing Tesco's of abandoning the cause of cheapo glory and thereby losing their true supermarket identity. Similarly, as we shall see, the development of French supermarkets in the early 1960s was much influenced by an imported philosophy of *Empilez-la haut!*

## The scientific salesroom

The rough supermarket has always enjoyed pitting itself against posher alternatives, initially not other supermarkets but other kinds of store, smaller and more expensive. But the 'smooth' supermarket – making a point of its architecture and decorations, indicating its willingness to offer personal service alongside the self-service system – has its own place in the early history of self-service. This is a tale of imagined self-service futures that for the most part were never to be.

In the 1930s, Carl Dipman of the American trade journal *Progressive Grocer* wrote a series of short books – in 1931, 1935 and 1940, the last co-authored with John O'Brien – exploring the possibilities suggested by new selling methods for food, chief among them self-service. Dipman's vision consciously combines scientific organization and aesthetics, with the first dominating. In 1931 he writes: 'The old-fashioned store was to a large extent a storeroom. The dealer was a storekeeper. But the modern grocery store must be a scientific salesroom. The grocer must be a modern sales engineer.'[12] This mention of the pre-commercial 'store' is common at the time in accounts of the new developments in food shopping. It draws on what is implicitly a three-phase history, touched on in Chapter 5. First, large quantities of non-perishable foods were preserved in the large storerooms or cellars of houses – always said to belong to 'our grandparents'. Then, as houses and households became smaller, and people started living in apartments, there was no longer any room to store food long-term, and the commercial 'store' came to serve that function for the neighbourhood. The old-fashioned store thus transferred the even older domestic storeroom or cellar to the communal space; people bought what they needed as they needed it. The third stage, now, is to make the shop into something other than a general storage space for items that are regularly required; it must be seen as actively promoting new things, treating the customer not as a known person with predictable needs, but – as Dipman put it four years later – as 'a bundle of sales possibilities'.[13] This is what has to be done by an applied scientist, a 'modern sales engineer'.

Aesthetics, in Dipman's scheme, is essential, but should not involve extra work or cost: 'The grocery store today must be both pleasing to the customer – a thing of beauty – yet so constructed that work and labor are reduced to a minimum . . . The application of sight and touch, coupled with efficiency of operation, are the most important factors in the new retail salesmanship.'[14] This minimalist mode, cutting out what can be cut out, is put in economic terms, with the implication that aesthetics might otherwise come into conflict with scientific efficiency. The word 'elimination' features too – in a 'time and motion' mode, aiming at 'the elimination of steps and lost motion so that the merchandise may flow through the store with the least expense';[15] and also in a slightly sinister way, referring to the benefits to be gained from a re-arranged floor plan, which will make possible 'the elimination of an employee or two'.[16] This is the brute economic version of *Shelf Appeal*'s packaging modernism where, as we saw in Chapter 5, the minimalism of display is first of all an aesthetic, and 'elimination' is about getting rid of over-ornate Victorian designs.

Scientific salesmanship is applied in particular to women, or more precisely American women:

> The American grocery buyer is the American housewife. And the American housewife is a woman of taste and refinement – a shrewd buyer – a woman who responds to cleanliness and orderliness – and one who evaluates the niceties of her environment to a far greater extent than do most of us men who operate her grocery stores.
>
> We must look at many of our problems through the eyes of the American housewife. We must take into account her peculiarities, her whims and fancies. We must remember that her senses are keenly developed – that she loves to browse about tempting foods – that she is happiest in the grocery store that surrounds her with merchandise in which she is interested – and displays it well.[17]

The future 'bundle of sales possibilities' is certainly a mixed one; but it is unclear whether the housewife's distinctive make-up is a result of (American) nature or nurture. At any rate, she is clearly endowed with aesthetic tendencies superior to those of Newsom's post-war British housewife (see Chapter 6); and she is certainly different from 'us men', who are less aware of 'the niceties' of their surroundings. But at the same time it is evidently possible for the male grocer to look at things 'through her eyes', in effect to become her for scientific purposes. 'Whims and fancies', it should also be noticed, are attached not just to 'that perfect duck of a hat' but also to 'tempting foods'. They are well on their way to being converted into the much more technical, scientific language of the supermarket 'impulse' purchase.

In the 1935 book, elimination is again at work, this time effecting the by now familiar removal of the counter, identified as a barrier:

> The properly arranged store . . . has no unnecessary barriers. It lets women and merchandise meet.
>
> As far as possible every square inch of the eyes' range

of vision, from the top of the shelving down to the floor, wherever the customer stands, wherever she looks, should display merchandise. Yet in many stores clumsy, antiquated fixtures and contraptions occupy more of the woman's range of vision. Women are not interested in woodwork and lumber – in boards, planks and tin.[18]

Which might be Dipman's retort to the rough pine fittings of Big Bear. All the same, the suggestion that eyes do not like to look at woodwork and lumber does not entail that they would prefer their field of vision to be occupied by merchandise, let alone *entirely* occupied by merchandise. Yet this is the plan. 'Every square inch' makes the space a territory for total coverage, and the phrase also conveys an unintended sense of oppression and imprisonment: '*wherever* the customer stands, *wherever* she looks', there is absolutely no getting away from it. At the same time, the fact that women and merchandise now 'meet' seems to take over from other kinds of meeting that are now ruled out – women and sales clerks, women and other women customers – and marks the growing interchangeability of shoppers and commodities as comparable types – each in their own way a 'bundle of sales possibilities'.

Soon, the floor-to-ceiling display would become the stock-in-trade of the average supermarket, but with the emphasis changing from proportion – the total (as opposed to partial) occupation of the customer's field of vision – to sheer size. As one of the trade journals puts it in 1953, 'The first principle in successful merchandising is to show merchandise – mountains of it.'[19] The relationship between prompt and purchase has shifted so that it is no longer a matter of 'merchandise in which she is interested', with the initiative hers, but rather the irresistible size and pressure of the merchandise massively bearing down on her, whatever her interest. Where 'whims and fancies' emanated from buyers themselves, 'impulse purchases' after the war appeared as the response forced out of them by the supermarket environment. The vast display overwhelms, physically and visually.

## The homely store

Such huge displays make it even more striking that early on, although self-service was being thought of as a matter for applied science, it was not assumed that the self-service store would be on a large scale: in fact, quite the contrary. In keeping with his concern for the indulgence of sweet feminine fancies, Dipman proposes a special kind of attentiveness, in a chapter of his earliest book called 'Charm – A Quality of Growing Importance in Food Stores'.

Dipman in no way envisaged the passing away of the window: 'Your store front, to be profitable, must attract people – must make passers-by feel "this looks like a nice store for me to trade with".'[20] So desirable are windows, in fact, that the store even has pretend ones inside it too:

> Little imitation window effects with mirror backings are another particularly successful wall treatment. These help greatly to give the store the appearance of a cheery cottage kitchen – and that is an atmosphere that makes a big appeal to the beauty-loving nature of women – it is the sort of atmosphere they like to be in, to linger in.[21]

Thus the 'scientific salesroom' of 1931 was based on an aesthetic not of grand scale and streamlining, but of cosiness and warmth; the interior is even 'packaged' with fake windows to make it look like home. The store is a place 'to linger in'; food shopping, as opposed to food selling, is not viewed in terms of efficiency. For the customer, time in this store is to be taken rather than saved.

And the customer's eyes may even be enticed with images that are not of merchandise:

> A third method of adding attractiveness above the wall shelving is by several pleasing pictures. Country scenes of meadows or brooks, or pictures of children at play, are always appropriate. So are pictures such as farming scenes that relate directly to the grocery business.[22]

It is just as well that the 'grocery business' reminder is there, because otherwise the customer might forget she is in a store altogether. That is more than likely in the case of Dipman's most whimsically delightful proposal:

*Women Appreciate a Rest Corner*

Many stores can afford a small space to be used as a customers' rest corner. It should be a friendly spot – a grouping of table, comfortable, colorful chairs, and if possible a telephone, fern stand, lamp, pads and pencils, a magazine or two. This is a good spot, too, for a radio or a canary, if the store has them.[23]

Here, in some golden age of the pre-supermarket imaginary, we find tucked away a little idyll of feminine domestic comforts, lovingly detailed down to the surrealistically perfect juxtaposition of the canary and the telephone.

But if this seated comfort seems a distant retreat from the big store pushing its customers round the aisles on their feet, then it is important to see it in another context, too. For here we have a suggestion that food shopping should have the relaxed luxury of department-store shopping, where reading rooms and refreshments were available to encourage the customer to spend the whole day in the shop if she so desired. In Dipman's small grocery heaven that was never to be, there is thus an inkling of a slower direction that supermarket shopping would also take. Dipman's store is a space 'to linger in' – not just to spend long trolley-pushing hours in; it offers a space for rest and reflection. From the late 1930s, the larger American supermarkets sometimes had lounges, and crèches for children. More recently, cafés and a wider range of non-food products and services have given supermarkets some of the features of the department stores from which they were initially so sharply distinguished in tone.

In the 1930s, food shopping was only just beginning to be classed as a matter of efficiency and time-saving, with the shopping trip notionally at least considered as a task to be finished as rapidly as possible, on the analogy of a monitored industrial job. Dipman's suggestions in one way do point towards this development, in pressing for scientific planning and efficiency in the layout of the store; but for the customer they imagine food shopping under quite a different rubric from the one that would become the norm with large-scale self-service. At the beginning of the 1930s, Dipman can develop an idea of the store as a second home, with the homeliness presented in the form of smallness and intimacy. Presumably there would be conversation between customers and with assistants, though Dipman does not make a point of this. The closest approach to an interaction is another kind of looking, in the recommendation that the rest corner be 'located where customers can observe store activity, for people like to watch others at work or play'.[24]

Never again was people-watching in stores to have such an innocent appeal; after the war, as Chapter 11 describes, the eyes of surveys and surveillance were turned towards customers, now regarded more as objects of distant study or potential suspicion than as house guests. Discussions in the 1960s about whether to provide supermarkets with rest rooms or toilets worry about their advantages for shoplifters. At this time, rest rooms are once again considered 'relatively new' as an idea; and despite the pilfering problem that is mentioned as an objection, some of the features of the 1930s 'rest corner' return with the accoutrements of the modern high-tech home: 'The lounges furnished in some of the supermarkets consist of an air-conditioned room; magazines, newspapers, and in some cases television sets, are provided.'[25] (Alas, poor canary!)

### The home a store

Yet while the store is sometimes imagined as a home from home, the home can just as easily take on the appearance of a store. We have seen how the pre-supermarket local food store was regarded as having taken on what used to be a household role of providing storage space for food. But with the coming of refrigerators and later on deep freezes – as with self-service itself, much earlier in the United States than in Europe – post-war advertising images would return to the earlier picture of the home as a storehouse.

There was an important difference, though. As with the store's own transformation into a 'scientific salesroom' for active promotion, in Dipman's manifesto, now the home could appear as a supplementary space for the aesthetic display of merchandise. In advertisements, the door of the refrigerator opens enticingly on to an array of technicolor produce; freezer compartments offer you a bright selection of instant meals. It is exactly the same shift as occurs with the shop, now to be seen as not just for storing but for showing and suggesting. As in the supermarket, you have only to take your pick of a wide range of products. Here is one description from 1957:

> The consumer has taken over the problem the retailer
> used to have, of making goods available frequently
> rather than infrequently. All he has to do now is to go
> and open his refrigerator door, and there his product is.[26]

The idea of the consumer having 'taken over the retailer's problem' is a particularly frank acknowledgement that the supply of a ready choice of meals for people imagined as always in a hurry – 'all he has to do now is . . .' – in fact depends on the same people taking over new tasks of planning and labour. As we have seen, the new arrangements of self-service and home storage transfer to customers functions that were previously performed by stores: people now do their own warehousing and their own distribution, in reverse order, travelling long distances to the store in their own delivery vehicles.

But even before the characteristic 1950s American combination of self-service, car and refrigerator, a conception of the housewife as an efficient stock-keeper and store manager was already in evidence. In her book *Household Engineering* (1920), Christine Frederick recommends the keeping of storage records for canned goods. These should show sizes, prices and the quantity in stock; 'then, as a can of peas or peaches is used, it should be crossed off the list, so that at a glance the number of cans on hand of any particular product can be seen without poking around the storage and actually counting the cans'.[27] The purpose of this procedure is to make the shopping list; the housewife is the manager of her own store, exercising a regular inventory control. Records, says Frederick, are to be kept in a special 'office corner' set aside for administrative purposes – the equivalent, in reverse, of the homely 'rest corner' in the Dipman cottage store. At this point, the crossover between home and store operates in terms of common principles of scientific management or 'engineering'. Frederick's housewife is as 'scientific' in her procedures as Dipman's storekeeper – and there is no mention of any feminine whims and fancies that might distract her from the business in hand.

After the war, the managerial housewife would reappear in military guise, armed to resist what were henceforth seen as the traps and lures of a supermarket trying to prevent her from behaving rationally. The next chapters look at some of the transformations brought about when that new kind of giant creature, the post-war supermarket, appeared, and Big Bear's childish pleasures had long been put away.

Frigidaire advertisement, 1935. Reproduced courtesy of the Bibliothèque Forney.

*The empire of the supermarket*

In the 1940s, supermarkets were well on the way to being established as the dominant food-selling form in the United States. But until after the war, the rest of the world dreamt on, ruffled only by the occasional rumour brought back by foreign visitors to America such as Jack Cohen, the founder of Tesco's, who prided himself on crossing the Atlantic twice in the 1930s to have a look at this new phenomenon called self-service.

The main source of the Big Bear stories, M. M. Zimmerman – 'Zim' to his preface-writer – was both perpetual propagandist and perpetual historian of new developments in food retailing; the supermarket was his pre-war cub and his post-war giant. He founded the journal *Super Market Merchandising* in 1936 and was the leading figure behind the Super Market Institute, inaugurated by the first national convention of supermarket operators in 1937. Before that, Zimmerman had worked for the advertising journal *Printers' Ink*, writing an important series of articles on chain stores in 1914 and another in 1930, which became a book. So did the 1936 series on the new supermarkets, published in 1937 as *Super Market: Spectacular Exponent of Mass Distribution*. Coming in the same year as the Super Market Institute and *Super Market Merchandising*, this book gave supermarkets a history at precisely the moment at which they were acquiring a solid future. From then on, and to a great extent through Zimmerman's own energy and eloquence, the supermarket was an established institution.

*The Super Market: A Revolution in Distribution* followed in 1955. The new book expanded on what was now called the 'pre-history' given in the first and added a whole generation of intervening events since the landmark year of 1937. It was intended for a wide international market; already, in the Zimmerman style of retailing history-in-the-making, there was a long account of how self-service had been spreading round the world.

After the war, when numbers of European businessmen started visiting America to see self-service for themselves, Zimmerman personally took them around. He visited Europe himself in 1947, and set about organizing the first International Congress on Food Distribution in Paris in 1950, attended by no less than two thousand delegates from all over the world.

Zimmerman's passion for supermarkets as a grand Idea he wants all to share involves little reference to the dull subject of profits; that they happen, as a result of the fast turnover, high volume and low prices, is part of the magical 'everybody bene-fits' effect attributed to the new stores. But when it comes to the Overseas Division of the National Cash Register Company, which was a major influence on the post-war international expansion of supermarkets, it is hard to forget about money, even though Zimmerman valiantly refers to their 'missionary effort'. He gives a suitably 'pick 'n' mix' choice of ideological approaches to what was actually going on in the company's gen-erous assistance in the supply of tills to foreign parts: 'acting with enlightened self-interest, it served its retailing clients in far-flung places by helping them in their initiation into American Super Market know-how, thus demonstrating the democratic co-operation possible in American private enterprise'.[1] Liberalism, philanthropy, community, capitalism – all are equal and equally benign in Zimmerman's happy supermarket philosophy.

Between them, Zimmerman and the National Cash Register Co. went about spreading the gospel of self-service to the rest of the world. Today, as more and more of the globe gets taken up with the growing of products to supply western supermarkets, so the same North American and west European companies are rushing to set up the universal superstore on every continent, especially in post-communist countries. In 1955 the process was already beginning. Zimmerman proudly lists figures not only from Switzerland or Sweden (the places with the highest per capita number of self-service stores in Europe) but from countries in every other continent as well; a photograph of customers at the checkout of the one Nigerian store bears the caption 'Shoppers are the same the world over' – as though already defying the accusation that if they are, it may be the National Cash Register Co. and friends that have made them so.[2]

Yet at the same time you cannot help sensing a tinge of frustration on the author's part at what he refers to as the 'slow' or 'modest' growth of self-service in the rest of the world: 'gradually, came word of self-service units, generally small in size, being opened and meeting with moderate success'.[3] This is partly, he acknowledges, because of local drawbacks that do not apply in America: in Europe, unfortunately, 'cities are centuries old and not only overbuilt, but overcrowded'.[4]

## Consumer society

Yet however slow the encroachments or advances of supermarkets in the retailing reality of some parts of the globe, they were seen in Europe as one symbol of the golden or glittering or ghastly post-war 'consumer society'. On both sides of the Atlantic, ever-higher standards of living and ever-increasing desires for more and more goods were singled out as significant features of the period, at the time as well as in later analyses. The identical catchphrases and slogans are bandied to and fro by enthusiasts and detractors alike, with only a shift of the moral connotation: celebration on one side, disapproval on the other. This was true in different ways in America and Europe; European countries, still subject to post-war rationing or the recent memory of it, looked to America as an image, whether feared or desired, of affluence soon to come.

Whichever the emphasis, the new consumer society was regarded as an American phenomenon making its way into Europe. It was seen by both sides as taking the form of an unremitting pressure on people to consume. President Eisenhower's response in 1961 when asked what Americans could do to help the economic situation – '"Buy!" – "Buy what?" – "Anything"'[5] – is matched with all due national differences by Prime Minister Harold Macmillan's equally notorious remark in 1957: 'Our people have never had it so good.'[6] Personal consumption per se can be represented as a national virtue in this American version; while in Macmillan's pseudo-demotic accents, affluence or the promise of it has the potential to take the place of traditional class concerns.

For the French, the critique of the new consumer society as *la société de consommation* was one of the spurs to the events of May 1968. But here it is a novel, not a ministerial utterance, that occupies the equivalent position to Eisenhower's and Macmillan's dicta, in this case setting off a fervent argument. Georges Perec's *Les choses* (1965) described a young couple whose desires and opinions are formed as changing lifestyle images of the 'things' that money can and cannot buy. Guy Debord's situationist critique, *La société du spectacle* (1967), was also a catalyst.

The French story of how the supermarket arrived is as dramatic as Zimmerman's American tales of Big Bear and his subsequent offspring. In France, the preservation of local, small shops was strongly fought for, while at the same time the Americans were effectively out-Americaned by the birth of the super-supermarket, the *hypermarché*. This was in fact very like what had happened in France a century before with the advent of department stores, *les grands magasins*, which were resented for their effect on small businesses but also welcomed as a sign of imaginative progress. French commentators on the first supermarkets refer to the parallels between these two moments all the time. They ask whether retailing history is like or unlike the history of modes of production; whether it is a matter of evolution or revolution, or (with elements of both) of repetition. Just as Perec's *Les choses* was animating arguments about contemporary consumer culture, so the text that is constantly cited in making the comparison between then and now is once again a novel, Emile Zola's *Au Bonheur des Dames* (1883), which was based on the rise of the Bon Marché department store in Paris.

More literally than elsewhere, the history of French consumer culture is inseparable from its fictions.[7]

## Tales of Trujillo

After 1957, when his famous seminars began in Dayton, Ohio, one of the biggest influences on supermarket development in France and elsewhere was an extraordinary figure called Bernardo Trujillo, known at the time – if believers are to be believed – as 'the pope of modern commerce'.[8] Born in Bogota, Colombia, in 1920, Trujillo came from a wealthy family who lost their money in the 1930s. He studied law and French at Bogota, then won a scholarship to the Sorbonne in 1939, but because of the war went instead to Springfield, Ohio. There he joined the National Cash Register Company, for which he translated brochures on self-service into Spanish, and argued for the need to adapt the new retailing form to conditions in different countries. After the war he was active in promoting self-service in Japan, one of the countries from which large numbers of delegates attended his seminars later on.

It was under the auspices, once again, of the National Cash Register Company, which was based in Dayton, that Trujillo gave his fortnightly five-day seminars on marketing methods to planeload after planeload of businessmen from all over the world. By all accounts, those who sat at his feet never forgot the experience – especially if they were French. It is hardly possible to open a French book on retailing from the early 1960s without immediately lighting upon some Trujillo soundbite, coupled with a marvelling account of the way in which, despite his un-French or un-European approach to things, he still managed to hold his very French or very European audience spellbound.

In his book of 1962 on the future development of supermarkets, René Uhrich says that he will attempt in his rendering to preserve the 'American' style and spirit, although they are 'always striking, even shocking sometimes, to a French mind.

Shamelessly, you will be got to "batter" prices and "murder" small shopkeepers. It isn't Shakespeare, but it is a drama.'[9]

According to Trujillo, supermarkets have to put on a permanent show, like a fair or circus; but the actual development of supermarkets is itself a drama on a grand scale, it turns out. Uhrich ends his book in style, or at least in full costume. He cites the bard of Dayton citing Shakespeare's 'All the world's a stage', and adds for his own part that there is also a drama of commerce in which the public is taking its seats, though the script is little known in Europe:

> In this European theatre of distribution the lights are being lowered. Behind the curtain, the actors are ready. We know the actors and the play.
>
> The three strokes ring out.
>
> The curtain rises.
>
> The show begins.[10]

Whereupon Uhrich signs off with a magisterial 'Strasbourg, 26 mars 1962' and, centre-line, 'FIN' ('THE END').

But Trujillo seems to have this kind of effect on even the most disciplined or sceptical members of his audience (Uhrich's book originated in a doctoral thesis). If supermarkets are to be the greatest show on earth, they will be hard put to supersede the drama of their own previews in Dayton. In the mid-1960s, Etienne Thil wrote two books on the development of French commerce that both feature the Trujillo experience in depth:

> Each seminar begins with a shock declaration from Trujillo.
>
> 'A million shopkeepers have died for not having been able to foresee the future . . . I ask you to observe a minute of silence in their honour.' Trujillo says nothing. Are we supposed to stand up or to smile? And suddenly, pointing his index finger at the audience, Trujillo adds: 'Another minute of silence for the millions of shopkeep-

ers who are in the process of dying . . . and who don't yet know it.'[11]

In the second book, for variation, Thil gives us instead Trujillo's 'rivers of blood which each new commercial revolution causes to flow' and 'the massacre of the small routine-bound shopkeepers by the discounters'; and this time he goes on to describe the beginnings of a counter-revolutionary protest among the audience:

> This dramatic fresco of commercial history overwhelms the audience. Some listeners are on the point of revolt. To calm them down, the 'prophet of distribution' without a word uncovers a placard. We read: 'We are presenting facts, not opinions. One can disagree about opinions. One cannot disagree about the facts.'[12]

Trujillo even provided an afterword to Thil's second book; but the written word evidently does not give him such dramatic or revolutionary scope as the spoken, for the only point of interest to be gleaned from it is that American supermarkets 'have such big parking lots that even a woman can park her car there without difficulty'. Still, there's no arguing with facts.[13]

In 1962, a special supplement of the *Revue des Deux Mondes* on supermarkets and their retailing forebears presented Trujillo's key points with the usual comment about his being an acquired taste for his visitors:

> His recipes are usually elaborated in such a tone, with accompanying mime actions, as not always to inspire confidence in European businessmen, who deliberately and systematically take themselves seriously. Among them, M. Bernardo Trujillo lays the most particular stress on the following:
>
> Pile high and bust your prices.
> Create little islands of losses amid an ocean of profit.
> Put on a permanent circus.
> No more shop windows, those merchandise-coffins.

Let the consumer do the work.[14]

These 'recipes' and others form the basis of Trujillo's famous MMM – Modern Marketing Methods, also known as Move More Merchandise and *Méthodes Marchandes Modernes* (and no doubt any number of other possible M-slogans that happened to strike him on the day). Sometimes other points or other versions of these ones are included, such as: 'dramatically low prices'; the giving of credit; self-service; increasing the surface area of stores; creating out-of-town stores – 'Nowadays, in the United States, you no longer find "sites", you make them.'[15]

### Bonjour, Carrefour

We will come back to some of the specific ingredients of the Trujillo recipes in more detail later. For the moment, let us consider the customers to whom they are being served. Immediately after the end of the war, there was some French interest in the new American way of selling. A book on packaging published in 1949 has a short section entitled 'Magasins sans vendeurs', shops with no salespeople, 'also called "self-service", "auto-service" or else "libre-service"'.[16] The author gives no other definition; he mentions that there are already some of these stores in France, as well as in other countries apart from America, and he describes their importance for packaging in the context of their likely future development: 'Visitors to the first International Packaging Fair [*Salon international de l'emballage*] opened in October 1947, were able to see an installation of a shop with no salespeople, which was presented under the heading "The Store of Tomorrow". Some magazines published photographs of it.'[17]

The first self-service store in France had opened in 1948, a Gourlet-Turpin shop in rue Letort in the 18th arrondissement of Paris; and the first supermarket – distinguished from a self-service by greater surface area – in 1957, in rue Pierre-Demours in the 17th arrondissement. By 1962, there were over a hundred supermarkets, and self-service had been growing steadily and slowly throughout the 1950s.

So far, so normal: not much, and not unlike Britain at the same time, as we shall see in Chapter 11. As late as 1961, we find the journal *Entreprise* providing a special section on 'Libre-service', which by then had become the standard French term, and feeling more need to explain its principal characteristics to readers than the writer of 1949. It's a precise and cold description, without enthusiasm:

> This new sales method is characterised by the presentation, for the customer's viewing and handling, with very clear display of prices, of generally pre-packaged products. We also recommend giving the customer free access to the merchandise, free choice of articles by the consumer without intervention of sales personnel, the provision of a container to customers to put their purchases in (trolley, basket or paper bag), a specially equipped checkout (generally constituted by a cash register worked by a female operator).[18]

But then along came something that had no parallel anywhere in Europe: a kind of post-supermarket or *Über*-supermarket, bigger than the biggest, before even supermarkets had got themselves well established in France. This was the phenomenon that journalists quickly dubbed the *hypermarché*, following the opening in June 1963 of a huge new branch of a chain called Carrefour at Sainte-Geneviève-des-Bois, just outside Paris. It was as if the French had leapfrogged the middle stage of the middle-sized supermarket, jumping straight from the beginner's self-service and small supermarket and moving on to something that was even bigger and better than its own American inspiration. Outdoing any transatlantic equivalent, let alone a European one, the Ste-Geneviève store had a selling area of 2,500 square metres; and it sold things that were not found in American supermarkets, like clothes and household appliances. It also had 450 parking places: long before out-of-town sites were on the agenda in Britain, France (which does have more land, with only half Britain's population density) had already gone down this American road.

In further anticipation of developments that were to come only much later across the Channel, Carrefour also had a cafeteria and sold cut-price petrol on site. Subsequent Carrefours maintained and expanded such features, providing traditional counter-service shops against the back wall – butchers of different types, fishmonger, dry cleaner, baker and so on. For these shops within the shop, all food preparation, including bread-making, was carried out on the premises.

The first weeks of the Ste-Geneviève Carrefour were planned as a big event, with staff reinforcements flown in from the other two Carrefours and a whole apartment block rented to put them in. The store was opened with great ceremony by Françoise Sagan, author of the celebrated mid-1950s teenage novel *Bonjour, Tristesse*. Only in France, we might think, would a literary star be thought appropriate to open a supermarket; only in France, perhaps, would there *be* in the 1950s a literary star of Sagan's celebrity status. But it also just so happened that Jacques Defforey, the man in charge of the building of the new store, was married to her sister.

Trujillo, of course, had something to do with it all. The local organizers of the new Carrefour had been sent off to Dayton for the treatment; and Michel Fournier, the leading figure in the founding of Carrefour in 1959, had also passed that way. Trujillo's demand for a permanent circus finds itself echoed in the response of a hapless housewife interviewed after the opening, who is quoted as saying: 'It was a holiday celebration [*la fête*] every day.'[19] It must have been gratifying to find this early communicant coming out with the party line so readily.

Later Carrefours staged ever more dramatic openings. On the first day of the Annecy event in April 1968, 'all Savoyards were invited' to come and drink ten thousand litres of vin de Touraine, served from a marquee on the parking lot; this was followed by a two-day programme of circus events and games, hosted by a TV personality.[20]

Inevitably, perhaps, the enthusiasms it provoked meant that Carrefour was straightaway likened, as the department store had been in the previous century, to a cathedral.[21] But in general, the comparisons were lighter than this. The Carrefour-Trujillo circus atmosphere revives the 1930s spirit of Big Bear, King Kullen, and the rest. Trujillo likened the supermarket experience to the European carnival or beer festival, the idea being that shopping was an outing (and for the whole family, not just the woman or the adults). The supermarket was also regarded as a descendant of, or return to, the traditional village market, 'where goods are freely offered to eyes eager to see, to hands desiring to touch, to nostrils ready to smell, to ears open to noises'.[22]

## The death of the window

Amid all this celebration of revolutions as forward progress and revolutions as coming full circle and returning to their points of origin, we might stop to shed a tear for the death of the window. Trujillo's often-quoted definition of the shop window as a 'tomb' or 'cemetery' for merchandise was in fact, and by his own account, another throwback to the 1930s. It was none other than Michael 'King' Cullen who had first pronounced the fatal words condemning the window as an 'obstacle' to selling in the same way as the counter; its purpose, like that of the old-fashioned store that the supermarket was ceasing to be, was to conserve goods rather than to sell them. Supermarkets were thus beginning their burial of the window in the very same decade in which, as we have seen, the art of display in 'the age of packaging' was showing it a very different future. In the end, the window was to survive to some extent on the urban street and inside the mall or shopping centre; but as far as the eyeless supermarkets were concerned, with nothing to be seen from outside but a line of checkouts or the odd blaring poster advertising the week's special offers, the beautiful display window might never have existed.

## Trujillo and Leclerc

Trujillo was not, it will be clear by now, much interested in aesthetics, which he said made little difference to sales. His counter-catchphrases – straight out of Zola, though he doesn't acknowledge this one – were *désordre organisé* and *désordre calculé*: ordered, deliberate disorder, with the idea, as always, of promoting the unplanned or 'impulse' purchase by taking the customer past goods she might otherwise not have looked at.

The 'no frills' emphasis on low prices marked out Trujillo's version of supermarket philosophy as in one respect similar to that of a second flamboyant figure in the development of French food retailing at this time: Edouard Leclerc. Unlike Trujillo, Leclerc became a kind of popular hero, and certainly a household name after the 'Centres E. Leclerc' became a feature of most large French towns. If Zimmerman was a missionary and Trujillo a pope, Leclerc was a crusader; he had, in fact, received a Jesuit education and had been destined for the priesthood. Like Trujillo, he was by no means a man of the people in his origins: his father was an army officer.

Leclerc set out to put an end to the unofficial system that fixed French grocery prices high to the benefit of manufacturers, wholesalers and retailers, but not of consumers. He started a small store in the mid-1950s in his home town near Brest by buying direct from manufacturers. Credit was not given, and cardboard boxes containing the goods were placed on the shelves without the contents being separately unpacked: the self-service customer acquired yet another job. The network of Leclerc stores that followed in the next few years was not owned by him, but run by managers who shared the same ideal of keeping prices down. There was no personal profit-seeking or wish to expand; Leclerc saw his stores as local catalysts that would force competitors to bring their prices down.

Trujillo and Leclerc were united in their contempt for small shopkeepers who refused to adapt, but the reasons for the scorn were quite different in each case. To Leclerc, the shopkeepers who pontificated about the virtues of old-fashioned counter service were failing to deliver the one service he acknowledged as a valid one, namely the lowest possible price; to Trujillo, they were failing to bring themselves up to date with new selling techniques. Trujillo habitually made fun of Leclerc as l'épicier (the grocer) in his seminars; he pitted le showmanship against Leclerc's insistence that what the customer really wanted was cheapness and only cheapness. In the same vein, Trujillo favoured loss-leaders as a spur to greater profits overall – 'little islands of loss in an ocean of profit' – while Leclerc wanted prices to be low in general and spurned the use of marketing as being against the real interest of consumers, which always came down to cheapness.

In their (radical) similarities and their (radical) differences, Trujillo and Leclerc were perfectly matched to fight it out – for ever. Their battle, one more version of the opposition between the 'rough' and the 'smooth' supermarket (see Chapter 7), is a symbolic one in the hundred-year war of supermarket development. Ironically, it became for some supermarkets a matter of dissimulation: the store must appear to spend nothing on its appearance.

This was articulated quite clearly when the eleventh Carrefour opened at Créteil new town, to the south-east of Paris, in late 1968 – this one had thirty-six checkouts, fifteen hundred parking spaces and a selling area of 7,000 square metres. Its chief architect spoke in Trujillo's language of the 'show where the customers are the actors', of how 'we give them a stage which conditions them, we put them in a can whose colours, smells and sounds set all their senses going'. The customer is 'conditioned' for buying as the product is 'conditioned' or packaged for selling. The reporter comments:

> What was particularly interesting in this store is that in fact this conditioning had to happen without giving the impression of investment in the décor. On the contrary,

the store has to give external signs of non-wealth, as the customer has to be conscious of being in a discount store, and thus of benefiting from 'slashed' prices. For the customer to 'believe' in this, he must not be basking in luxury.[23]

In the moral rhetoric, if not the moral standpoint, the economy versus embellishment argument between Leclerc and Trujillo sounds distant echoes of the flaunted provision by present-day British supermarkets of very cheap, plainly packaged own-brand goods that customers can take or leave instead of the more expensive competing lines, including smarter own-brand goods. The cheapness card – low prices, manifestly no expenditure on unnecessary packaging or display – is played alongside, on the very same aisle as, the offering of quality and attractiveness. Two supermarkets for the price of one; and an argument that has all but disappeared in the sea of 'choice' as the universal medium. It is as though it were no longer necessary to fight about price versus display, access versus aesthetics or showmanship, if all these things can be presented as options that are equally and freely available in the same place – if you have the transport to get there.

Front cover image from *Which?* magazine, September 1959.

*Two-person salesmanship psychology*

'Every customer presents a minor problem of psychology.' So reads the first sentence in a British book on starting a shop of your own published in the late 1940s.[1] Its presence in such a textbook, for would-be small shopkeepers, shows how far a consciously scientific and psychological approach to selling had made its way since the beginning of salesmanship theory at the turn of the century. Placed under the heading 'Personal Relationship with the Customer', which might suggest the local picture of two people who know each other talking across the counter, the statement implies that the personal relationship should be abstracted into a formal question of 'psychology'.

Yet at the same time as the sentence moves from the individual to the general, it also moves back in the other direction. *Every* customer presents a psychological problem of their own; each one is in some sense a unique person, who will not exactly fit existing descriptions and cannot be known in advance. Psychology is not proposed as a prefabricated, unchanging system through which every case can be interpreted; instead, each in its own 'minor' way can change psychology, challenging or adding to it.

The scientific vocabulary makes every selling encounter into an experiment, which will result in the confirmation or the modification of existing hypotheses. But the shopkeeper's role as scientist is not one-sided: he is not presumed to confine his researches to observing the customer from an objective distance. Like psychoanalysis, which also began at the turn of the century, salesmanship theory is based on a two-person psychology revolving around a conversational exchange; and in both instances, emphasis is laid on the salesman or analyst not regarding himself as aloof from the prospect or patient. Instead, as we saw with Dipman's proposals for a new kind of store interior in Chapter 7, the salesman is advised to *put himself in the customer's place.*

This change of position can take a number of possible forms. In one mode, it amounts to a role-play of cross-identification. The salesman is encouraged to imagine himself in the customer's shoes – her situation in general and her situation this minute as she stands before him – in order to discover how she might feel about life in general and about the proposed purchase in particular.

A second version also requires a conscious identification, and also considers the customer's likely ideas and opinions; but this time the opinions concerned are the ones that relate directly to himself: the customer that the salesman becomes in imagination is the customer looking at him. So we have the poor salesman instructed by a 1927 textbook to examine his appearance in the mirror every morning before he departs, and 'scrutinize' every feature with the eyes of a female prospect who must not be put off her purchase by the image of the man in front of her.[2]

The third, and most common, form of the salesman's identity-swap is both territorial and psychological. He is supposed to go around other stores, comparing other kinds of display, other ways of selling. But the suggestion normally is not that he place himself as an outside observer, watching how fellow salesmen deal with their customers, but rather that he adopt the position of customer himself: 'Whenever the opportunity arises, he should visit other stores and let other clerks experiment on him, and he should analyze the feelings aroused in him by different kinds of selling methods.'[3]

In this combination of identification and separation, emotions and analysis, the salesman treats himself as a case for his own observation. On the one hand, he allows himself to experience passively the emotions of someone put in the position in which he is used to putting others; and feelings are given a place as a part of the scientific method. On the other hand, the interchangeability of the positions of customer and salesman, and the capacity to stand outside both, enable the salesman to see his job as a role, and thus to take a distance from his exchange with any individual customer. She is a case for study more than she is an impossible, or likeable, or timid woman; at the same time, like him, she is acting in accordance with the position she is presently in, that of customer. For both reasons, there is no need to *take her personally*, in other words to take either himself or her as their private selves.

## Mass marketing

For all the scientific ambience of salesmanship textbooks, the two-way, identificatory practices they recommend are very different from the versions of scientific consumer psychology that came to be familiar in the decades after the war. The first change was that the textbook presentation of consumer psychology became more formalized and technical; it was no longer for the practitioner on the job but for business studies students. The psychology is laid out as given and fixed, predictable according to certain laws; it is not suggested that it might be open to modification, whether case by case or in any other way. The second, related change was that there was now a clear demarcation between the position of researcher and that of the customers under observation. This is obviously the case for statistical and other calculations at a distance, but it also applied to what was in fact a peculiar new form of two-person engagement, the ubiquitous clipboard survey of post-war market research. Clipboard surveys either chart customers' movements without them knowing it, or present a set of questions and possible answers that are already settled and planned.

In the pre-war manuals, it is as though there was a *hesitation* about the process of selling. Nothing can ensure its outcome; the passage from the point of offering your wares to the point of the customer buying them is a sequence that may or may not proceed, and all sorts of explanations and hypotheses, mainly taking a psychological form, can be invoked as a way of understanding what goes on in the transaction between the two of you, which is primarily a *mental* transaction. There is a tentativeness about the classic four-term sequence that is supposed to constitute the successful 'drama' of selling – Attraction, Interest, Desire and Sale – not least because there *are* four separate stages and nothing ensures the progression from one to the next. The buyer starts off as though in a state of free-floating attention that, if a purchase is to ensue, must be arrested or captured and then focused. Something detachable as desire or impulse for this particular item or service must be set going; and parallel to this, something that, in view of the end that is sought, can be construed as a 'resistance', must be overcome.

We have seen how inter-war discussions of the package and the shop window, two kinds of 'silent salesman', sometimes suggested that they were more reliable in their effect on the buyer than the personal salesman with his human failings and, for that matter, human qualities. With his talk and his mere presence as a third party between what now appeared as the primary relationship – not buyer and seller but buyer and goods – the salesman is an obstacle rather than a facilitator. But what he is obstructing is a process that in the 1950s came to be seen as potentially *automatic*: it occurs when certain 'responses' to universally effective aesthetic stimuli can be set in motion. If only buyer and goods can be given the chance to 'meet' in private, without the need for words or the presence of a third, then the requisite purchase-desires will be aroused in the buyer *as though by nature*, by the sheer force of sensory attraction exerted by the product or its display.

After the war, then, the 'science' of salesmanship psychology started to appear to work, infallibly, at the same time as the dominant paradigm of selling ceased to be the two-person exchange. Salesmanship practices had become marketing 'techniques', with results supposed to be predictable in advance because based on identifiable and repeatable conditions. Customers were no longer seen individually, each imagined as passing the window or crossing the threshold of the store with her own particular personality to be 'dealt with'. They have multiplied into a 'mass', and the mass is conceived of as undifferentiated, divisible into identical units, and much the same psychologically wherever you tap it. In applications of behaviourist psychology in the 1950s, all customers are thought of as reacting in the same way to the same 'stimuli'; some things they will automatically want, and others they will find they want once their resistances – often described as the 'inhibitions' formed by their culture – have been removed.

In discussions of two-person encounters, as we have seen, the active/passive polarity is regarded as being relatively flexible – the upper hand can move about between salesman and buyer during the exchange leading up to the sale, and the salesman can imagine himself in the buyer's position. For critics, collective persuasion is perceived as inherently more insidious in its effects, less amenable to negotiation or resistance, than the one-to-one model of selling that predominates in salesmanship manuals and consumer psychology before this time. The psychology of 'mass' consumption assumes an involuntary loss of individual subjectivity, through a response that is 'mindless', as are the devices that bring it about. The 'techniques' of persuasion – 'techniques' suggesting artifice as well as efficiency – act upon a mentality that is thought of as uniform across individual manifestations, constant and predictable in its reactions. Where a mind is understood to reflect on or otherwise modify what comes its way, this is a mentality that merely reacts to prompts. It is, precisely, 'mindless', like the mechanical techniques that address it or manipulate it.

The diffusion of loudspeakers and radio in the 1930s had led to new 'mass' forms of speaking and hearing in which the voice of an unseen speaker addressed a vast collective audience, at a distance. As war approached, the power of such a voice came to be seen less as a marvel of the modern world than as dangerous and uncanny: Hitler's voice in your own home.[4] In the 1950s, the malign effectiveness of the new mass communications technologies is normally taken for granted by their critics.

It is at this point – where the mindless masses of consumers match the mindless techniques that operate upon them – that the prevailing images of 'manipulation' or 'brainwashing' derive their force; such terms were already clichés in their own time, as though in reinforcement of the automatic effects they assume. Paradoxically, American capitalism is converted into the image of its ideological opposite, as the same insidious techniques are attributed at once to the Russians and to the advertising men of Madison Avenue and beyond. Criticism of advertising during the Cold War period is directed not against its understanding of human nature but against a forceful and idiosyncratic conjunction of the illegitimate and the effective. There is no disagreement about the psychology: the critics too imagine that the techniques work, which is precisely why it is immoral to apply them.

In a talk given to fellow advertising people in 1963, Georges-Marie Tronquet makes an interesting additional point:

> Many people are scandalized by psychology being placed in the service of business in this way. Some feel anxiety at the idea that this popularization enables the 'sorcerers' apprentices' to multiply ad infinitum, just when modern techniques – radio, cinema, television – are giving them the means of acting simultaneously upon millions of minds. They state that the multiplication of those who are thus in a position to influence and guide opinion is happening to the detriment of their selection, their quality.

The ungifted crowd is not only the mass of consumers, but the newly large number of 'persuaders', as Tronquet calls them, in English, using what he curiously dubs 'the old French word dug up by Vance Packard'.[5]

## The package in the supermarket

Packaging and supermarkets went together like a car and

garage. But it wasn't exactly a marriage of equals. For one thing, their backgrounds were very different. In the 1930s, as we have seen, packaging had been linked to new possibilities for modern design aesthetics – whereas the American supermarket, though it settled down into purpose-built smoothness, had begun in a rough-and-ready way, with no thought for the art of display.

There was also a difference in what each of them took from the relationship. Self-service for food products could not have proceeded very far without packaging, which was already quite well developed as a science and practice by the time the first supermarkets appeared. Self-service depended on customers and checkout staff being able to handle goods easily and identify them; without these two conditions being met, customers' service of themselves would have been virtually impossible.

Packaging, on the other hand, could have done without the supermarket (and might have had a much happier life as a result). Supermarkets radically altered the retailing situation for which packages had to be designed, since even if some packages were still going to non-self-service outlets, the increasing dominance of supermarkets made it impossible to disregard their particular selling conditions. Tins and packets were now thought of as having to get themselves noticed among thousands of similar products, as having to make an appeal that – in the ubiquitous word of the time – would be 'instant'. And the instant appeal now took the sensory self-service psychology of the 1930s a step further, or a step lower: it implied a *simple* form of address to a simple mind that basically, underneath, worked through automatic reactions to given stimuli. Though it could have been otherwise – there is no reason why large scale and mass display had to mean bad aesthetics – the effect of supermarkets was, to begin with, to deprive packaging of the aesthetic halo that had accompanied some of its pre-war incarnations.

*The instant and the impulse*

In 'The Taste of the Age', an essay written in 1953, the American poet Randall Jarrell takes 'instant' food products as the sign of a wider cultural malaise:

> One sees in stores ordinary old-fashioned oatmeal or cocoa; and, side by side with it, another kind called Instant Cocoa, Instant Oats. Most of our literature – I use the word in its broadest sense – is Instant Literature: the words are short, easy, instantly recognizable words, the thoughts are easy, familiar, instantly recognizable thoughts, the attitudes are familiar, already-agreed-upon, instantly acceptable attitudes.[6]

The objection to Instant Literature thus involves its consumption as much as its production: no one has to think, or think twice, because it already corresponds, in a 'recognizable' way, to their ready-made opinions.

This usage of the word 'instant' entered the language specifically in the context of brand-name consumer goods and the vocabulary of package labelling; it is given separately by the *Oxford English Dictionary* as 'of a processed food that can be prepared for use immediately'. The first recorded example is from a 1912 advertisement in the American *Ladies' Home Journal*. The second is from a book published in 1915: 'I wish I had drunk less of that hog-wash that my wife calls instant coffee' – which neatly reflects the association of distasteful consumer goods with women, the wife somehow becoming identified with the hog-wash because she's dumb enough to describe it as coffee.

From these two early instances of 'instant', the *OED* jumps to the late 1950s, when it appears in an almost paradigmatic role: 'Your grand new world of jet airplanes, nylon stockings, frozen food, instant coffee and brainwashing'.[7] This heterogeneous list as a mode of characterization is itself akin to what Jarrell means by 'instant' literature. Such a list derives its rhetorical force from its own deployment of the linguistic devices of a quick-fire, instant-impact advertising slogan. The implication is that there is no time to say more, and the keyword or buzzword must serve as a snappy shorthand.

With its associations of speed, modernity, consumer abundance and technology, this 'grand new world' is not just indicated by instant words, it *is* itself a series of instant things – instant in their effects, their availability, their indifference to sequential time. Coffee and nylons are easy, artificial substitutes for the quality of the real thing. Jet planes and frozen food do without the restrictions of natural time by speeding it up in one case and suspending its slow seasons and gradual decay in the other. They make places and products immediately and eternally available. Finally, 'brainwashing' applies to the mind required to fit with instant things: a programmed, quickly fixed reactor to the stimuli that strike it at each moment.

The instant product abolishes the gap between origin and end, wish and satisfaction – abolishes time altogether, in reducing it to the infinitesimally small unit. The cessation of time is also the end of causality and connection: there is only a series of unrelated instants, with nothing carried over from one to another and always the illusion of starting over as though for the first time. Hannah Arendt characterized the consumption of modern mass culture as precisely this: using up with no residue.[8]

The instant product also has connotations of a speed and efficiency that are to function in the face of time conceived of as full, overloaded – as rush and hurry, too much to do. Avoidance of waste is the usual and acceptable criterion for efficiency in economic theories, and time is one of the quantifiable resources to which it is applied. In the transfer of this model of time as a scarce resource from production to consumption, and from the factory to the home, the consumer is placed in an equivalent position to the entrepreneur: she is addressed as someone who, in the interests of maximizing efficiency, has no time to lose. This is a development of the Christine Frederick managerial model of housekeeping discussed in Chapter 7, but with a new emphasis now on a pressure of 'shortage' and urgency associated with time.

In advertising terms, the portrayal of the housewife as over-worked and short of time is also a way of warding off the adverse associations that might be attached to the notion of an instant food as *too* labour-saving, avoiding the effort that the housewife ought to be putting into her productions. A favourite textbook example from the 1950s was the introduction of cake mixes, which were first of all marketed with all the ingredients, already mixed, in a single packet, and then in a 'just add an egg' variety – the reason for the change, supposedly, being that housewives preferred to think of themselves as supplying some necessary work and creativity to the preparation.[9]

Looked at from another angle, 'instant' also has associations with magic. The product simply *is*, with no evidence of a process of time or labour involved in getting it either into the smooth hygienic neatness of its package, or from its package into the situation of its consumption. The 'instant' product just pops up, is no sooner here than vanished, and is always potentially available, to satisfy your every random whimsical want.

This is the point at which the 'instant' product meets the 'impulse' buy in the full coincidence of their perfect psychological match. The impulse purchase became a cornerstone of everyday supermarket psychology after the war. It depended, with disarming simplicity, on an assumption that actions can be neatly divided into the planned and the unplanned. From this point of view, the ideal customer is normally thought of – though surveys at this time never tire of reopening the issue – as the one who comes in unprepared, without a list, and whose passage through the store will take her through unfamiliar or unnecessary paths where she may be attracted to products she had no intention of buying when she came in.

The impulse that prompts the picking up of the product is the exact subjective correlative of the instant object. It appears as an immediate response to the sighting of the thing whose acquisition instantly lays it once again to rest. The expression 'impulse buy' also transfers the initiative away from the purchaser, since it can refer either to the act or to the thing bought, but appears to be quite detached from the buyer herself.

The impulse buy had made its first appearance in the trade literature of the 1930s. There, its associations are in every sense light. Speaking of manufacturers' display material, a writer in the late 1930s says: 'Properly designed, it offers the dealer an incentive to place the package within easy sight and reach of the customer, saves the time of the sales clerk and incites impulse purchases.'[10] The impulse buy involves a small, cheap item you can casually add to your main purchases – there is no suggestion here of a pressure on customers to buy against their better judgement. But even so, with hindsight the impulse purchase looks like the avant-garde of self-service to come: with clerks and counters still in place, it is something you pick up yourself.

## The package in the jungle

It was not just that packages lost their looks, or that supermarkets smartened up their circus acts. Something called 'consumer society', as we saw in Chapter 8, was beginning to be identified and deplored as such, and supermarkets and packages came to stand for all that was bad in it. In the post-war decades, the pair of them, yoked together as never before, could appear as positively wicked. So, at the beginning of one of many 1960s anti-supermarket tracts, we read:

> The supermarket, glossy symbol of our affluence, is today the scene of the greatest swindle since the serpent sold Eve on the forbidden fruit . . . The villain is the grocery package, sitting mutely on the shelf like an insidious booby trap, waiting to spring its devilry on the unwary.[11]

The images are parallel: the superficial, deceptive exteriors of both supermarket and package – 'glossy', 'sitting mutely' – in each case hide the reality within, the infernal 'swindle' or 'trap'. And what a transformation has happened to our old friend the silent salesman, 'mutely' now clearly a sign of devilousness. The package does not give you something extra, whether an atmosphere or an extra sensual pleasure or, more straightforwardly, protection for its contents; quite simply, it is there for the purpose of hiding the rottenness inside. As part of the supermarket environment, it is meant to deceive; and the language has moved decisively from the aesthetic to the psychological and the moral. Packages have become 'hidden persuaders', in the title of Vance Packard's famous critique of contemporary marketing techniques in 1957.[12]

Gone are the days when Big Bear and his chummy pals cavorted with the family; all this pretence of jollity is past, and what we see now is not a menagerie but a 'jungle', with the word suggesting aggression, danger, big bears against little ones, and customers at risk rather than at play. The jungle is populated by the huge creatures evoked in the hyperbolic adjectives on the enormous packets, 'the shrill chaos of "giant," "economy," "jumbo," and "NEW."'[13] Loud and disorderly, the 'silent' salesman has now become that offensive oxymoron of the senses, a visual noise:

> Americans found themselves in a jungle of goods, which seemed to have grown up around them overnight and was filled with strident macaw voices, screaming the claims of each of them.[14]

In the predatory jungle are hunters as well as wild beasts; and in another of the ubiquitous supermarket metaphors of the time, they leave 'traps' everywhere for the 'unwary' visitor, as in the 'forbidden fruit' passage above. The giants of 'big business' are out to get you, ruthless males bent on exploiting helpless females.

### The female computer

Another contemporary villain emanates from a very different world from the jungle. Decades before the advent of barcode technology, the computer was already being mentioned in connection with supermarkets: the *Progressive Grocer* survey in the middle of the decade makes much of the current 'electronic age', in which it features prominently. In negative accounts, the computer was one image for machines that were out there with (mindless, mechanical) 'minds of their own': beyond control, a potential threat to personal autonomy through their sheer size and supposedly infinite powers. The computer fits with the post-war image of marketing techniques as impersonal, inexorable, dauntingly powerful.

It is in this context of the computer as a sign of the supermarket's insidious control that the following remarkable piece of advertising copy (for Scott Paper) appeared in *Life* magazine and various American newspapers in March 1963, under the title 'The Original Computer'. This radical new account of the female consumer was prompted by the first hearings on Senator Hart's controversial 'Truth-in-Packaging' bill, an initiative itself responding to widespread protests about deliberately misleading labelling practices:

> Somewhere in that head, among the bobbypins, the hairdo, the perfume, and the problems, there is a thing that makes calculations and decisions. This tricky little thinking center is the oldest instrument of progress in the human race; it is never satisfied with today's cut of meat or cut of skirt. Day in and day out, moment by moment over the years, this feminine computer is concerned with one thing above all others: Value . . . A strange change comes over a woman in a store. The soft glow in the eyes is replaced by a steely financial glint; the graceful walk becomes a panther's stride among the bargains. A woman in a store is a mechanism, a prowling computer. . . . At first the whole epic struggle seems no contest. On one side we have this frail creature. On the other side we have her surrounded by some twenty thousand square feet of branded canned goods, branded dry groceries, nonfoods, dairy products, and hosts of other items. In the background are the unseen masses of manufacturers try-

ing to bewitch and bedazzle her into buying. But when our girl starts down the aisle, her defenses are massive. Jungle-trained, her bargain-hunter's senses razor-sharp for the sound of a dropping price, our girl is the easy winner almost every time.[15]

The passage brilliantly inverts all the by now standard criticisms of supermarket selling techniques. The image of the prowling computer keeps but transforms the two principal metaphors used to criticize the bad supermarket and its tactics: the jungle and the machine. The woman is now all brains and aggression rather than stupidity and vulnerability. 'This frail creature' is still an animal but a predatory one. 'Her bargain-hunter's senses razor-sharp', she is both a natural, instinct-led, and also prepared for the job. She still looks like a dumb blonde, but the silly bobbypins, hair-do and the rest are just the external cover for the inner driving intelligence. 'A strange change comes over a woman in a store', just like Rupert's mother or the fazed housewife behind the trolley; but unlike the first she gets what she wants by herself, and unlike the second she is not so much bemused as ruthless: 'The soft glow in the eyes is replaced by a steely financial glint.' The manufacturers are indeed trying to seduce and overpower, 'bewitch and bedazzle' her, just like the critics say; but 'our girl' can't be beaten. Attack is the name of the game; so 'defenses' are what she provides, not pathologically but strategically.

The prowling computer was invented by the industry to counter the critics of manipulation by showing a shopper well able to cope, thus in no need of legislative protection; but ironically, it was then adopted as a positive image by the critics themselves. Jennifer Cross's *The Supermarket Trap* was published by an American university press in 1970; it is an indication of the popularity at the time of anti-supermarket texts that it sold well enough to be reissued as a mass-market paperback soon afterwards.

Cross begins by describing the supermarket as:

that bewildering, enticing, craftily packaged trap that awaits every housewife during her weekly shopping expeditions, which all too often leave her numb, fatigued, and slightly poorer than she anticipated. The contest is not an equal one, largely because most people are unaware that the trap exists, and of the competitive conditions within the food industry that sprung it, the marketing techniques that bait it so cunningly, or the waste that is one by-product of all this effort.[16]

In her dramatic language of bad magic, entrapment and deception, Cross sounds like the more popular anti-supermarket literature. But her claims tend to move from the sensational to the common-sense. The housewife goes from 'numb' – a severe condition – to just 'slightly poorer than she had anticipated', and the exotically described trap – 'bewildering, enticing, craftily packaged' – dwindles in relation to much plainer economic statements about competition and waste as a by-product. It's a see-saw style, shooting up into a wicked fairy-tale world of bewilderment, enticement and craftiness, then pushing itself back down on to the flat ground of ordinary economics.

Cross's language verges on the melodramatic, but she asserts, magnanimously, that 'If there is any villain it is the bind into which corporations are forced by the pursuit of profit.'[17] No baddies, only a bad system; and the appeal throughout is for what she calls 'balance', which turns out to mean weighting the odds in the other direction. The trap and its enticements are real, and so overpowering that they appear to be beyond resistance; but it is up to the poor shopper (and definitely, as we shall see, the housewife rather than any other individual) to see to maximum damage limitation: 'By learning the rules industry has made, we can turn them to our own advantage and make food shopping an intelligent expedition instead of a casual safari.'[18] As the 'safari' indicates, the jungle is still present in the background as the environment that has to be negotiated, with the 'prowling computer' now taken up as a positive model to imitate: 'If industry could be persuaded that the housewife really preferred to be a prowling computer, it might give in more gracefully' to demands for more informative packages.[19]

Cross's tone sometimes becomes almost dictatorial, as readers receive their instructions for the counter-campaign. First rule – no children, since they are likely to influence buying decisions as a result of what they have seen on TV: 'If possible preschoolers should be left at home, perhaps with a neighbor on a reciprocal basis, or parked in the kiddie korral.'[20] Second rule – no men: 'Husbands need more tactful handling, particularly since 41 percent of them regularly do some of the marketing, or accompany wives on evening or weekend shopping trips.'

At this point it apparently strikes Cross that it may not seem entirely obvious to readers why the presence of 41 per cent of husbands is automatically to be considered a dreadful problem. So she elaborates: 'Such trips are fun – but they can add up to 40 percent to the bill, partly because of the husband's sweet tooth, his liking for gourmet foods, his weakness for high impulse items, and also because a family in a relaxed, sociable mood tends to overspend.'[21] Obviously, such an expensive, childish creature must not be tolerated, nor the supermarket trip be allowed to deteriorate into an enjoyable occasion.

Although the field is now relatively clear, with the weak troops removed as unfit for service, the housewife has to make sensible preparations as regards her own defences. Chief among these is a list. Cross's faith in the dissuading power of this appurtenance outweighs some evidence to the contrary, most strikingly at the time from *Progressive Grocer*'s 1963–4 survey, which found that list-endowed shoppers in fact bought *more* than the others.[22] Nevertheless, Cross's shopper is enlisted with severe discipline: 'The shopper's most important countermove is to *make a shopping list and stick to it*, allowing only for the genuine (*occasional*) oversight or the unexpected bargain.' She even has her own version of the Christine Frederick domestic management plan:

You should make your own record of current food prices.

> Keep a small notebook with each week's shopping list in
> the front and a permanent alphabetical reference section
> at the back . . . Prices should be entered in pencil, and a
> pencil with an eraser top should accompany all major
> shopping trips for piecemeal revisions.[23]

With all these preparations arming her for the expedition, the
risk or the hope is perhaps that the housewife may never in
fact arrive at the point of making a single purchase. Cross has
created a time-scheme and a pattern of restraint which is the
symmetrical opposite of the one promoted by the supermarket
psychology of the period. Where Cross has fortifications, the
supermarket has 'instant' access. Where Cross's time takes the
form of a strict agenda, the supermarket's time is one discon-
nected moment after another, with nothing to limit or structure them. Against the aberration of uncontrollable impulse
purchases, Cross offers the hyper-rational madness of planning without end.

### Hidden persuaders

Two other common images for the supermarket, closely
related to the jungle, the trap and the computer, are the prison
and the labyrinth. The supermarket does not let you out, and
in it you can only get hopelessly lost. When you do find the
exit, you are stopped in your tracks and your purchases exam-
ined. You are constantly under surveillance; over and above
all, in some nebulous and unreachable elsewhere, is a 'system'
or 'them' that is in control. In the most extreme version of this
extreme version, there is no exit because all the world is a
supermarket.

This is the position fictionalized in J. M. G. Le Clézio's novel
of 1973, *Les Géants* (*The Giants*), in which the hypermarket sym-
bolizes a world of pure system, entirely covered by the seam-
less network of the electrical grid. It is Plato's cave in reverse,
not a darkness that hides the light of truth but a blaze of totally
artificial illumination. Le Clézio's novel is scattered with repro-

ductions of advertisements and allusions to *The Hidden Persuaders*, a testimony to the way in which this book had itself taken on the role of providing a universal grid through which to interpret the forces governing the contemporary world.

Packard's book was a bestseller; it was, and still is, the first reference for critics pointing to the devious operations of marketing psychology at the time, a book that almost everyone has heard of and many have read. It is not, however, an angry exposé, although it is often remembered as that. The chapter on supermarkets, 'Babes in Consumerland', gently teases researchers who solemnly spend their time calculating shoppers' eye-blink rates as much as it also infantilizes the housewife allegedly subject to aisle-induced 'trances'. Packard speaks of 'the new jungle called the supermarket', but he also describes it as 'this fairyland': if the jungle is not especially friendly, it is not menacing so much as childishly cute and unreal. When Packard describes the scene of enchantment, he is paraphrasing the findings of a motivational psychologist; and his own language – 'Some had a sort of glassy stare' – seems to hesitate, as if he doesn't quite know whether he is seeing the same thing or mocking the tone of the other observers. He seems to be saying the women really are in a trance, and so the psychologists are scientifically right in their findings but morally wrong to apply them; but his pastiche also debunks the trances and eye-blink rates as nothing more than the invention of misguided boffins who are really no threat to anyone.

The wit and readability of *The Hidden Persuaders* are no doubt part of the reason for its success; and there is, evidently, an appeal in reading about just how thoroughly we are or might be being manipulated without our knowledge. Yet given his own lack of trenchancy, it is ironic that Packard's fate cast him at both extremes of the manipulation thesis attributed to him: involuntarily, he himself became the most powerful of hidden persuaders. It was Packard's book that made its way into every level of discussion about consumer society, persuading people that formidably effective scientific conspiracies were working to control their behaviour and their choices with ever greater success.

Like Le Clézio's hypermarket, Randall Jarrell's rueful metaphor for his essay of 1959, 'A Sad Heart at the Supermarket', makes the modern world into a commercial machine, one that leaves no place for the poet. As the next chapter will explore further, literary representations of the supermarket and its uses as a metaphor for the state of the world have a particular resonance because of the way that commerce in general has often been seen as antithetical to cultural values. But the brief exhibition in this chapter of traps, prisons, circuses, jungles and other such oddities should already indicate that there is no reason for thinking that non-literary supermarkets are any less metaphorical than literary ones; and when, as with many literary supermarkets, the image is a negative one, writers' rhetorical problems are the same: the supermarket is bad, and metaphorically *so* bad – Evil, Prison, Exploitation – that it seems that there can be no possible amelioration.

JUNE, 1954

Front cover of *Talking Shop* magazine, the W. H. Smith in-house journal, June 1954.

In Ian McEwan's novel *The Child in Time* (1987), a physicist speaks of the multiplicity of models of time in her subject: 'There's a whole supermarket of theories these days. You can take your pick. They're all written up for the layman in books of the "fancy that" variety.'[1] Where once there were readers, now there are consumers; and where once there was a field, academic or agricultural, now there is a supermarket. In it, choice is false choice, all the books on the same lowered level, and all presented with the same superficial appeal, represented by the knowing use of hackneyed marketing phrases: 'take your pick'; 'the "fancy that" variety'. The supermarket combines multiplication with trivialization. More theories, more books, more readers; more choices, less distinction.

This metaphor of the academic supermarket is itself a contemporary commonplace that can pass with no special emphasis into a novel. But this is a novel which begins with a harrowing scene in a supermarket in which a child disappears at the checkout. It is against this background that the casual, metaphorical 'whole supermarket of theories' occurs – without comment from the narrator, or indeed from the physicist's interlocutor, who is the father of the lost toddler and whose life, two years after the event, remains fixed in the memory of that supermarket. The supermarket as unbearable loss; the supermarket as smooth multiplication of choices. It is left to readers to wonder if there is meant to be connection, or irony, or anything at all.

For some time, as we have seen, the supermarket has been visible as a powerful cultural image as well as a place to get the groceries or a public space. The boundary between the building and its exemplary constructs is blurred from the start, as the supermarket appears in all sorts of differently shaded guises: a place of work or diversion, of exploitation or opportunity; a place where lovers might meet or children be lost. This chapter considers a particular case of this ordinary blurring of the real and the way it is represented: the literary supermarket. This is meant to suggest three overlapping senses. The literary supermarket is the supermarket as it appears in writings about culture; the supermarket as a place of reading; and lastly – this will be the principal focus – the supermarket as it appears in literature.

## The anti-cultural supermarket

The intellectual supermarket of banal, easy choice is the latest in a fairly long history of images of the supermarket and its precursors as the antithesis of culture. Across the spectrum of critiques, Plato's myth of the cave (from Book VII of the *Republic*) is usually somewhere in the background; the supermarket's darkest hours, from this point of view, were the 1950s and 1960s. Customers are seen as being deprived of the power of critical thought, or as never having had it in the first place; they live in the half-light of deceptive images, which they take for reality, never realizing that they are being produced elsewhere; they do not imagine a world beyond the checkout. In the supermarket equivalent of the cave, the doors seductively swing round to make the illusion of a self-contained environment, and the population either drifts about in a daydream or else is chained unknowingly to a perpetual round of trolley-stacking or shelf-stacking whose logic is beyond them.

For my money, the *locus classicus* in this matter, not to say the key to all supermarket mythologies past and present, is an extraordinary footnote near the beginning of Coleridge's *Biographia Literaria* (1817), which reads as follows:

> For as to the devotees of the circulating libraries, I dare
> not compliment their pass-time, or rather kill-time, with
> the name of reading. Call it rather a sort of beggarly day-
> dreaming during which the mind of the dreamer fur-
> nishes for itself nothing but laziness and a little mawkish

sensibility; while the whole material and imagery of the doze is supplied *ab extra* by a sort of mental camera obscura manufactured at the printing office, which *pro tempore* fixes, reflects and transmits the moving phantasms of one man's delirium, so as to people the barrenness of an hundred other brains afflicted with the same trance or suspension of all common sense and all definite purpose. We should therefore transfer this species of amusement (if indeed those can be said to retire *a musis*, who were never in their company, or relaxation be attributable to those whose bows are never bent) from the genus, reading, to the comprehensive class characterized by the power of reconciling the two contrary yet co-existing propensities of human nature, namely indulgence of sloth and hatred of vacancy. In addition to novels and tales of chivalry in prose or rhyme, . . . this genus comprises as its species, gaming, swinging or swaying on a chair or gate; spitting over a bridge; smoking; snuff-taking: tête-à-tête quarrels after dinner between husband and wife; conning word by word all the advertisements of the *Daily Advertizer* in a public house on a rainy day, etc. etc. etc.[2]

In drawing a psychological distinction between active purpose and distracted relaxation, with the latter 'manufactured' or 'supplied *ab extra*', the primary commodities Coleridge targets as the source of such substitutive pleasures are books, in the form of the ephemeral literature of the circulating libraries. Questions about the psychology of reading and the psychology of mass consumption go together; Coleridge begins by distinguishing what 'the devotees of the circulating libraries' do from 'reading' in the real sense of the word. Here, the mass consumption of 'beggarly day-dreaming' and 'an hundred other brains afflicted with the same trance' is already the prototype of the 1960s image of the zombie housewife dumbly drifting round the store, succumbing to the commodity fantasies prepared for her by unseen manufacturers. In psychological terms, the circulating libraries are the first supermarkets.

We have already (in Chapter 4) encountered Sartre experiencing a sense of disorientation at the sameness of all the five-and-dime Woolworth's stores in New York. In 1932, Q. D. Leavis's *Fiction and the Reading Public*, her critique of the decline of reading quality with the coming of the mass market for print, takes us inside a British Woolworth's, the 'three-penny and sixpenny store':

> Here, while passing from counter to counter to buy cheap crockery, strings of beads, lampshades, and toffee, toys, soap, and flower-bulbs, and under the stimulus of 6d. gramophone records filling the air with 'Headin' for Hollywood' and 'Love Never Dies', the customer is beguiled into patronising literature.[3]

The literature in question is not the literature that Leavis would like to purchase or read – she mentions the new 'film books', and she would also have seen things like Rupert books selling for sixpence. The complaint is at the debasement of literature both internally, to the level of film books, and in its external relations, as a commodity: here it is mixed up with a heterogeneous assortment of items from toffee to crockery, with nothing in common except their cheapness. 'Passing from counter to counter to buy' introduces a casual customer, but one with some purpose 'to buy' this or that. By the end of the sentence, the casualness has become more like vulnerability. 'Stimulus' and 'beguiled' make this a mildly dangerous atmosphere; shopping – and reading of this kind – involves addiction or seduction. In fact, 'novel-reading is now largely a drug habit,' she says later on.[4] For Leavis, literature has become sadly muddled with a cheap mess of other things, and Woolworth's can stand for a lack of discrimination between literature and other commodities, or between proper and commercial literature.

Only a year or two later, though, Woolworth's customers really would be 'beguiled into patronising literature' in Leavis's sense. In 1935, Allen Lane launched Penguin Books at sixpence each. For Lane, the possible inclusion of books among everyday purchasable pleasures was not a source of regret but an opportunity: 'For the first time a British publisher had made a bid to brand a "line" of books at a price that made reading competitive with smoking, the movies, or a cheap magazine.'[5] Lane first made sure of securing advance orders from Woolworth's, 'who could be counted on to rate six-penn'orth of Aldous Huxley at the same valuation as six-penn'orth of soap'.[6]

By 1940, Penguins were selling a hundred thousand a week and rising; the long hours of confinement in air-raid shelters during the Blitz were increasing the demand for reading material. With the headline 'War on Penguins', *Shelf Appeal* reported that a group of major publishers – Jonathan Cape, Cassell, Chatto & Windus, Dent, Faber, Heinemann, Harrap and John Murray – had got together to market their own line of cheap books for popular outlets.[7]

In France, the growth of supermarkets coincided with an expansion in the market for cheap paperbacks. Even the tiniest *superette* should have its 'livres et disques' section for books and records, says an article of 1965 in the trade journal *Magasins*, pointing out that three and a half million Livres de Poche – the most popular brand – had been sold in outlets other than bookstores the previous year.[8] Publishers like Hachette, and other suppliers, undertook to operate the books section, with carefully chosen fast-turnover books and a sale or return policy. Because they cost less and people had more money for little luxuries, pocket-money pocket books were seen as ideal self-service sales items. Like any other rectangular package, they were displayed with covers outwards, not spines. The *Magasins* piece pointed out that many people did not have the time or the inclination to go into designated bookstores, so that supermarket book sales were less an alternative than an addition to the total.

But while serious books could sometimes be cheap commodities, the separation between literature and the mass market intensified in some forms of cultural criticism. In Randall Jarrell's 'A Sad Heart at the Supermarket' (1959), the supermarket stood for a madly excessive and meaningless consumption that had all but obliterated the cultural places for serious writing and reading. By this time, the negative Woolworth's image had evolved along with Big Bear's supermarket descendants; and the antithesis between culture and the supermarket was enough of a cliché to be open to parodic reinforcement in the form of a sublime literalization and reversal. Here is the literary critic Leslie Fiedler, concluding his conspectus of American cultural prospects in 1964, which bore the doom-laden title *Waiting for the End*:

> For a long time the index of literacy has crept inexorably upward, the paperbacks in supermarkets have proliferated until there is scarcely room for bread and milk; and the boards of directors of large corporations have invited intellectuals to lecture their junior executives on Dostoevski and Kierkegaard and Freud.[9]

Well, perhaps. But this deliciously daft and desperate fantasy of food for thought displacing ordinary staples on the shelves should not mask a minor historical fact. For in the history of shop design, it is bookshops, strangely enough, that were the precursors of supermarkets. They, alone of all types of shop, made use of shelves that were not behind counters, with the goods arranged for casual browsing and for what was not yet called self-service. Also, when brand-name goods and their accompanying packages were non-existent or rare in the sale of food, books had covers that were designed at once to protect the contents and to entice the purchaser; they were proprietary products with identifiable authors and new titles – not just any novel, but the latest by such-and-such a writer. And in recent years, bookstores like Borders in the United States or Waterstone's and Dillon's in Britain, following the FNAC in France, have been taking a leaf or two out of the supermarkets' trade manuals: piling high their volumes and thereby defying the conventional wisdom according to which this particular commodity should be sold in ways that have nothing in common with the display techniques associated with other goods.

The peculiar history of the relations between book-selling and food-selling, and between readers and eaters, took a further turn in Britain with the ending, in 1996, of the long-standing Net Book Agreement protecting the price for the retail sale of books. The papers were full of speculations, soon forgotten, that within a few weeks the Asda supermarket chain would be putting up special end-of-aisle displays of discounted Booker Prize finalists. It was only a matter of waiting for the happy fulfilment of Fiedler's prophecy, with perhaps the smell of freshly printed paper wafting out over the aisles to add a distinctive 1990s touch.

Reading could even be presented as the reward for economical supermarket shopping. In 1999, a poster for Ed l'épicier, a descendant of Leclerc's discount stores, showed a classic image of a young woman reading in front of a window. 'It's good,' says the slogan, 'when I leave here I have money left to buy nourishment for my mind.'

## Reading in the supermarket

In a more practical sense, supermarkets have always been, in one respect, a place of reading: the marked prices and the labels on the packages take the place of the verbal exchange with the sales clerk. In the early 1960s, when self-service first became part of the social landscape in Britain, W. G. McLelland, the head of a chain of stores in the north-east, confidently linked its success to 'the increasing importance of the written word amongst an educated population'.[10] Less talk, more print; a customer who, instead of engaging in conversation with store assistants or her peers, becomes a solitary, silent reader of innumerable printed texts on packages offered for her perusal.

The sensible, undramatic tone of McLelland's account matches its picture of plain, informative supermarket literature. With these positive 'uses of literacy', McLelland implicitly answers Richard Hoggart's regret for the displacement of local oral cultures, like the corner-shop chat, by mass-produced American-style images such as movies and cartoons.[11] From one point of view, the supermarket provided further evidence to support Hoggart's fears: it was another post-war American import, and embodied the kind of insistent selling that was by now associated with television advertising, which started in 1955. But in McLelland's representation, people are not fooled by the images; on the contrary, they exercise their intelligence through the written word. Indeed, all this talk of manipulation is exaggerated, because we can rest assured that 'the common man and his wife quickly build up some resistance to gimmicks and over-slick advertising'.[12]

## The supermarket in literature

Supermarkets can be regarded as places for reading, of packages and lists, while their open shelves resemble the layout of the bookshop. But what happens when supermarkets themselves appear in literature? In fact, they seem to have done so with extraordinary infrequency, given their prominence in daily life and in cultural metaphor for nearly half the century. There is no supermarket classic to compare with what Zola's *Au Bonheur des Dames* did for the department store in 1883.

John Updike's short story 'A & P' (1960) makes the supermarket a scene of moral claustrophobia. Three girls turn up in 'bathing suits', to the different amazements of female customers and male staff. When a manager ventures to tell them off – 'Girls, this isn't the beach' – the checkout clerk walks out into an uncertain freedom: 'my stomach kind of fell as I felt how hard the world was going to be to me hereafter'.[13]

A crucial section of Christine Angot's autobiographical *L'inceste* (1999) takes place in a Codec supermarket in Nancy after the end of the author's sexual relationship with her father. Invited by him to charge the groceries to the family account, Angot is wrongly denounced at the checkout by the woman behind, who does not know of this daughter's existence. She pushes through anyway with the goods; this transgression is like a banal echo of the one that took place between her and her father.

Supermarket beginnings, as in *The Child in Time*, are not uncommon. Adam Mars-Jones's *The Waters of Thirst* starts at the checkout with 'a funeral procession of groceries'. Anne Tyler's *Ladder of Years* (1995) has a wonderful play on the supermarket's curious combination of anonymity and co-shopping intimacy. A woman is accosted by a recently separated husband and asked to pretend to be with him while he shops; the performance is meant for his wife and her new man, sighted in another part of the store.

Still, it's a surprisingly sparsely stacked aisle of literary supermarkets from which I have chosen three novels and a poem to look at in more detail here. The four texts offer very different supermarkets, and equally divergent pictures of the consumerly condition. Two of the novels, Ira Levin's *The Stepford Wives* and Joanna Trollope's *The Rector's Wife*, would not be out of place in the paperback section of the stores that they contain, whereas Don DeLillo's *White Noise* and Allen Ginsberg's 'A Supermarket in California' have more pretensions to a longer literary shelf-life. This division is intriguingly repeated in relation to the sexes. In DeLillo's and Ginsberg's literary supermarkets, the significant actors are men. Levin's and Trollope's novels, on the other hand, are feminist fantasies with female stars; but the supermarket's role is very different in each of them.

### 'A Supermarket in California'

In Allen Ginsberg's mid-1950s poem, the speaker, 'in my hungry fatigue', sad and gay heart, goes 'shopping for images' in the aisles full of bright fruit and happy families. He cruises through a homoerotically literary emporium, spotting the playwright Lorca 'down by the watermelons', and Walt Whitman, 'poking among the meats in the refrigerator and eyeing the grocery boys':

I wandered in and out of the brilliant stacks of cans
following you, and followed in my imagination by the
store detective.

We strode down the open corridors together in our
solitary fancy tasting artichokes, possessing every frozen
delicacy, and never passing the cashier.[14]

Ginsberg's poem comes from the same period as Randall Jarrell's laments for the fate of literature in the sad supermarket of
contemporary American culture (see Chapter 9). But something more suggestive than a deadening, anti-literary supermarket is being activated here, as though this impulse poem
from *Howl* could remake the figure of the poetic *flâneur* in the
fantasy of a deviant shopper.

Yet in both his wandering images – of following or being followed, and of having it all and encountering no barrier – Ginsberg in fact neatly captures or falls in with what are themselves
already well-worn paths in the annals of supermarket psychology, if not of supermarket poetry. In the first case, following
recalls the surveillance not only by detectives but also by the
assigned surveyors mapping shoppers' movements around a
store. In the second, the 'solitary fancy' suggests what self-
service is deliberately designed to foster. It is the model
customer as well as the transgressive one who drifts about taking all the things that take her fancy; until the arrival at the
checkout, the store is like a fantasy space where you really can
pick up anything you like, letting the trolley pile high with
whatever happens to find its way in, with no obligation to purchase.

Ginsberg's speaker parodies these perverse norms of
deviance and surveillance, some of whose official versions will
appear in more detail in the last two chapters. But in Ira Levin's
*The Stepford Wives* (1972), which draws on 1960s arguments
about the manipulation of women as domestic consumers,
there is no escape from (or humour in) the madness of supermarket sanity.

## The Stepford Wives

Joanna and her husband and children have just moved from the city to a small town called Stepford. The novel opens with the regulation visit from the Welcome Wagon lady, come to dispense coupons and free samples from local supermarkets – just an ordinary scene of community integration. But our heroine soon comes to think that there is something suspiciously flawless about the town of Stepford, where all the women seem to be indistinguishable from the housewives in TV commercials. They spend their time shopping in the supermarket and cleaning the house, they have the bodies and the make-up of models, and their conversation is limited to friendly recommendations of brand-name goods. The husbands, meanwhile, appear equally unusual, spending their evenings at a Men's Club from which strange chemical smells emanate in the depths of the night.

Joanna makes friends with the only women in the town who seem willing to do anything other than housework and shopping; like her, they are recent arrivals. Then the one who has been there longest suddenly becomes like all the rest, after a weekend alone with her husband. The other two begin to wonder about the peculiar skills and interests of some of the men in the club, including one who used to work at Disneyland.

The first black family in the neighbourhood moves in, and Joanna begins to make friends with the wife, Ruth, while she and Bobbie, the remaining friend, become increasingly desperate as they see their time running out. Bobbie is on the point of actually leaving when she too disappears for a weekend and returns transformed into a vision of domestic docility. Joanna panics; there is a visit to a therapist followed by a visit to the library, where old newspapers reveal that the Disneyland man used to make the life-size, walking, talking figures of presidents. She confronts her husband with her discovery; there is an attempted escape and an equivocal dénouement in Bobbie's house, where Joanna is about to witness a demonstration knife-cut to prove that her sometime friend Bobbie is flesh and blood after all. She suddenly sees that the big kitchen knife is meant for her as the first stage in her transformation, at which point the narrative cuts to a final scene in which Ruth, who has implicitly taken over the role of surviving real woman in Stepford, is pushing her trolley round the supermarket and wondering, just as Joanna herself did a hundred pages ago, at the meticulous order and neatness of all the women and their trolleys, including a now immaculate Joanna. The book stops there, in the supermarket, with the unstated expectation that the serial murder makeovers will continue.

The text is studded with references to prominent feminists and the women's movement. There is an epigraph from Simone de Beauvoir; Kate Millett and Gloria Steinem are mentioned by name. Joanna's suspicions of present-day Stepford are initially fuelled by her discovery of an old newspaper cutting in her basement describing the visit of Betty Friedan to the local branch of a feminist organization. And it is her type of feminism that comes to stand for the novel's bedrock of normality and reasonable thinking, for men as well as for women. As in Friedan's book *The Feminine Mystique*, the novel's version of a natural woman is one not too bothered about keeping house, who combines motherhood with a creative career. Ruth writes children's books; Joanna is a 'semi-professional' photographer; frequent visits are made to the library as opposed to the supermarket.

On the other hand, the Stepford wives embody in perfect caricature the kind of femininity that was the object of Friedan's critique. Published in 1963, her book begins with the identification of 'the problem with no name', the dissatisfactions she had sensed among suburban housewives.[15] Most of what follows is an attempt to track down the cultural culprits – advertising, magazines, psychoanalysis, educational policy – in what Friedan regards as a general conspiracy to make feminine homemakers out of would-be feminists, to make women in an image that will never make them wholly happy, and to which, she argues, they will never be able to confine themselves completely in any case. The book has elements of the detective novel – who did it? – while it remains undecided as to whether the men and their institutions were definitely behind it, or whether – since she wants to hold on to a notion of individual responsibility – the women are in some sense complicit in their own imprisonment.

Levin's book amounts to a novelistic vindication of Friedan's already novelistic plot. In *The Stepford Wives*, there are women who seem to have no 'problem', to be happy living out the cultural image of femininity, but lo and behold, they aren't real, they are robots! Men really did make them for their own convenience, so as not to be troubled by feminism! The women are naturally feminist, as they are in Friedan's book, and the men had them swapped for docile dolls.

Many of Friedan's themes reappear in Levin's novel, often in hyperbole. Friedan elaborates an eccentric history of feminism. Before the war, the major battles were won, but now women have re-enslaved themselves and feminism survives only as a term of abuse. Levin has his feminist heroine digging among the newspaper archives to find that, not long ago, the women who now spend their days between the kitchen and the supermarket were active members of feminist organizations. As in Friedan, an erstwhile thriving political movement has been mysteriously blotted out, overwhelmed by the renewed demands on women to be full-time wives and mothers.

Advertising, personified as 'the men of Madison Avenue', is one of Friedan's primary suspects for women's brainwashing. Television advertisements are the model for Levin's zombie women, and this is the first clue to their being actual robots. Lest it escape us, the point is underlined via Joanna's reflections: 'That's what they *all* were, all the Stepford wives: actresses in commercials, pleased with detergents and floor wax, with cleansers, shampoos, and deodorants. Pretty actresses, big in the bosom but small in the talent, playing suburban housewives unconvincingly, too nicey-nicey to be real.'[16]

Friedan also turns her accusations against psychoanalysis. In *The Stepford Wives*, a therapist interprets Joanna's suspicions as a personal conflict between old and new conventions of female identity, the housewife and the professional; but the novel validates the feminist fears as reality. Friedan derides the mutation of sex into what she calls 'pseudo-sex', as practised by teenagers, male homosexuals, and bored adulterous house-wives; it is distinguished from real sex by its strong component of 'fantasy'. Levin makes an equally straight demarcation. We know there is something funny about Stepford when we hear about the rubber gear that the husband of one not yet subdued wife likes her to wear, but the really telling sign is that after her husband's first visit to the Men's Club, Joanna wakes up to find that 'He had been – masturbating?' (p. 26).

This is about as close as the novel gets to an explanation of why the men want the women to be robots. And indeed the masculine side of the novel's psychology is peculiarly enig-matic in this would-be feminist novel written by a man. When they first arrive in Stepford, both Joanna's and Bobbie's hus-bands are carefully shown to be sympathetic to their wives' impatience with the old-fashioned ways of the exclusive Men's Club. The women's metamorphosis into angels of housework is accounted for by the sufficient fact that they have been mur-dered and rebuilt; but the husbands' metamorphosis into men who are part of the male conspiracy is not explained at all. Nobody, apparently, knocks their brains out; their transforma-tion occurs as though spontaneously.

So it turns out that the novel might carry an underlying mes-sage about men and women and reality and fantasy that is rather different from its overt one. In the same way that the perfect feminine woman is nothing but a figment of fantasy, so is the feminist man. Take away the female tyranny that makes men into feminists too, and the men will revert to misogynist type. Scratch a male feminist sympathizer, and you get the red blood of a brute straight out of a horror movie (which the novel duly became). In The Stepford Wives, the women who conform to the stereotype are man-made, but the men acting out the equivalent stereotype of maleness are real.

Yet the fantasy satisfied by the novel may be one that can be shared by feminists of both sexes. It is the idea that the happy homemaking woman is quite literally mindless, a zombie or a robot. The particular configuration of this period brings together the sexy body and the full-time shopper and cleaner as all-in-one image of femininity to be repudiated by the feminist woman as impossible and unreal.

Still, the tussle over real womanhood in the novel is strictly confined to the youngish, educated middle class; in this category alone does the division between zombies and real women take place. Working-class women make an occasional appearance as full-time or temporary maids, and so does a scattered population of walk-on older widows or spinsters, such as the librarian weirdly named Miss Austrian. These women are clearly not candidates for the robot treatment.

The exceptional category, after age and class, is race, as the novel takes pains to make it clear that a black victim, Ruth, is acceptable, just as a black family can nowadays move into Stepford. But the deliberate emphasis on racial inclusiveness only highlights the other variables that are continuing to function as usual in the conflict over real versus fake, living or dead women. Leaving aside the nasty men, Levin's world of attractive, middle-class women is not, after all, so different from that of the TV commercials of the time.

## The Rector's Wife

In Joanna Trollope's novel of 1991, the supermarket has come a long way – to England, for instance, where life for women seems a lot more promising than it did in Levin's novel. Nice Anna Bouverie is untidy, educated and erstwhile urban, just like a new Stepford wife. But far from being the death of her, the supermarket is the scene for this heroine's first step out into a world of independence. As a rural clergy wife in early middle age, married to a failure and resentful of her parish obligations, she is all set to plunge into a liberation of love and work, marked by the adoring attentions of conveniently eligible men, and a part-time job at the supermarket in the local town. Anna's confidence grows as she resists the crude attentions of suitor no.1, a rich businessman who has just bought the beautiful old rectory next door to the 1960s box where she and her husband live, and as she falls in love with suitor no.2, the glamorous don who is spending a few months living with his brother, the new archdeacon. When Anna's emotionally dead husband is conveniently killed in a car accident, some readers may begin to suspect that this is *Middlemarch* racily rewritten for the 1990s, as Anna is now free to leave her parochial prison and establish a life on her own terms with the romantic Will Ladislaw figure.

In *The Rector's Wife*, the men are not misogynist conspirators so much as ineffectual, at various points on a continuum that runs from helplessness at one end to aggressive assertiveness at the other – with a large warm area left for sensitivity, Christian and non-Christian, in the middle. They appear individually to be in various kinds of subservience to female attractions and demands. The real male problem, though, is identified as being the church, which works to keep women in their domestic, ancillary places.

In contrast to the church, the supermarket is given the role of benignly enabling institution. At Pricewells, Anna's good work on £3.21 an hour is rewarded almost instantly by the offer of management training. The Stepford world in which brand-name goods and advertising symbolize women's subordination to men has been turned upside down. Here, the supermarket is the place for satisfying work, as opposed to unpaid domestic labours; obscurely named goods, though not especially objects of desire in themselves, are a means of liberation, not exploitation, through the joys of shelving.

Yet Anna's role in the supermarket is in fact almost a hyperbolic replica of her situation as the rector's wife. Instead of the unspoken agreement that she should be always available to answer callers and engage in various forms of unpaid, semiskilled work, now she wears a badge that says: 'I'm Anna. Can I help you?' The difference between the two situations seems to be constituted firstly by money – now she is paid for her work – and secondly by sex. For this new version of availability to all-comers coincides with her new place as an object of interest to no less than three men, the suitors and the husband. One of the more peculiar features of Pricewells as a supermarket is that virtually the only customers shown to set foot in it are men desperately seeking Anna, who then comes to seem like the store's unique attraction.

Right from the start of her job in the supermarket, it seems that Anna cannot get enough of it. She demurs when told it is time for the ten-minute coffee break – 'I'll just finish the teriyaki sauces'[17] – and muses on her second day: '"It's only the beginning, this arranging of soy sauce, it's only a start. I wonder," she said to herself with a sudden lurch of the heart, "I wonder if I'm embarking on something I shall not be able to stop?"' (p. 71). But with proper feminist good sense, she doesn't immediately agree to marry the man she has swept off his resolutely unattached feet; instead, she keeps him waiting while she sets up home with her children and takes a full-time teaching job. Anna makes her choices and settles for independent domesticity, a sexier man than her husband, and a good job that suits her education and class. The supermarket has served its purpose as a thrilling interlude.

## White Noise

In Don DeLillo's *White Noise* (1985), the supermarket is everywhere. It is the scene for every kind of activity from sexual play to philosophy to shopping, all of them happily contiguous and overlapping; it is something between symbol and actualization of a host of ancient, modern and postmodern states: love, desire, death, life, and the difficulty sometimes of distinguishing between them.

The novel is narrated by Jack Gladney, who teaches in a

prestigious small-town American university. Jack and his wife Babette have four children living with them, who slip in and out of the narrative, as do other children of one or other of them who are not part of the present household. Despite the recent formation of the family – none of the four is the child of both parents – they worry about which of them is going to die first, as though death alone might part them, and as though the death of the other is the only source of fear.

Into this group, as a kind of participant-observer who joins in the shopping and sits taking notes while the kids watch TV, there enters Murray Jay Siskind, a visiting professor. Murray's discussions with Jack and with fellow teachers of American popular culture, a medley of theories and trivia quizzes, are barely distinguishable from those between the children, whose dialogues flip about, with greater or lesser degrees of apparent connection, from one verbal or factual soundbite to another. 'The family is the cradle of the world's misinformation,'[18] says the narrator, pseudo-authoritatively; and the book is partly concerned with the impossibility, in a world of multiple media, multiple theories, multiple families, of maintaining any kind of workable distinction between misinformation and anything that might positively count as its opposite, let alone as truth. Reality here is nothing more or less than the 'whole supermarket of theories' of McEwan's novel, and as we shall see, death is part of it as well.

Amid these confusions, the supermarket occupies a double position. It is a relatively stable site in the narrative – like the home, it is a place in which the major characters congregate – and it is a characteristically unstable, malleable theme for interpretation in the men's intellectual discussions. Jack's representations of it fluctuate between identification and cynicism. Like its own equivocal commodities, the supermarket is a matter of entirely artificial contructions; and it is also, without contradiction, a matter of life and death.

Plots of various kinds, novelistic or conspiratorial, are constantly invoked. In a parodic thriller climax, Jack, prompted by a kind of 'tempter' speech from Murray, goes in search of a for-lorn motel. He means to murder a man he thinks slept with Babette; the man had been supplying her with top-secret pills for countering the fear of death. The status of these pills – as real or fictitious, effective or not – is itself one of the minor pseudo-plots of the novel. But the whole narrative is seasoned with hints and incidents pointing at the indistinguishability of truth from false information, or real from simulated events, in a world whose 'white noise' of media announcements and expert scientific languages seems to leave no space – linguistic, psychological or familial – that might be clearly differentiated from it.

The supermarket is the nearest thing in *White Noise* to a com-munity space. Far from being impersonal, it is regularly the occasion of encounters between friends. It is a kind of public forum, where serious discussions may take place, and where people seem automatically to go in times of need or crisis. It is in the supermarket that Murray tells Jack that he has just heard that a colleague has died: 'Lost in the surf off Malibu . . . I found out an hour ago. Came right here' (p. 168). The glorious non-sequitur, or unexplained sequitur, of 'Came right here' purports to take it for granted that the supermarket is the nat-ural place to share or react to the news of death.

Shopping does not seem to be marked as a female activity. Rather than Babette, it is Murray and Jack who visit the super-market most. For them, the supermarket has become the post-modern scene of philosophy: Plato's academy, not Plato's cave. On a long walk together through the campus and the town, the two men drift into it as a natural continuation of their outdoor stroll. It is where, with more or less irony, they expound their theories of life, death and shopping.

In an early scene, Murray is holding forth in the aisles to Babette about the supermarket as a place of spiritual renewal, going into details about the technological perfection of the sealed-off supermarket interior, and comparing it to Tibetan rites of dying and rebirth. Jack, who as narrator reports the whole speech, is also an eavesdropper on Murray as a seducer; in what appears to be a traditional scenario, the woman is on the receiving end of the lecture, but does not speak herself. If the knowledge of the mysteries of life and death is now to be found in shopping, it is the men who parade it.

Various theories and observations about the supermarket are entertained as Murray, Jack and the children pass through the aisles. Jack's reflections circulate between interpretation of and identification with the marketing techniques of the store. In this passage, he moves away with his daughter:

> Steffie took my hand and we walked past the fruit bins, an area that extended about forty-five yards along one wall. The bins were arranged diagonally and backed by mirrors that people accidentally punched when reaching for fruit in the upper rows. A voice on the loudspeaker said: 'Kleenex Softique, your truck's blocking the entrance.' Apples and lemons tumbled in twos and threes to the floor when someone took a fruit from certain places in the stacked array. There were six kinds of apples, there were exotic melons in several pastels. Everything seemed to be in season, sprayed, burnished, bright. People tore filmy bags off racks and tried to figure out which end opened. I realized the place was awash in noise. The toneless systems, the jangle and skid of carts, the loudspeaker and coffee-making machines, the cries of children. And over it all, or under it all, a dull and unlocatable roar, as of some form of swarming life just outside the range of human apprehension. (p. 36)

The passage begins with facts – the precise length of the wall, the arrangement of mirrors – and then changes direction with a complaint about the placing of the mirrors, to be echoed further on with the mention of practical difficulties with another vision-enhancing material, 'filmy' plastic bags. The loudspeaker intervention may or may not interrupt Jack's thoughts – it simply hangs there in the middle of them, recorded but uninterpreted, despite its incongruity: naming a brand as usual, but seeming to address the commodity itself rather than its potential customers. In this supermarket stream of consciousness, or unconsciousness, it is impossible to tell what place the announcement has or what difference it makes to the direction of his thoughts.

After this, Jack's musings change gear, becoming almost lyrical with their jingly poetic devices of alliteration, repetition, and conscious rhythm: 'tumbled in twos and threes'; 'There were . . . there were'; 'seemed . . . season, sprayed, burnished, bright'. The last sentences move to an almost transcendental plane, 'over it all, or under it all', gesturing unknowingly, as at many other moments in the novel, towards what might or might not be some deeper or higher human or non-human elsewhere, concealed or invented or both by the bits and pieces of modern machines and their sounds.

This 'roar' beyond the white noise is maybe more than human, maybe just a machine gone wrong. Triviality and tragedy can't be separated. In the closing scene, chaos comes again when . . . the supermarket layout is rearranged. A liturgical voice intones:

> In the altered shelves, the ambient roar, in the plain and
> heartless fact of their decline, they try to work their way
> through confusion. But in the end it doesn't matter what
> they see or think they see. The terminals are equipped
> with holographic scanners, which decode the binary
> secret of every item, infallibly. This is the language of
> waves and radiation, or how the dead speak to the living.
> And this is where we wait together, regardless of age,
> our carts stocked with brightly colored goods. (p. 326)

Limbo as a checkout, the checkout as limbo: there is bathos and parody from the mix, and there is also a serious reflection on modern conditions of experience.

But in another sense, the supermarket is a Garden of Eden, and Jack can look nostalgically upon three-year-old Wilder's interest in its multifarious colours and shapes as an enjoyment of 'fleeting gratifications' that maintains, as yet, or in the eyes of a parent, a kind of innocence. In this, the child is fresher, more natural, than the modern fruit of Paradise:

> I took Wilder along the fruit bins. The fruit was gleaming and wet, hard-edged. There was a self-conscious quality about it. It looked carefully observed, like four-color fruit in a guide to photography. We veered right at the plastic jugs of spring water and headed for the checkout. I liked being with Wilder. The world was a series of fleeting gratifications. He took what he could, then immediately forgot it in the rush of a subsequent pleasure. It was this forgetfulness I envied and admired. (p.170)

The fruit is posed, prepared as a conscious display; far from deceiving or tempting or offering itself, as when it merged into its own mirror image in the other passage, here it is seen by Jack as though on a page in a book, isolated not merely as an image, but as a representative image of an image, how to photograph fruit. It looks looked at, 'carefully observed'; it has the self-consciousness of the adult that can then make Wilder's world the picture of a lost innocence, the source of envy and admiration, spring water not yet seen through plastic.

The passage is also in some respects a loving, cynical, nostalgic rewriting of Ginsberg's poem of 'shopping for images'. Here, all the pleasures are manifestly normal, the very ones that the supermarket means to offer its customers. It is the fruit, not the grocery boys, that is for eyeing up; it is the toddler, not the man, who enjoys 'fleeting gratifications'; and the 'whole families shopping' that Ginsberg's poem views at an ironic distance are here centre-stage.

In *White Noise*, the narrator is not on the margins of the scene; he invokes no critical or subversive place. He describes himself and his family in the role of ordinary consumers, which means speaking as someone both aware of and formed by the psychological solicitations of this strange modern space. So he examines the fruit in one aspect of its presentation as a commodity; his own experience of the supermarket takes the form of a series of interpretations, most of them in the styles of marketing aesthetics and psychology. There is no difference, for Jack, between identification and resistance, or between enjoyment and critique. Like the supermarket's own multiplication of lines, he seems to be energized by, to survive on, the proliferation of theories about what the supermarket is.

Jack moves on after the fruit bins to another completely different representation, in which he erects the supermarket into a symbol of urban stability and progress, in contrast to the decay and disrepair of the buildings and streets around it: 'But the supermarket did not change, except for the better. It was well-stocked, musical and bright. This was the key, it seemed to us. Everything was fine, would continue to be fine, would eventually get even better as long as the supermarket did not slip' (p. 170).

The level of detachment or irony in Jack's resoundingly positive commentary here is impossible to measure, as he unwittingly or wittily repeats the language of 1950s marketing triumphalism. Perhaps the funniest illustration of the 'better and better' mode comes at the beginning of this same shopping trip, when Jack informs us: 'There were two new developments in the supermarket, a butcher's corner and a bakery, and the oven aroma of bread and cake combined with the sight of a bloodstained man pounding at strips of living veal was pretty exciting for us all' (p. 167). This deadpan extravaganza, the blandness of 'two new developments' immediately fleshing out into an image of primitive butchery as a bit of fun for all the family, mocks the hyperbole of advertising imagery, but at the same time it does not deny reality or validity to the pleasure it promises. Perhaps this double reading of the modern supermarket is one way of living with it.

## 11  The Shopper in the Survey

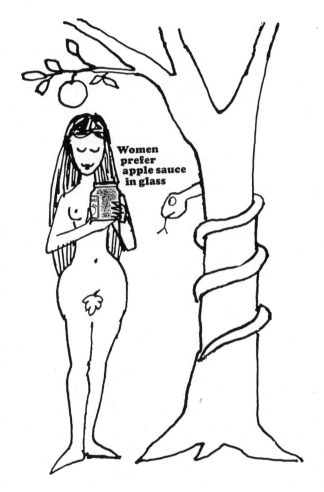

Women
prefer
apple sauce
in glass

'Nothing tempts Eve's daughters like apple sauce in glass. A 1963 consumer survey among 833 housewives shows that 2 out of 3 women prefer apple sauce in glass jars. And for good reasons: glass is its own refrigerator jar, opens easily, reseals tightly, keeps flavour fresh and unchanged. Isn't it just good business to give your customers what they want?'

From *Progressive Grocer*, January 1964.

In the 1930s, as we saw in Chapter 6, the American trade literature about the present and future arts of food merchandising was speculative and optimistically anticipatory. After the war, the sense of change was gone, other than as an expectation of perpetual growth: more of the same. The supermarket was a settled institution, and food stores a subject for policy and planning rather than for curiosity. At the same time, the sheer scale of the enormous store selling thousands of lines was out of all proportion to its predecessors. In light of both these differences, customers ceased to be seen – as in Carl Dipman's delicious descriptions – as one or two individuals making their way round a small, familiar space; or as the lively, bargain-seeking crowds out to enjoy something new and cheap at Big Bear or King Kullen. They became a species for study and investigation in the mass, its behaviour and habits to be recorded and analysed scientifically in order to predict what changes in its environment would get it to do more of what it was put in the supermarket world to do: buy.

Thus it was that a dreary new genre of writing arose: the supermarket survey. Beginning in 1950, the American trade journal *Progressive Grocer* got into the habit of running extensive reports on the present state of the supermarket art, based on studies of particular stores and their typical customers. As supermarkets themselves went on expanding, the surveys also got longer and longer and more and more elaborate, their endless figures and findings eventually running to hundreds of pages. They were presented in the form of serial reports that went on for months, in seemingly indefatigable attempts to give the impression of being able, still, to stop and 'take stock' before the figures and projections were out of date and it was necessary to begin all over again with yet another study –

always announced as 'the most comprehensive yet'.

It is a strange and a wearying experience to pass by the shelves of all these discarded displays of supermarket history. Ever more vast and multifarious documents are seen to emerge each time to replace smaller-scale antecedents. But what these surveys do offer is a record of different ways of asking questions about why shoppers do what they do, and different ways of seeing whatever it is that they do. I have no wish to try to offer the most comprehensively dreary survey yet, the survey of all the surveys, by attempting to provide a recapitulation of the lot. Instead, I'll concentrate on one of them, chosen because it presents itself, deliberately, as departing from previous ways of imagining what a supermarket shopper is. The shoppers in the American survey will then be compared with those that emerge through the very different perspectives of a British survey of supermarket shopping conducted at the same time.

*Progressive Grocer's Consumer Dynamics in the Supermarket*, the sixth survey since 1950, took eighteen months to do and a whole year to report on, from October 1965 to October 1966; it was preceded only the year before by the *Colonial Study* (of supermarkets in the Colonial chain), whose six-month run ended in March 1964. *Consumer Dynamics* focused on stores in the Kroger chain in the Cleveland, Ohio region; its proclaimed 'unique selling point', as a survey, was that for the first time it was considering the supermarket's customers not as a homogeneous mass, but as distinct demographic groups with their own characteristic features.

In previous studies, some variables had in fact been implicitly deployed, since the 'mass' of shoppers was assumed to be women – not men and not children. In the most recent survey, sex and age had been explicitly marked: for the first time there was a range of adult age-groups, and for the first time men shoppers – who may or may not have been present before – came statistically into focus. A quite different type of variable was also considered: the contingent fact of whether or not the shopper comes with a list. Against expectations, the *Colonial* survey found that it was the listed not the listless who bought more; and since listedness, unlike age or sex, is a characteristic open to modification, it was possible to make recommendations accordingly – for instance, for supplying customers with ready-printed lists to be used on the next visit.

*Consumer Dynamics* goes in for a much more elaborate scheme of differentiation, which draws (though not consistently) on criteria including race, income, life events, age, neighbourhood. It divides its sampled world into seven groups, as follows: Movers; Newlyweds; Upper Income; Industrial Neighbourhood; Negro; Young Married; and Small Town Rural.

The change of perspective is represented in several ways, not exactly compatible with one another. On the one hand, it is supposed to be the recognition of a long-standing fact: consumers never have been all the same. On the other hand, it is supposed to be a recognition of a new social phenomenon: nowadays, people are seeking to express differences in their identities, and they do this partly through the stores they shop at. Thirdly, there is an argument in relation to economic saturation. Now that supermarkets not only dominate the food retailing field but are almost too many to be able to survive against each other, they have to find new ways of differentiating themselves to increase their market share. So, long before the 1980s reinvented it as niche marketing, we are said to be entering a period of 'pinpoint merchandising' targeted to 'fragmented and localised markets'.[1]

The designated social groups are each made the subject of their own long section, listing – ad infinitum – the precise statistics of their buying habits with regard to hundreds of different products, and analysing data to do with their opinions in general and about food and supermarkets in particular. Descriptions and data go on and on, prosaic chunks of fact and figure. There is no longer any halo of mystery surrounding the store and the shopping. But human interest is generated elsewhere, as the survey moves away from the supermarket itself to present an overview of contemporary American society.

The groups into which the population is heuristically divided have no statistical neatness, since it would be quite possible to belong to several or to none of them. 'White' is an unstated assumption for all but the one racially marked category, but it is noted that 'Industrial Neighbourhood' customers are likely to be second-generation immigrants from various European countries. 'Young Marrieds' refers only to couples with children, where one parent is under forty. 'Newlyweds' is the species that appears most exotic a generation later. At the time, as the survey tells us, the *average* age of 'first-time' marriage was eighteen, and the number of people who married each year – for the most part children of the post-war baby boom – was over two and a half million. 'Movers', too, are numerically an enormous group: 20 per cent of the population – thirty-six million – each year.

## The moving mystery

The movers are treated first, and they are in every sense the vanguard group, acting out literally the character traits ascribed to 'this fantastically mobile, restless nation' (K37). The mover personifies mobility in its many senses, and so it is claimed that movers are 'psychologically as well as physically more predisposed to change' (K38–9). 'Mobility breeds more mobility', and the mover is someone who 'keeps his bags packed mentally' (K38), which is both good and bad for supermarkets. They want customers who are open to change and to new things, but they also want customers who will stay with their particular store. The study also notes, however, that many who move within one city do not in fact change their store. One theory is that it is too much trouble, or one trouble too many, to 'learn' a new one even if it is now nearer to home. Or the store becomes the familiar territory that stays the same even when the domestic space is changed: it is a home more stable than home.

Movers may be enticed into the store for a first visit by a figure who acts as a sort of hired neighbour. Paid for by supermarkets and other businesses whose services she promotes, the Welcome Wagon lady – who made a momentary appearance in *The Stepford Wives* (see Chapter 10) – acts as a go-between or interloper, taking the store right into the home: 'A cheerful, sympathetic woman, usually wearing a hat, she rings the door-bell and introduces herself; it's an unusual person who will not invite her inside.' (K56). Unusual indeed: there she is, with her pretty basket of free gifts, and coupons for more free gifts if the newly arrived resident would care to make a visit to her gen-erous local supermarket. But the nice lady has a sinister side. She is also being paid to take careful note for her sponsors of 'such information as the newcomer's number of children, year of car, type of residence, attitudes and preferences in food shopping, etc.' (K55). Even before she enters the store, the cus-tomer is the object of a survey; she needs to be known so that her needs can be anticipated.

This idea of the customer as fundamentally unknown, a mystery, is the premise here and in other *Progressive Grocer* surveys. But elsewhere it applies not specifically to the large numbers of unfamiliar customers in a moving population, but to the way that self-service differs from the over-the-counter selling it supplanted. Then, supposedly, the customer knew what she wanted and was known to the clerk; exchanges between the two were marked by a perfect directness of com-munication: 'The product either was there or it wasn't. And if it didn't suit her, she told the grocer off on the spot and stomped off down the street to his competitor. He didn't have to guess why she left him' (K109). A simple story of an angry woman who walks out. But now, the world has changed and the woman is being aggressively wooed not by the grocer but by far more products than she can ever deal with:

> Back in the 1930's she made her choice from about 700 items. Now she is bombarded from all sides by nearly 7,000 brightly colored packages calling: Buy me! No, buy me!
>
> As she browses through the newspaper or magazine or drives through town, alluring supermarkets also vie for her attention, each promising her the Land-of-Plenty-at-a-

Bargain. And the question is, what makes her choose one brand, or one super market over another? Most of the time, we don't really know for sure. She seldom tells us when she leaves – she just folds her tent and disappears into the night, or appears magically like the morning sun, shopping cart firmly clutched in hand. (K109)

The contemporary shopper is in a continual state of passing through or passing by: walking up and down the supermarket aisles, browsing through the newspaper, driving through town. There is an indistinct relationship between a vaguely questioning general observation by 'us' who wonder about her (while the goods bombard her), and a vaguely enigmatic woman who 'seldom tells' what makes her magically appear or disappear in her nomadic way: 'More and more we are realising that we don't know nearly enough about our customers – how they live, what they consume, why and where they buy . . . most important of all, what a consumer really is' (K109; ellipsis in original). And so the survey follows, with its various devices – questionnaires, interviews, purchasing statistics – attempting to pin down the customer as perpetual mover.

The unpredictability of the modern shopper – now you see her, now you don't – provides one prompt for surveys. But another description of the situation makes the consumer's mobility into an answer not a question, part of a life on the move. The car is taken as a symbol of a life lived in a perpetual present of constant innovation:

Time and distance have altered so radically as to produce en masse that novel phenomenon, the housewife with an automobile. Yesterday's newspaper has become ancient history . . . Quality in the old sense of 'the tried and true' has lost much of its value. To some extent, it has come to be regarded as the antithesis of value, since to the modern housewife, the symbol of quality is 'change', 'improvement', 'newness' . . . Goaded by new affluence, more leisure time and the possession of an automobile,

the American housewife has become almost obsessed by
the pursuit of the new, which has become a symbol of
quality, particularly in the area of food. (K91)

This is very much the attitude ascribed to the 'High Income'
shopper, a demanding woman whose regular custom is that
much harder to secure because her automobile always gives
her the freedom to move on. But the presumed ubiquity of this
generic 'American housewife' moving confidently into
modernity is in fact contradicted by the survey's inclusion of
other types or groups whose interests and psychology are not
regarded in the same way.

## The 'Negro'

With civil rights activism at its height, the justification for discussing 'the Negro' as a category apart is curiously contradic-
tory in its cynicism. It is that Negroes are *not* different, because
they spend a lot, and 'Nobody is going to segregate that much
money' (K196). The crude economic point is put another way
with the argument that the whites have all moved off to the
suburbs while the blacks have moved into the inner cities; if
urban retailers want to do any trade at all, they had better look
to this market.

Ironically, the approach in this section manages to make
black people more white than the whites. When their buying
preferences are surveyed, 'Negroes' are found for instance to
show more preference than other groups for well-known
brands, and generally to like the same things about a store as
people in other groups. Yet because it is assumed that this
behaviour does not make sense in relation to lower incomes
(named brands cost more), a special technical vocabulary of
conditioning, status-seeking and defensiveness is brought in to
explain it:

The urban Negro, largely because of his socio-economic
background, has become acutely quality- and brand-

conscious. It might truly be said that the restrictions that make the Negro feel he is a second-class citizen also have tended to make him a first-class customer. His insistence then on brand names and quality-products reflect [sic] a need commonly referred to as 'status-seeking'. (K197)

Status-seeking, enshrined in the title of Vance Packard's *The Status Seekers* (1959), was indeed 'commonly referred to' at the time. A watered-down version of Thorstein Veblen's notion of 'emulation' in *The Theory of the Leisure Class* (1899), it was mainly about the white middle classes. Yet 'status-seeking' is not the diagnosis that the *Progressive Grocer* report applies to them, or indeed to any of its other groups.

The different approach in this case can also be seen in a tacit change of sex. Throughout the main section, as in the quotation above, the article talks in terms of a type character in the masculine singular, 'the Negro'. Except in the two photographs, and in the introduction, where the focus is on shopping and the shopper is a she, the woman disappears altogether; the rising social subject is not her.

## The 'Industrial Neighborhood Shopper'

In all groups, the basic household unit is a married couple and the primary shopper is the woman. But some men, it is noted, either share the shopping trip or do some of the shopping on their own. 'The male, blue collar shopper', for instance, gets a column of his own in the 'Industrial Neighborhood Shopper' section. His existence is seen as requiring explanation:

There are many probable reasons why the male shopper is so conspicuous in the industrial neighborhood. One that stands out most vividly is the lower income status of this group, which makes it plausible that the male might want to keep a tighter, personal rein on the family purse strings and stem the purchase of items which he may consider superfluous. (K177)

Other possible reasons are that wives who have jobs themselves will 'relegate [*sic*]' the shopping to their husbands while
they 'keep house in their off hours'; or that since the family may
not have a car (a situation mentioned euphemistically as 'the
high percentage of pedestrian traffic in this type of neighborhood'), the husband is needed to help carry the bags. These reasons are heterogeneous – maybe he wants to keep an eye on the
spending, maybe she gets him to do it, maybe she just can't
manage on her own. They are of a quite different order from the
'status-seeking' interpretation offered in a parallel case – to
explain a surprising fact – in relation to 'the Negro customer'.
The blue-collar man going shopping elicits a bunch of would-
be common-sense suggestions; the buying of brand-name
goods by the Negro shopper is treated as a symptom of a collective disposition that has nothing to do with the shopping.
But what if the Negro shopper buys brand-name goods for the
same reasons as everyone else (they are advertised, they are
familiar)? Or what if the men shopping has more to do with the
beginning of the end of this particular sexual division of
behaviour?

## The 'Newlyweds'

It is noted that over half the newlyweds also shop in couples;
yet the 'brides' alone are regarded as targets for special marketing attention. Newlyweds are truly the newborns of supermarket shopping, getting lots of love and attention to provide
them with a secure environment which, hopefully, they will
not want to leave. As the section's caption reads: 'That bumper
crop of babies hatched after WW II is altar-bound . . . Here's
how to woo and win the youngest of the young adults before
they start to "settle down"' (K59).

The newlyweds get their own special equivalent of a Welcome Wagon lady. This takes the form of a 'brides-to-be pro-
gram' on wedding planning, attended not only by the bride
but by her mother, plus sometimes her mother-in-law-to-be;

and also 'occasionally a girl friend who also has matrimony in mind' (K70) – and what girl friend wouldn't have, for better or worse, in a world where 90 per cent of her peers will be married by the age of twenty-five? The whole entourage, apparently, tends to finish up as 'grateful' customers, whether or not they previously used the store (K72).

All those interviewed in every survey group respond to 'prompts' in the questions put to them. As with the products they are offered in the supermarket, they can say yes or no to opinions proposed to them, choose this one rather than that one; but the words and ideas are standardized, put together elsewhere. With the newlyweds, the spoon-feeding process is gently exposed, as they learn to repeat their grown-up consumer language, with or without a meaning: 'newlyweds do want value, but just aren't sure what value is' (K68).

The great advantage of newlyweds is their malleability; and happily, the store is there to show them the way, reassuring with helpful advice about how to prepare meals and with what cuts of meat: 'The biggest blank these kids face is in the meat department – they don't know what to buy, how to fix it, what constitutes quality. A common question is: "London Broil – what's that?"' (K74).

Newlyweds are favoured children: with young women working nowadays, they have double incomes, which is why they can set up home so early. They don't seem to have any worries or indeed any aspirations beyond how to become the sort of housewife who will be able to make her husband's dinner with confidence: after all, 'it's unpleasant when it does not go well' (K68). For all the emphasis on change and mobility in relation to other groups, it is a constant finding, or assumption, with regard to the newlyweds that what they want, above all, is to settle, to grow up, to cease to be 'inexperienced'.

## The 'Small Towners'

The other group whose settledness functions as a counterpart to the mobile orientation of the movers and others is, predictably this time, the small town sample, who are put at the end of the survey. From the beginning of the introductory text, they are cast as a dream of old-time rootedness:

> If you stepped into a Norman Rockwell painting, you might find people who are more heart-of-America-looking than the faces you encounter among super market customers in the small county seat type of communities that dot central and southern Ohio. Short of that improbable step, we doubt that you'll find them. (K251)

These characters are said to be a 'microcosm' (K252) of all the population groups to be found in a big city, including those that the survey has covered, and some in specifically rural occupations that it hasn't. But they are 'geared to live at a slower pace than their city cousins' (K252), and happy with that:

> While the typical small-towner may agree that his provincial existence is at best a two dimensional slice of life, he wouldn't think of trading it for the 'Three-D' world of the big city. Especially when the three 'd's' are drugs, discotheques and drudgery. (K253)

Better to stick with the Norman Rockwell surface and miss out on the counter-caricature of the city, with its assortment of downsides.

More local colour is provided in the form of a bit of would-be down-home dialect:

> They may flock to a spanking new store in the community because they are as interested in new things as anyone, but within the shiny facade they'll not feel completely comfortable until someone greets them with a 'Howdy, neighbor, glad to see ya' or 'Welcome to our new "diggins".' (K253)

As with the flash modern furniture store described by Richard

Hoggart (see Chapter 3), there is the movement of curiosity to see something new – an interest that is common to 'anyone' – and then the 'comfortable' settlement provided by the friendly greeting. First the glitzy decorations, then the heart of gold. After all the moving and status-seeking, and all the careful differentiation between social groups, it is the small-town customers who are brought on to provide a very ordinary, inclusive conclusion. On the one hand, be new; at the same time, be familiar.

## Shopping in Suburbia

In the American survey of the 1960s the supermarket itself is a given, as much a part of the landscape as the small town or the factory. It is as if it had always been there. In Britain at the same time, supermarkets were seen as new and as far from established. Their image, as we shall see, could sometimes suggest the 'drugs, discotheques and drudgery' of the American small-towner's imaginary big city: supermarkets were dangerously appealing; they were fun; and they made you work. But compared to the United States and France (see Chapters 6 and 7), their history and development in Britain makes a drab, uneventful tale, marked only by bungled attempts at planning the future of shopping in relation to community needs. There is just one flamboyant, famous personality to compete with the likes of Michael Cullen or Edouard Leclerc: Tesco's Jack Cohen, who started as a barrow boy in Hackney and became a household name when Tesco's battled for the abolition of legally maintained manufacturers' retail prices in the 1960s.

The pilot Tesco self-service store in St Albans in 1947 was one of the earliest; but the first in the country, in 1942, was a co-op inside a department store in Romford, Essex. This came about through the efforts of Harold Wicker of the London Co-operative Society, who later formed the Self-Service Development Association. It measured all of twenty-two by eight feet, which gives some idea of the scale of European self-service at the beginning.

For the most part, British supermarkets developed in the country's time-honoured slow, unrevolutionary way: small then larger stores gradually occupied existing sites on the high streets. Unlike in France and America, large stores away from city centres were not built for many years in Britain, partly because of concern about how they would alter the pattern of everyday life. Planning restrictions were added to existing obstacles: the shortage of available land and the relatively low percentage of car-owning households. Then, in the 1980s, came a change of policy, and large edge-of-town and out-of-town stores began to appear all over the country. And then, in the 1990s, as the stores continued to multiply and to increase in size, the policy shifted again. Superstores were found to have had just the effects that the earlier restrictions had been designed to prevent. They had taken away trade and thereby community focus from town centres and, for that matter, from villages, few of which now retained even a single local shop.

At the turn of the 1960s, though self-service was gaining in popularity, it did not seem to pose any significant threat or to offer any excitement. A writer on the planning of shops and shopping in British towns, while noting the new development, could calmly state, in 1959: 'We can, I feel, safely assume that the development of self-service will not affect seriously our plans for the foreseeable future even in respect of the large centres.'[2] The premises behind the prediction are interesting:

> Local shopping is often an occasion for gossip and meeting friends . . . Shopping in this country, as no doubt in others, is not for many women one of those chores to be done as quickly and easily as possible. Shopping is more than buying an article, and it is difficult to see any substantial alteration in this state of affairs even though, as a nation, we are becoming more scientific in the house as well as the factory.[3]

The suggestion that increased efficiency is the general direction of change is here used as an argument *against* the super-market: shopping is not this kind of job.

The sentiment that shopping serves an important social function for women has an illustrious history. In *The Second Sex* (1949), Simone de Beauvoir provides a passionately exhaustive account of all the constraints and dullness in a housewife's daily life. Yet the one moment of break-out is when she goes shopping:

> While they are doing their shopping, women exchange remarks in the shops, on the street corners, through which they affirm 'housewifely values', where each one derives a sense of her importance: they feel they are members of a community which – for a moment – is opposed to the society of men as the essential to the inessential. But above all, buying is a profound pleasure: it is a discovery, almost an invention . . . Between seller and buyer a relationship of tussling and ruses is set up: the point of the game for her is to procure herself the best buys at the lowest price; the great importance attached to the smallest of economies could not be explained merely by the concern to balance a difficult budget: the thing is to win a round. For the time she is suspiciously examin-ing the stalls, the housewife is queen; the world is at her feet with its riches and its traps, for her to grab herself some loot. She tastes a fleeting triumph when she empties the bag of provisions onto her table.[4]

The shopping interlude is the one time in Beauvoir's description when life is something other than the stifling repetition of itself in solitude, as housewives move outdoors to take a breath of col-lective fresh air and to enjoy what is practically the only pleasure that she recognizes for them. They are not prowling computers but old-fashioned hunters, players, queens; and their female community is a micro-revolution in values every day.

But by 1969, ten years after the shrugging off of self-service's British future, a Consumers' Association report on 'Shopping', published in its magazine *Which?*, took it for granted that super-markets were an established part of life; and the assumption about what food shopping means had changed as well:

> Most of the women interviewed made it clear that general food shopping was something to be carried out efficiently . . . On the whole, they wanted to get the job (which has to be done at least once a week) over fast, so preferred to do it alone, without small children, and without too many other shoppers around.[5]

A desperately solitary shopper here – not only away from the children but, it seems, as near as possible alone in the shop. No need here for the Cross instructions, outlined in Chapter 9, about keeping the family out of the way. Shopping is no longer a social occasion when you chat to your friends; it is a private, asocial chore for which the shopper makes herself into an efficient operator for the (minimized) duration. It seems to take place in an indeterminate environment, characterized only by the negatives of what is not in it (children, other shoppers). The presence of other people, who might take up time, is simply a distraction.

Some years before this, in 1963, there appeared *Shopping in Suburbia*, commissioned by a supermarket chain and some high street stores, including W. H. Smith's. It is described as 'a report on housewives' reactions to supermarket shopping'; in it, supermarkets are presented as a new, unfamiliar phenomenon. Utterly different from the American surveys of the time, this one is very little concerned with what women actually do or buy in supermarkets. For instance, in place of the American calculation, based on thousands of observations, of twenty-nine minutes as the average shopping time, the British method is to ask women on their way out about how long they think they have just spent in the store – a method glossed as 'not entirely accurate perhaps'.[6] There is anecdotal evidence to show that in Britain supermarkets were regarded, by planners and shoppers alike, as American in origin: 'It *is* an American idea, isn't it? I believe some people go to America to get ideas sometimes' (p. 32). What the survey does offer as statistics are mainly related to opinions and feelings about supermarkets gleaned through interviews; and the interviews are not only with those who shop in supermarkets but also with those who don't.

But *Shopping in Suburbia* does resemble *Consumer Dynamics* in its sociological approach. In both cases, a high proportion of the space is given to the presentation of broadly sketched information and speculations about recent social changes, with the idea that these have effects on the psychology of customers, considered individually or in groups. Pockets of purely psychological analysis appear too, but the emphasis is not so much on individual dispositions as on groups considered like natural species, their lives conditioned by a particular social world: they are settled, but at the same time they are adaptable. Again, as with *Consumer Dynamics*, there is a broad notion of mobility: 'Shoppers are on the move – psychologically as well as physically' (p. 15).

In its low-key way, the rhetoric of *Shopping in Suburbia* is quite dramatic, referring to 'this post-war revolution in retailing' and even, moving beyond the shop itself, to 'a minor revolution in social habits' prompted by the arrival of self-service and supermarkets (pp. 47, 15). But the use of the word does not lead, as it does in France, to discussion of revolution or evolution as appropriate terms, or of how the present change is to be understood in relation to previous moments in the history of shopping. *Shopping in Suburbia*'s revolution means the importing of ideas and practices which may or may not turn out to be compatible with different conditions: questions are raised about the difficulty of following directly in the footsteps of American practice, where cars and supermarkets are fundamental to the newly built post-war suburbs. Britain's older 'suburbia', with its local shops for customers on foot, was built in a different world, for which the desirability or even feasibility of supermarkets is not self-evident.

The continuing growth of supermarkets in Britain is thus

seen to be a matter of some delicacy. So far they have been sited on main shopping streets, with the idea that women are not going to take themselves out of their way. This jars with the *Consumer Dynamics* assumption that however conservative they may be in other respects, people will always at least want to see or try out what is new. The chief obstacle to British supermarket development, though, is that people do not (yet) shop by car. It is thus no use upgrading the housewife from basket to cart in the hope that she will buy more, as she is not going to be pleased to find herself out on the street with no means of getting the stuff home – 'left to sag on the pavement', as the report rather graphically puts it (p. 42).

It is also said, though – a point rarely mentioned in the American literature – that many American women in fact shop by bus, when their husbands have taken the car to work; this might be a possible solution to British carlessness and pavement-sagging. But ultimately, it is expected that cars will be the only way forward, and this will involve 'another social revolution'. This is glossed, however, as 'enough "home-makers" . . . eventually allowed by their husbands to use the family car for shopping' (p. 42). It is not clear whether the revolution is in the car use or in the husbands' capitulation. But in any case, it didn't happen, since the women continued to sag for another decade. A House of Commons seminar in 1976 on the planning of large stores was informed: 'The main weekly shopping visit results in the average housewife attempting to carry home no less than 1 cwt. of groceries – just imagine carting round a sack of coal!'[7]

Even if transport problems were dealt with, the big out-of-town store would still have to get built in the first place. This involved the dual problems of land prices – cheaper in America – and planning restrictions – tighter in Europe. In a rare anecdotal, if not mythological moment, the report characterizes the American difference by citing the case of 'a well-known [supermarket] operator' at a conference in New York, who 'said that if he found his ideal site was on land "zoned" for some other purpose, he approached the Authority and had it "re-zoned"' (p. 38). Somewhat wearily, it is concluded that 'if and when larger supermarkets appear, they will be the fruit of the well-known British capacity for compromise' (p. 40).

The description of the supermarket's social environment sits at an angle to the survey's main focus, ostensibly a psychological investigation of customers' perceptions of the new retailing form. The individual customer starts off by appearing, like her American counterpart, as something of an enigma:

> People enter the supermarket, seem to indulge first of all in perimeter shopping and then in most cases make for the centre or subsidiary aisles, criss-cross in maze-like fashion, read notices, pick up products, sometimes choose quickly but at other times read pack directions, take the pack in the hand and weigh it up, shake it, smooth the cellophane wrappers, try to see what is inside – indulge, in fact, in any number of miscellaneous actions all indicative of certain states of mind . . . But the key to such actions is not always obvious; and if shoppers take articles and then replace them on the shelves, it is, in most cases, only possible to guess at the underlying motive. (p. 16)

The actions are distracted, all over the place; but rather than being seen as derived from the 'maze-like' layout of the surface of the store itself or the multitude of articles for sale – or, for that matter, from the presence of an over-interested observer – they are ultimately attributed to an 'underlying motive' at which, from watching alone, it is 'only possible to guess'. More will be known about why she does one thing rather than another, prefers one shop rather than another, 'the more deeply we can probe the mind of the shopper' (p. 30).

It is clear that this new environment is not always a happy one for the British housewife. If something like detective work is deemed appropriate to find out what she really thinks, deep down, then that corresponds, it turns out, to a common experience (for one in six of those interviewed) of the supermarket as a place where you are being watched in case you take anything without paying. Combined with 'the feeling that "nobody knows you in supermarkets"', it is easy for customers to feel 'lost, lonely or under suspicion' (p. 18).

Yet another problem is that the supermarket is thought of as 'the shop where impulse purchasing is at its height' (p. 13), a phrase that manages to suggest both the fear of entering a den of iniquity – it's going on all around you – and, at the same time, the fear that individually you will be unable to resist the lure. It is striking too that when supermarkets have not yet established themselves definitively in Britain, 'impulse buying' has already entered everyday language, in the form of an infection to be avoided – or even a latent instinct to be resisted.

Loneliness comes up as a particular form of distress associated with supermarket shopping; but when others do enter the picture, they may well be an aggressive species of sister. In British supermarkets, it isn't so much the slow checkouts – an eternal theme of American surveys – that cause annoyance (though they are duly mentioned), but 'pushing and shoving from other customers' (p. 19). This is regarded as a problem by almost a third of those interviewed: 'some of the women push and push with wire baskets and once I was pushed into some butter and then I swore I wouldn't go there again – but I was there the next week!' (p. 17).

This last statement, nicely suggestive of the pull as well as the push of the new kind of store, is attributed to a 'Working-class housewife. Aged 47'. Age and class (in the three categories of working-class, lower middle-class and middle-class) are the two principal variables used to differentiate responses in this survey. There is also the straightforward division between those who do and those who don't shop in supermarkets. Housewives who have jobs are differentiated from those who don't, though contrary to expectations that working women would like supermarkets more, the survey cannot find any marked difference in their attitudes (p. 25).

All shoppers are described as 'housewife', a title that starts at the age of sixteen and applies, universally, to the female sex. There is not a non-housewife, male or female, to be seen among the survey's respondents. Unlike its contemporary counterparts in the United States, where they are given special mention as a growing category, the British survey simply turns a blind eye to men shopping in the supermarket. This is in spite of the acknowledgement, from a question about 'shopping companions', that 'in seven out of every hundred shopping journeys, husband and wife shop together . . . The husband and wife figure presumably builds up at times when the husband is more easily available – in the evenings and particularly at weekends' (p. 12). From the same table, though unremarked in the main text, we can also glean the information that in one trip out of every hundred, the housewife is accompanied by 'dogs'.

Men cannot be seen as shoppers; the reverse side of this situation is that women, as shoppers, have to be distinguished from the category of those who study and plan for shoppers. Perhaps a transitional stage is indicated by the opening to the 1969 *Which?* investigation: 'Fifteen men and two women sat around a vast table on the fifteenth floor of Millbank Tower discussing the shopping needs of the future in this country.' In comparison with the pictures of apparently all-male conventions in the food merchandising journals, the fact that there were even two women present is significant. More so, perhaps, is the fact that *Which?* should start off by stating the composition of the group in gender terms, and gently mocking 'the men' who 'seemed to be exceedingly well informed about exactly what type of shop and shopping centre would bring the most trade and make the most profit'. One of the two women was *Which?*'s Eirlys Roberts, 'aware of knowing nothing whatever about the kind of shops, or shopping centres, shoppers would like to have planned for them'.[8] In her signed column at the start of the issue, Roberts is not just ironic but explicit, giving the object of the exercise as: 'to find out how the planners could discover what shopping facilities women shoppers actually want – as distinct from what male planners think they want'.[9]

In the early 1960s survey, supermarket shopping in Britain was still regarded as a skill to be acquired: 'Supermarkets mean *learning* and not everyone will make the effort. But the idea of supermarket shopping meets with interest and curiosity; and if shoppers persevere through a few visits they seem to adapt quite quickly to new conditions' (p. 16). The organism may or may not be intelligent, and in this sense the supermarket can be represented as a kind of comprehensive school: 'people feel free to find their own level – the quicker thinker acts at once and the slower thinker can browse and take her time' (p. 16) – which is certainly a novel way of interpreting variations in the length of the shopping trip.

From this perspective, it is to be expected that the younger housewives will find supermarkets easier to grasp, because there is less to unlearn; but there is frequently an element of *work* implied in the suggested statements about what supermarket shopping involves. Only in the British context does 'self-service' seem to carry this particular connotation. Unlike Zimmerman's exuberant Big Bear customers, like ducks to water 'content to wait on themselves', British housewives are struggling to cope. To a British economist, in 1962, 'self-service is . . . a process of "hiving off" certain operations from the retailer to the customer'. And that's all there is to say, since 'the general idea of self-service is, by now, so familiar that it requires no more detailed description'.[10]

The same idea could be used as a criticism of self-service as lazy shopkeeping. In 1937 the *Listener* reported a debate about the future of shopping under the heading 'Big Business v. Small Shopkeeper'. Captain Harold Balfour, MP, after a dramatic opening worthy of Trujillo – 'I do not believe the uncontrolled killing of the small man would be in the interests of consumers' – rejects the argument that big stores are better because they are cheaper: 'The big people skim the shopping cream. They will sell easy things which need no service behind them. For instance, they will sell kipper in cellophane but not handle wet fish.'[11] Supermarkets are not yet the issue, but some of the objections against them are already in place: through pre-packaging and lack of individual service, large stores are cutting out work and making things 'easy' for themselves. What they are not yet said to be doing is passing the work on to the housewife: that would be the post-war, self-service addition.

A comprehensive manual on retailing published in the late 1940s presented self-service in quite a different light:

> Already in operation in a number of shops and stores in Great Britain, self-service has the advantage of eliminating the queue, of reducing overhead costs, and of allowing shoppers to make their purchases at high speed or in a leisurely manner, as they wish, without impeding the movements of other shoppers.
>
> After taking a shopping cart or basket at the entrance to the self-service shop or department, the customer moves about with perfect freedom, helping herself where and when she pleases.[12]

Jostle-free, 'at high speed or in a leisurely manner', self-service shopping here promises the choice between the two modes of shopping, fast or slow, as 'perfect freedom'.

But the early suggestions of liberty gave way to a contrary stress on effort. *Shopping in Suburbia* does talk about something called 'fun', and trawls through the old debating point about whether food shopping is or might one day be regarded as more of a pleasure than a task to be got through, in supermarkets and elsewhere. Though such high jinks find no place in the sensible survey, Tesco store openings at this time had an echo of the carnival atmosphere of Big Bear and King Kullen in the early 1930s, or hypermarket openings across the channel. According to David Powell's history of Tesco's, these occasions, more than fifty of them in the single year 1966, were characterized by 'promotions, gimmicks and glitz'. They often featured a knight by the name of Sir Save-a-Lot who made his entrance dressed in medieval armour, mounted on a white charger – until he came to an unfortunate end at an Essex opening in 1969, when the horse 'reared at the sight of a biscuit display, dumped the unhappy knight into a pyramid of corn-flake packets, then collapsed on its back amongst piles of Cad-bury's chocolate rolls'.[13]

Such antics, though, could be put down to the vulgarity of Tesco's, with its 'Pile it high, sell it cheap' image and its Green Shield trading stamps. Predictably, class divisions between supermarket chains were stronger in Britain than elsewhere. A company like Sainsbury's, if only in contrast to Tesco's, man-aged to promote a certain middle-class aloofness from class with its conscious lack of flash and its shiny white bags bearing the plain message 'Good food costs less at Sainsbury's'. In this regard, the extra work of self-service could mean the imposition of unladylike labour. There is a story that Lord Sainsbury was once 'accosted by a judge's wife in Purley', who said that he 'had no right to expect the customer to do the work the assistants had done in the past'.[14] Right or not, there was no alleviation of the judge's wife's sentence; and if she is still alive (or ever had an existence outside supermarket legend), she may well have found herself in the 1990s parking her BMW outside the local Tesco's, now in every respect the social equal of Sainsbury's.

# 12 The Deviant, the Checkout and the Future

'Back from a trip to the grocers! Future stores will be designed to accommodate new trends in transport. Vertical take-off craft will speed shoppers to market with no traffic problems and land in reserved parking areas no more than about 250 feet from an entrance. To match convenience and relation of transportation, stores will provide facilities for supervised entertainment of children.'

From *The Grocer Centenary Number*, 1962.

*The shopper in the abstract*

'At 9.36 one morning an average woman customer walked into a five-checkstand Super Market. Each step she made was watched by a market research man from a vantage point that overlooked the whole store. He had instructions to record her every action.'[1] The year is 1957 and the lady's crime, it turns out, is well hidden: 'What showed up was a seemingly aimless shopping route whose purpose was apparent only to the shopper.' And there are thousands like her: 'a group of research people all turned up similar "erratic" patterns of shopping'.[2]

Nothing better illustrates the post-war relationship of distance and scrutiny between the supermarket and its customers than traffic-pattern surveys. These formed a part of the grand 1960s American survey of the type discussed in Chapter 11; but in more modest forms, as we shall see, they also went on in other places and for other purposes too.

The traffic concerned was a mystifying, if not suspect species, these strange women wandering around the store with motives known only to themselves. To and fro, round and round, the surveys try to make sense of their movements. But as with the larger surveys, the study is almost by definition never-ending – in this case because erratic routes and unplanned purchases are precisely what the stores are trying to encourage.

The shoppers are not always observed from on high. The most common method involves a form of discreet tracking, whereby individual customers are shadowed by someone who notes all their movements, everything they put into their trolley, and everything they pick up or look at but don't, after all, choose to take. This is literally 'customer-led' behaviour. At no other time in self-service shopping is such comprehensive, one-to-one attention bestowed on the otherwise self-reliant, solitary shopper

– and she doesn't even know it. The other becomes her double, her covert fellow shopper, following every one of her actions in the minutest, most faithful detail. It is an entirely mute relationship, silent salesmanship turned secret scrutiny. Once again, there is a third party beyond the customer and the merchandise.

The person following is usually someone just like the customer, a locally recruited housewife. She carries a clipboard with a plan of the store on which she plots her data. Presumably, she is meant to look as if she is checking the stock, for her real task must not be guessed. Here are the instructions from the traffic pattern section of the 1966 *Progressive Grocer Consumer Dynamics* survey:

> Personnel should try to maintain a distance from the subject which allows the customer to be observed without that customer's being aware of being followed. This is desirable so that nothing inhibits or influences the customer to deviate from her normal shopping pattern. Remaining unrecognized is surprisingly easy because of most customers' intensive concentration on their shopping.[3]

'Normal' and 'deviating' are supposed to be clearly separable forms of shopping behaviour. Normal, however erratic, is what the customer does and what the surveyor won't stop her from getting on with; it includes an absorption so intense as to make her oblivious to the constant proximity of another person. But ultimately, the purpose of the information gleaned by this method is to change the route and make the normal customer wander from her course. In parts of the store where 'a dropoff of traffic' occurs, 'there must be a careful choice of product categories . . . to tempt the customer to deviate from the beaten path' (K77).

Deviation is valued because it prompts equally out-of-the way purchases, departures from whatever shopping plan the customer may have had. Some goods, such as health and beauty products or sweets, are thought especially likely to be the subject of unplanned purchases; they are even known generically as 'impulse items'. As a general rule, these things need to go where the customer does so that she will find herself in front of them and the impulse will have its chance. The important thing is 'to expose them to as heavy a flow of traffic as possible' (K80), while the planned items that the customer will seek out deliberately can be put in the aisles that might otherwise be overlooked. This policy is meant to maximize what is known as the 'passing—buying ratio'. However, it is important not to go too far in putting the necessary items out of the way; otherwise you may not achieve your aim but simply further distress an already distressed woman. For an incongruous moment the report turns solicitous, with the sententiously pious reflection that 'life is involved enough without a store layout which confuses' (K77). The thought seems to lead the language into its own bizarre confusion of images when it is stated that 'All of the pressures which the housewife brings with her into the super market plus the added challenge of the store layout may not make a Greek tragedy of her shopping excursion but the combined result may make it something less than a picnic' (K77).

If the shopping trip is not a picnic and not a Greek tragedy, then what is it? Answer: an abstract expressionist painting. Look at the plotting of shoppers' movements, and that is what you see. It is nothing less than a new aesthetics of shopping resulting from the transition to self-service stores:

> Two decades ago, the path of a customer shopping the grocery store usually consisted of a straight line from the store entrance to the nearest clerk who filled the customer's grocery order . . .
>
> But the advent of the super market and of self-service brought fringe challenges . . . The simple one-line concept of the shopping pattern began to evolve into a complex zig-zag, in-and-out design rivaling an abstract work of art. (K75)

The said artwork is reproduced in all its complexity, thick and thin black lines winding erratically in and out over a grid map

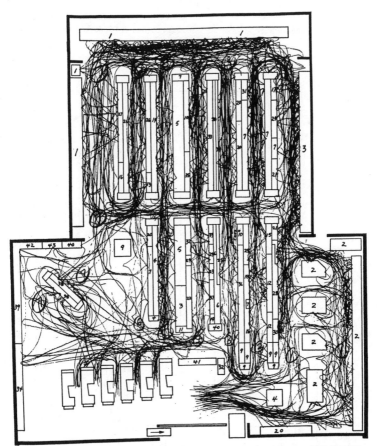

**The Illustration** above may look like an abstract artist's impression of the song "Show Me The Way To Go Home," but actually it is the result of plotting the paths travelled by 100 weekend customers in a typical Colonial Super Market. While each customer's path was originally traced on a small replica of the store layout, this total picture of 100 shoppers' tours superimposed one on top of the other provides a graphic portrait of the maze-like routes travelled by super market customers to fill their shopping carts with food and groceries. For specific passing-buying ratios see pages C90 and C91.

SKETCH 1.   SHOWING MOVEMENT OF 3 CUSTOMERS IN STORE A PRIOR TO ANY ALTERATION
IN AISLE DISPLAYS

of the supermarket's aisles; a similar illustration, larger in scale and also said to resemble the work of an 'abstract artist', had appeared in the previous study in 1964 (see p. 239).[4] What presents itself is a fairly intractable task of interpretation. 'The importance of understanding the shopper's in-store wanderings' (K75) is one thing; providing a plain rationale for the randomness of the lines on the painting, another. In the absence of any other kind of landmark, the report resorts to its historical comparison with the pattern of twenty years ago. Instead of the simple A to B to A again – entrance to counter to exit – the customer is now a figure in a 'maze' or 'labyrinth', winding her way around something that actually has no beginning or end or discernible logic at all (K86, K76).

Thus it was that a thousand Ariadnes found their way in and out of the labyrinth; all their investigators could figure out was that there had been a 'sudden change in the role played by the customer. From the position of being a virtual observer in the selection of items from the shelves in service stores, the super market shopper was cast as an active participant' (K75). Which is one way of looking at it, but not one that seems especially to follow from the evidence, or to require it. The customer's 'wanderings' are a mystery, so solve it by surveying her; the survey shows the customer's wanderings to be an insoluble mystery; so survey her again; and so on, round and round.

As we saw in Chapter 11, supermarket surveys in America virtually became an industry in their own right. This particular traffic-pattern study, a tiny part of the vast *Consumer Dynamics in the Supermarket* project, did indeed follow a thousand customers in Cleveland supermarkets over one weekend. Elsewhere, however, the numbers were not on so epic a scale.

### The biscuit

Lost in the pages of a little pamphlet from the early 1960s is a small record of a contemporary British customer survey undertaken in two co-op branch stores, in which the scale of things is rather different. The objective: to improve the sales of that quintessentially British commodity, The Biscuit. The number of customers in the sample? Three.

The enterprise is lovingly detailed:

> It was recognised that, in the choice of biscuits by the customer, there is a large element of impulse buying and that the decision to buy can include considerable examination time. From this knowledge of the customers' habits in relation to the purchase of this commodity, it is obvious that biscuits need a site in the store where they are easily seen, readily accessible and are at a place reasonably free from congestion.
>
> Naturally purely visual inspection of the biscuit site revealed a great deal as to whether these requirements for high biscuit sales were being met in this store.[5]

But 'purely visual inspection', although it may tell you everything you need to know, is nowadays not enough, even when just looking is given this technical name. Like biscuits, biscuit customers too deserve 'considerable examination time' and there are new American ways to do it:

> To aid this inspection and to record quickly what was happening in the vicinity of biscuits a customer flow plan of the movement of three customers was prepared.
>
> It is conceded, of course, that the path of only three customers does not necessarily reveal the general movement of customers within the store, but in this instance it was sufficient to confirm previous impressions gained about the biscuit site. (p. 44)

So far so good – everything is ready for proving that everything is as it always has been; but just to make sure – and to make sure that the plan of action is understood – we are further informed that 'the movement of three customers coming into the store in fairly quick succession was plotted on a sketch of the sales area' (p. 44).

Two maps follow (one is reproduced on p. 240), and then an account of how certain changes were made in the positioning of the biscuits. It remains to see whether the changes will have the desired effects. Three more customers are duly observed:

> The second batch of three customers now are encouraged to, and in fact do, move more freely in the biscuit area. They have shopped the whole of that aisle more comprehensively than the first three customers did. (p. 46)

This is indeed a triumph of applied science. But conclusions must be cautious: 'Of course the proof of the success of the venture would not rest on the behaviour of three customers, encouraging as this was' (p. 46).

No drama about the mysteries of ladies' movements here. But lest anyone be tempted to think that the sweet little survey might be a less extravagant and more pragmatic way of conducting things than the *Progressive Grocer* version, it could be pointed out that if the same number of words had been devoted to each of the thousand Kroger customers as was, on average, to each of the three co-op biscuit buyers, then that particular fragment of the American survey would have run to some fifteen hundred pages.

## The checkout

Even when the tills are in working order, as they weren't at the start of Chapter 1, there remains a point in self-service shopping when the 'straight line' can return with a vengeance; it is also the only point at which the customer necessarily comes into communicative contact, however minimal, with another person. Whether the passage round the aisles has been muddled or drifting or simple, the checkout is the place where no customer wants to linger, and where there is only one way through.

Beginning shortly after the war, a continuous stream of American supermarket literature investigated the problem of how to abolish the cruel contrast between open wandering round the aisles and the obligatory, stand-still lines at the end. This literature reached its height in a spate of Ph.D. dissertations in business studies and economics at the turn of the 1950s and 1960s, with the ultimate aim of making proposals for how to hasten a customer's passage past the tills and therefore give her a more contented exit.

The *Consumer Dynamics* survey quotes representatives of all its customer groups predictably reporting, in what is by then a well-worn repertoire of phrases, how they prefer a store where the checkout lines are short, where their groceries are bagged or carried out for them, where the staff at the end show courtesy or even know them by name. It is not a matter that lends itself to variation or deviation – basically, the customer at the checkout wants out, and I will come to the end of the subject as quickly as I can. But still, my heart goes out to the man whose youth was passed in the research for a Cornell University Ph.D. on 'A Comparison of the Turnover Per Customer and Rate of Checkout between Three Ithaca Supermarkets, 1959–61'. (And my heart goes out even more to the gratefully acknowledged wife whose youth was spent in typing the thing up.)

Not until the 1980s did computer technology provide the breakthrough in the perennial checkout impasse, with the coming of barcodes. Standard items no longer had to be individually marked with a price individually entered at the till by the checkout cashier. The barcode, combined with related innovations such as computerized inventories and ordering, made possible data-keeping on the miniature, infinitely detailed scale to which the *Consumer Dynamics* survey was already gesturing in the 1960s with its appeal to 'fragmented, local markets'. In the 1990s, almost every product is identifiable by its barcode specifications; so is every purchasing transaction recorded on the till. In places where 'loyalty cards' have become the norm, the identification number provides precise information on what is bought not just on a given shopping trip, but on every shopping trip across a given period of time. You are what you have bought, no more, no less. And each customer is unique, with a different profile from every other one.

It does not follow from this that more is known about why customers buy what they buy, either in general or in relation to any particular visit to the supermarket. As was suggested in Chapter 1, two shoppers with quite different ways of making their choices may come out looking identical from the till receipt. And the unique customer profiled by the record of purchases with the loyalty card may well be a composite figure of more than one individual, sometimes shopping together and sometimes separately.

But despite these uncertainties, the choosing customer is often portrayed in a newly definite and high-tech way. As though to match the data that are now available, customers themselves are seen as computers. The computers they resemble are nothing like those 1960s symbols of power discussed in Chapter 9, impersonally overseeing the world of big business from some unidentifiable place. Now, the computer has come down to the level of friendly, reliable reason; it is portable and 'customized' to everyone's personal needs and desires. In contemporary supermarket psychology, the customer-as-computer means someone with all the information necessary to make the decision that is right for them individually; he or she moves through the aisles picking out this and ignoring that, processing data with superlative efficiency.

The consumer-computer is very different from the poor passive being unable to hold out against those irresistible packages that drew out a matching 'impulse' to buy them. Gone for ever is that image of the feminine automaton of the aisles, robotically blinking along, making choices that were characterized by compulsion and unconsciousness. This new customer does not much resemble the enigmatically drifting shopper of the 1960s surveys who didn't know where she was going or what she really wanted and nor did anyone else. The smart new portable knows just what sort of thing it wants and how to find it.

What the computer and the automaton do have in common

is that they are both machines. But the significance of the machine has been turned around. That zombie housewife of the early supermarket years was thought to be acting mechanically – she couldn't resist the techniques that were forcing the goods upon her, and her responses to bright displays and colours could supposedly be charted by scientifically precise measurements. Shopping psychologists today are still deploying a mechanical model, but now the customer as machine is highly intelligent – able, just like the scanner that will read the barcodes, to process a vast amount of simultaneously presented information.

In the new image, the machine connotes not mindlessness but intelligence, not passive susceptibility but individual agency. Where once the technology of marketing was imagined as a form of sinister control, imposing itself ineluctably on masses of receptive, choiceless consumers, now – in a world of 'user-friendly', 'hands-on' personal machines of all kinds, from videos to mobiles to personal computers themselves – consumers themselves can be seen as a specially well-programmed variety, carefully or playfully selecting what they want from the range of options available, and moving about at will between different dispositions: one moment you buy the routine stuff on the list, another you allow yourself the purchase of a little luxury or surprise. The old opposition between the rational purchase and the induced 'impulse' purchase has given way to a model of well-adjusted coordination between different modes or moods, in which the consumer-computer is ultimately the one who is in charge of the whole enterprise. The machine is still in the picture; but it has become an image of 'empowerment' and 'flexibility', not automation or brainwashing.

This transformation of the machine-customer from mindless to brainbox exactly parallels the change in the gendering of the customer, now no longer assumed to be a woman. That the shopper-machine has ceased to be strongly gendered is not incidental, and there is more than one irony here. Men shop more than they used to, and it would no longer make sense – if indeed it did in the 1960s – to classify all shoppers as women, or all women as housewives. Women have ceased to be seen as the shoppers to the extent that they have also ceased to be seen as 'the housewife'. And the shopper has miraculously got brighter, insofar as he or she is no longer seen first of all as a woman in the stupid, frivolous or drudge-like mode. That woman shopper, marked as such, seems to have departed the supermarket aisles for ever.

This development is inseparable from the two fundamental changes to the ways that shopping and shoppers are imagined. First, the revaluation of shopping itself, now regarded as not necessarily trivial or silly, but as a legitimate pleasure or practice for the multi-faceted postmodern person (triviality itself acquires a kind of ironic legitimacy). And second, the turnabout in the dignity of the consumer – from dupe to paragon of the individual in control. These shifts cover both ends of the shopping spectrum – fun at one extreme, good sense at the other; the irony is that the newly positive image in both instances goes together with the fading of the shopper's femininity.

Yet there is a place where the woman shopper survives in more or less splendid isolation: on the lunatic fringes, where she appears or suffers as 'fashion victim' or (more seriously) shopaholic. 'Retail therapy' is an expression used jokingly, as though to counter the image of excessive shopping as semi-pathological by reclassifying it as a cure. The problem is elsewhere, and leaving it behind by temporarily letting yourself go (shopping) is thought to operate as a pleasurable equivalent to 'pulling yourself together': you find the happier self through buying a new image. In the picture of retail therapy, shopping is seen as a drug, but the drug is either addictive or therapeutic, oscillating uncertainly between the two.

Where shopping addiction has the force of an illness, requiring psychotherapy or other forms of treatment, it is almost exclusively a female source of suffering. This has not changed in the more than a century since 'kleptomania', the department-store disease, was first clinically identified as a psychiatric condition. In the medical literature too, it was seen as being fostered by the new conditions of shopping: a psychological condition with identifiable social causes.

In this regard, it is interesting that Barnabooth, Valéry Larbaud's fictional turn-of-the-century millionaire (see Chapter 2), is not exempt from the pathological as well as the pleasurable associations of female shopping. '*Crises* of *boutiquisme*' begin to suggest this: there is something compulsive and addictive about the bouts of shopping he engages in.[6] The urge comes on him and he can't stop himself. At one point the suggestion of illness tips over into its clinically defined form, when Archie goes in for a bit of kleptomania (his word for it). He starts filching exquisite little handkerchiefs from boutiques where he has spent enormous sums of money. Archie's stealing, like his shopping, is characterized by there being *no need* for it – he doesn't lack the money any more than he wants the things. He hopes that shoplifting will give him a thrill, as he has heard that it does; but in fact it doesn't, and he keeps on doing it partly in the hope that the promised experience will eventually follow. Yet from one point of view, Archie's self-styled kleptomania is a more restrained form of behaviour than his shopping: it involves control and limitations (not much can be concealed), whereas the buying sprees need neither of these.

On a smaller scale, kleptomania continued to be a recognized condition, often regarded, as it was on its first appearance, as a convenient excuse for shoplifting: she helped herself because she couldn't help herself; she really *didn't* have a choice. Both the taunts and the typical traits identified have remained remarkably consistent across the other changes in shopping over the past century. A French article of 1963 was still referring back to Zola's novel of 1883 for its paradigm of department-store shopping, both the paying and the non-paying varieties. 'A "distinguished" woman doesn't steal, she kleptomanizes':

> The true kleptomaniac is very rare: the outstanding characteristics are: attraction for a particular object, the capacity to pay, immediate admission, absence of remorse,

collecting the stolen objects or else systematically destroying them. It is gratuitous theft, theft for its own sake, which belongs to psychiatry.[7]

The commoner shopping affliction of the present-day 'credit-card junkie' does not involve the thrills or fears of criminal behaviour that were always identified as part of the structure of kleptomania; and if only for practical reasons, the kleptomaniac did not necessarily take very much. But the common factor for both kleptomaniac and shopaholic is their taking literally the invitations of stores and catalogues – choose anything you like – and the suggestion that there is always something more to want: why ever stop shopping? As we have seen, floor plans for both department stores and supermarkets were deliberately designed to get the customer to 'lose herself', to deviate whether she wishes to or not, in order to find other things on the way to whatever she might be looking for.

## Supermarket futures

In 1962, the British trade journal *The Grocer* published a centenary number that included a fanciful feature on 'The Grocery Shop of the Future?'. The accompanying illustration, a black-and-white drawing (see p. 235), shows mother, daughter and dog returning from the supermarket in their flying-saucer-shaped helicopter. Outside a ranch-style suburban dwelling, father and son stand waving a welcome in the distance.[8] This private helicopter fantasy had some currency at the time: in France, René Uhrich's book, also published in 1962, imagines that in the United States at least, 'the civilisation of the automobile' will soon give way to 'the civilisation of the helicopter'.[9]

In the article, Howard Fox runs through possible prospects for stores that in the 1970s will move from rectangular to circular designs, perhaps with 'a series of little personal shops' round the perimeter. The customer stands on moving aisles, getting off whenever she wishes. In the dim distance that can be glimpsed beyond the 1970s, the shoppers have come to a complete standstill as the goods circulate to offer themselves for her inspection: 'Eventually, the entire perimeter of a store may be arranged in lounges, with the shopping area a huge revolving island. The housewife would sit, talk with her friends and pick items as they pass by.'[10]

This passage is quoted from an American source on which the whole article is based: characteristically, the future of supermarket shopping is imagined in an American mode. And in numerous respects, the piece returns us to earlier histories – of supermarkets themselves, of their antecedents, and of the first projections of their futures. With those little shops round the edge, the old high street or Main Street is back, now inside the single store. Shopping, we learn, is to be 'a pleasure rather than a chore'.[11] The homely lounges might almost include the odd canary.

From the perspective of 1990s Britain, these 1960s fantasies, in their own time echoing futures past, become strange in another way, comfortably and uncomfortably familiar in their partial anticipation of our own present. There is the out-of-town site reached by private transport; the deli and fresh fish and bakery counters round the edge to signify service along-side self-service, the best of all worlds under one roof; the place to sit and talk. Supermarkets may not have changed their clas-sical four-sided structure, to transform themselves into circles with moving aisles. But in certain ways, they have almost gone further than Fox's projections. It is as though they were turning the wheels of retailing revolutions full circle, coming to be all shops to all people, to recapitulate all the phases of retailing history under their single roof.

Evoking the fonder memories of the small shops and the street market they have supplanted, supermarkets parade their counters with personal service – the baker, the fishmonger, the butcher, the dry cleaner, and even, in England, the post office and the bank. In the wake of their general upmarketing, as they come to sell more and more expensive, recherché lines, they loudly proclaim their fidelity to their cheap origins, still piling it high and selling it low with ranges of minimally priced own-brand goods. At the same time, like the grand department stores in their heyday, they now present themselves as fashionable as well as cheap. Where the department stores collected the exotic products of the colonies, supermarkets sell 'ethnic' cuisine and plant out the former colonies to supply them with esoteric tropical vegetables. And where they were once associated solely or primarily with the selling of food, supermarkets have extended their range of non-food lines and services so far that they have come to resemble the department stores in contents as well as in forms. American supermarkets offer e-mail facilities, catering and restaurants. In Britain too there are cafés, inviting the slower time of an outing. Now, you can be doing the shopping and going shopping, getting the basics and enjoying yourself, all in one place and one time.

Or indeed, it might seem, at all times and everywhere. For supermarkets in Britain have risen in the 1990s to a position of unprecedented prominence in that blur between media representations and actual behaviour that makes up the fabric of daily life. They seem to be occupying every possible space and time, from daytime and prime-time TV advertising to Sunday morning family shopping in the wake of the relaxation of the laws on opening hours in 1994, and now all-night shopping as well. In their metamorphosis into out-of-town superstores, they have become the focus for a new environmental argument about the decline of urban centres and the growth of a car-dependent culture. The old image of the supermarket shopper as a female zombie has given way to a diverse population: anyman, anywoman and especially anybaby – for we all have our special trolleys now, thoughtfully provided to meet our aisle-cruising needs from Pampers to eternity. And not a deviant in sight.

Meanwhile, across the turn of the new century, the computer has become not just the model of the efficient consumer but a new means and medium of consumption (and sometimes itself an object of desire). Internet shopping has taken off – as a constant topic of discussion as much as in reality. Supermarkets and other stores are experimenting with many kinds of 'e-tail' and home delivery, sometimes linked. As so often in the history of shopping, there is speculation that 'the high street' will suffer. Malls or shopping centres, the first poachers of town trade, are rarely mentioned. It is as though this atmosphere of ultra-modernity somehow prompted a return to the older symbols of a long-gone continuity. The high street has not been the high street for a long time now; perhaps it was only ever stable as the standard image of lost or threatened locality in an ever-repeated simple story of usurpatory change.

When Bernardo Trujillo and his followers quoted 'All the world's a stage', they saw a drama without end, the permanent showmanship of commerce and the lights of the supermarket never going down. On the computer screen or in the mall, the ghosts in the windows never show up in a blaze of unearthly light because the shop has never closed and there is no street outside to grow dark. There is nothing outside the supermarket.

Yet in another kind of development, big supermarket chains in Britain are reversing the movements of half a century by experimenting with small stores in city centres. And in less obvious ways, some other new forms of shopping can also be seen as returning to long-established practices. At the beginning of the last century, telephone shopping was an early prototype of internet shopping: the wealthy housewife could deal directly with the store by ordering goods herself and avoiding the mistakes or misdemeanours of the servant who would otherwise shop on her behalf. A century ago, mail-order catalogues played a vital part in the dissemination of consumerly habits and desires – to rural America and to Europeans in the colonies. Now, they appear as a first form of virtual shopping: images of merchandise for browsing at home. At the same time, at the functional rather than the imaginative end of shopping, home delivery restores one of the tasks of distribution that self-service took away. It also takes the private car that had served as a delivery vehicle for so much of the twentieth century off the road once more. And in an ironic repetition of the history of self-service itself, where bookselling can be seen as the forerunner of the open display and browsing of the supermarket, it is currently books that are the products most commonly bought via the internet.

Against the sense of shopping's incessant encroachments and extensions, echoes and mutations like these suggest a more complex history, one in which earlier moments resurface in the context of new developments and new arguments about shopping's future.

> Two jolly bears once lived in a wood;
> Their little son lived there too.
> One day his mother sent him off
> The marketing to do.
>
> She wanted honey, fruit, and eggs,
> And told him not to stray,
> For many things might happen to
> Small bears who lost the way.[12]

Not even Big Bear, let alone poor Rupert and his parents making their first appearance in 1920, could have known into what strange ways the humble food-shopping errand would lead them by the end of the twentieth century.

# Notes

## 1 The Haunted Superstore

1 Emile Zola, *Au Bonheur des Dames* (1883; Paris: Garnier Flammarion, 1971), p. 258.
2 See Jennifer Cross, *The Supermarket Trap: The Consumer and the Food Industry* (Bloomington: Indiana UP, 1970), and Marion Giordan, *The Consumer Jungle* (London: Fontana, 1974).
3 Paul Morand, *New York* (Paris: Ernest Flammarion, 1930), pp. 88–9.
4 Frank Pick, Foreword to Major G. Harrison and F. C. Mitchell, *The Home Market: A Handbook of Statistics* (London: George Allen & Unwin Ltd., 1936), pp. v–vi.
5 Pick, p. v.

## 2 The Mobile Shopper

1 Valéry Larbaud, *Journal intime* d' 'A. O. Barnabooth' (1913), in *Œuvres* (Paris: Gallimard, Pléiade, 1957), p. 87. Further page references are given within the text.
2 See Marcel Arland, 'Préface', p. xviii, and G. Jean-Aubry and R. Mallet, 'Notes', p. 1150, in Larbaud, *Œuvres*.
3 Theodore Dreiser, *Sister Carrie* (1900; New York: Penguin, 1981), p. 327.
4 Dreiser, p. 326.
5 M. Jeune, 'The Ethics of Shopping', *The Fortnightly Review*, vol. LVII (1895), 124.
6 Evelyne Sullerot, *La vie des femmes* (Paris: Gonthier, 1965), pp. 103–4.
7 Sullerot, p. 104.
8 Elizabeth Gaskell, *Mary Barton* (1848; Harmondsworth: Penguin, 1970), p. 61.

## 3 The Silent Salesman

1 Paul H. Nystrom, *Retail Selling and Store Management* (New York: D. Appleton and Company, 1925), p. 11.
2 Milton Alexander, *Display Ideas for Super Markets* (New York: *The Progressive Grocer*, Butterick Publishing Co., 1958), p. 29.
3 *Progressive Grocer Colonial Study*, *Progressive Grocer*, January 1964, p. C 82.
4 Nystrom, p. 55.
5 Nystrom, pp. 56–7.
6 William L. Butler, *How to Make Grocery Windows Pay* (New York:*The Progressive Grocer*, Butterick Publishing Co., 1932), pp. 1–2.
7 Ellis E. Somake and Rolf Hellberg, *Shops and Stores Today: Their Design, Planning and Organisation* (London: B. T. Batsford Ltd., 1956), p. 111.
8 E. D. McGarry, 'Marketing Research in the Academic Field', *American*

*Marketing Journal* 1:2 (April 1934), 77.

9  R. Freulon, *Pour faire des affaires dans l'alimentation: L'art de vendre, de diriger et d'organiser au service du détaillant, du grossiste, du fabricant* (Paris: Editions Publis, 1924), p. 52.

10  D. E. A. Charlton, *The Art of Packaging* (London: The Studio Publications, Inc., [1938]), p. 96.

11  'Super Markets and the Packager', *Modern Packaging*, 11:1 (September 1937), 45.

12  *Super Market Merchandising*, April 1953, 9.

13  Floyd L. Vaughan, *Marketing and Advertising: An Economic Appraisal* (Princeton: Princeton UP, 1928), p. 94.

14  *Shelf Appeal, Omnibus of Marketing and Packaging* (London: Creative Journals Ltd., 1938), n.p.

15  Richard Hoggart, *The Uses of Literacy: Changing Patterns in English Mass Culture* (1957; Boston: Beacon Press, 1961), p. 90.

16  Pierre Herbin, *Comment concevoir et rédiger votre publicité* (Paris: Editions de la revue, *La Publicité*, 1938), p. 305.

17  A. S. J. Baster, *Advertising Reconsidered* (London: P. S. King & Son Ltd., 1935), p. 20.

18  See *Shelf Appeal*, 3:4 (October 1935), 24–39.

## 4  The Passer-by and the Shop Window

1  Virginia Woolf, *The Years* (1937; Oxford: Oxford World's Classics, 1992), p. 316.

2  See Rachel Bowlby, 'Walking, women and writing', in *Still Crazy after all these Years: Women, Writing and Psychoanalysis* (London: Routledge, 1992), pp. 1–33.

3  Samuel Taylor Coleridge, 'Reflections on Having Left a Place of Retirement' (1796), lines 9–18, in *Selected Poetry and Prose* (San Francisco: Rinehart, 1971), pp. 16–17.

4  Virginia Woolf, *The Waves* (1931; Oxford: Oxford World's Classics, 1992), pp. 52–3.

5  Luke, 10: 31–2.

6  Friedrich Nietzsche, *Thus Spake Zarathustra*, trans. R. J. Hollingdale (Harmondsworth: Penguin, 1969), p. 198.

7  Beverley Pick, 'Trends in Window Display in Great Britain', in Walter Herdeg (ed.), *International Window Display* (London: Cassell and Company Limited, 1951), p. 55.

8  *Parade* 6 (juin 1927), 3.

9  Herbert N. Casson, *Window Display Above All* (London: The Efficiency Magazine [1934]), p. 62.

10  Paul H. Nystrom, *Retail Selling and Store Management* (New York: D. Appleton and Company, 1925), p. 61.

11  Casson, p. 78.

12  Richard Harman, 'Window and Interior Display', in W. G. Copsey (ed.), *The Practical Grocer* (London: The Gresham Publishing Company Ltd.,

[1933]), vol. I, p. 50.

13 Cyril C. Freer, *The Inner Side of Advertising: A Practical Handbook for Advertisers, Those Engaged in Advertising, and Students* (1921; 2nd edn London: The Library Press Limited, 1925), p. 257.

14 Casson, p. 41.

15 Casson, pp. 29–30,

16 C. L. T. Beeching, 'Window and Shop Dressing', in Beeching (ed.), *The Modern Grocer and Provision Dealer*, new edn (London: Caxton Publishing Company Limited, [1937]), vol. II, p. 204.

17 Casson, p. 14.

18 Harman, 'Window and Interior Display', p. 33.

19 Casson, p. 67.

20 Gaston Fournials, *L'Etalage: Bases théoriques et méthodes pratiques* (1949; 2nd edn Paris: Dunod, 1956), p. 20.

21 William L. Butler, *How to Make Grocery Windows Pay* (New York: *The Progressive Grocer*, Butterick Publishing Company, 1932), p. 14.

22 Casson, p. 72.

23 Casson, p. 66.

24 See, for instance, Gustave Le Bon, *Psychologie des foules* (1895; Paris: P.U.F., 1983); W. Trotter, *Instincts of the Herd in Peace and War* (1916; London: The Scientific Book Club, 1942); Sigmund Freud, *Group Psychology and the Analysis of the Ego* (1921), trans. James Strachey, in *Standard Edition of the Complete Psychological Works of Sigmund Freud*, vol. XVIII (London: Hogarth Press, 1955), pp. 65–143.

25 Walter Dill Scott, *Influencing Men in Business: The Psychology of Argument and Suggestion* (1911), 3rd edn, revised and enlarged by Delton T. Howard (New York: The Ronald Press Co., 1928), p. 159.

26 Richard Harman (ed.), *The Practical Display Instructor* (London: Blandford Press Ltd., 1937), p. 14.

27 Bournville Studio, *Sweet-Shop Success: A Handbook for the Sweet Retailer* (London: Sir Isaac Pitman & Sons, Ltd., 1949), p. 112.

28 Harman, 'Window and Interior Display', pp. 33–4.

29 Harman (ed.), *The Practical Display Instructor*, p. 9.

30 E. Rachinel and M Buisson, *Vente et publicité*, Agenda Dunod (Paris: Dunod, 1936), p. 317.

31 E. Rachinel and M. Buisson, *Vente et publicité*, Agenda Dunod (Paris: Dunod, 1930), p. 369.

32 Emile Zola, *Au Bonheur des Dames* (1883; Paris: Garnier Flammarion, 1971), p. 87.

33 See Lou Taylor, *Mourning Dress: A Costume and Social History* (London: George Allen and Unwin, 1983).

34 Charles Eyre Pascoe, *London of To-day: An Illustrated Book for this Season, and for all Seasons: 1892* (London: Hamish Hamilton, 1892), p. 382.

35 *Parade* 4 (avril 1927), 9.

36 *Display for the Man's Shop*, published by the magazine *Style for Men* (London: The National Trade Press Ltd., [1938]), p. 4.

37 *Display for the Man's Shop*, pp. 4–5.

38  Harman (ed.), *The Practical Display Instructor*, p. 10.

39  Harman, *loc. cit.*

40  Harman, 'Window and Interior Display', p. 50.

41  Casson, p. 18.

42  F. P. Bishop, *The Economics of Advertising* (London: Robert Hale Limited, 1944), p. 48.

43  Richard Hoggart, *The Uses of Literacy: Changing Patterns in English Mass Culture* (1957; Boston: Beacon Press, 1961), p. 120.

44  Morris Ketchum, Jr., *Shops and Stores.* (New York: Reinhold Publishing Corporation, Progressive Architecture Library, 1948), p. 239.

45  *Parade* 5 (mai 1927), 1.

46  Jean-Paul Sartre, *Situations* III (Paris: Gallimard, 1949), pp. 117–18.

47  Ketchum, p. 148.

48  See Walter Benjamin, *Das Passagen-Werk* (1982); trans. Howard Eiland and Kevin McLaughlin, *The Arcades Project* (Cambridge, Harvard University Press, 1999).

49  Raymond McGrath and A. C. Frost, *Glass in Architecture and Decoration* (London: The Architectural Press, 1937), p. 147.

50  Louis Aragon, *Le paysan de Paris* (1926; Paris, Gallimard, 1933), p. 18.

## 5  The Package

1  Gilbert Russell, *Advertisement Writing* (London: Ernest Benn Ltd., 1927), p. 38.

2  Richard B. Franken and Carroll B. Larrabee, *Packages that Sell* (New York: Harper & Brothers Publishers, 1928), n.p.

3  Franken and Larrabee, p. 1.

4  Franken and Larrabee, p. 277.

5  Floyd L. Vaughan, *Marketing and Advertising: An Economic Appraisal* (Princeton: Princeton UP, 1928), p. 28.

6  Harry Jones, *Planned Packaging* (London: George Allen and Unwin, 1950), p. 33.

7  *Shelf Appeal*, 3:9 (March 1936), 22.

8  *Shelf Appeal*, 8:2 (August 1940), 20.

9  *Shelf Appeal*, 8:3 (September 1940), 21.

10  See *Shelf Appeal*, 3:3 (September 1935), 17.

11  *Modern Packaging*, 11:10 (June 1938), 63.

12  *Shelf Appeal*, 2:2 (August–September 1934), 102–3.

13  *Shelf Appeal*, 1:7 (January 1934), 278.

14  J. de Holden Stone, 'Beautiful Pictures', *Shelf Appeal*, 1:8 (February 1934), 282–3, 289.

15  A. S. J. Baster, *Advertising Reconsidered* (London: P. S. King & Son Ltd., 1935), p. 47.

16  *Shelf Appeal*, 5:3 (September 1937), 20.

17  *Shelf Appeal*, July/August 1941, 19.

18  *Shelf Appeal*, 1:2 (August 1933), 45.

19  *Shelf Appeal*, 1:2 (August 1933), 46.

20 Walter Dill Scott, *The Psychology of Advertising: A Simple Exposition of the Principles of Psychology in their Relation to Successful Advertising* (1908; 5th edn, Boston: Small, Maynard & Company, 1913), pp. 192–4.

21 Walter Benjamin, 'The work of art in the age of mechanical reproduction' (1935), in *Illuminations*, trans. Harry Zohn (New York: Schocken Books, 1969).

22 *Shelf Appeal*, 2:9 (March 1935), 434.

23 *Shelf Appeal*, 1:9 (March 1934), 378–9.

24 *Shelf Appeal*, 2:1 (July 1934), 32.

25 Franken and Larrabee, p. 14.

26 Franken and Larrabee, p. 17.

27 *Shelf Appeal*, 2:1 (July 1934), 63.

28 *Shelf Appeal*, 3:3 (September 1935), 46.

29 *Shelf Appeal*, 1:9 (March 1934), 329.

30 *Shelf Appeal*, 3:3 (September 1935), 7.

31 *Modern Packaging*, 11:1 (September 1937), 42.

32 *Shelf Appeal*, 2:1 (July 1934), 63.

33 Georges Blond, *J'ai vu vivre l'Amérique de New York à Hollywood* (Paris: Librairie Arthème Fayard, 1957), p. 53.

34 *Shelf Appeal*, 3:5 (November 1935), 41.

35 *Shelf Appeal*, 2:8 (February 1935), 343.

36 *Shelf Appeal*, 3:6 (December 1935), 4.

37 *Shelf Appeal*, 1:9 (March 1934), 341.

38 *Shelf Appeal*, 5:3 (September 1937), 41.

39 *Shelf Appeal*, 3:10 (April 1936), 28–9.

40 *Shelf Appeal* 5:2 (August 1937), 31.

41 *Progressive Grocer*, March 1966, p. K139.

42 *Shelf Appeal*, 1:7 (January 1934), 269–72.

43 Jacket blurb for I. O. Evans, *The World of To-morrow: A Junior Book of Forecasts* (London: Dennis Archer, 1933).

44 *Shelf Appeal*, 1:5 (November 1933), 130.

45 *Shelf Appeal*, 1:3 (September 1933), 86.

46 See Virginia Woolf, *Orlando* (1928; Oxford: Oxford World's Classics, 1992).

## 6 The First Shoppers

1 Henry Foster Adams, *Advertising and its Mental Laws* (New York: Macmillan, 1916), p. 256.

2 *Shelf Appeal*, 8:9 (May–June 1941), 19.

3 *Shelf Appeal*, 8:2 (August 1940), 20.

4 *Shelf Appeal*, 3:10 (April 1936), 49.

5 *Shelf Appeal*, 3:10 (April 1936), 47–8.

6 *Shelf Appeal*, 1:1 (July 1933), 19–20.

7 *Shelf Appeal*, 1:1 (July 1933), 26.

8 Stuart Chase and F. J. Schlink, *Your Money's Worth: A Study in the Waste of the Consumer's Dollar* (New York: Macmillan, 1927), p. 9.

9 'Rupert and the Winter Sale' (1960), in *Rupert: The Daily Express Annual*

(London: Beaverbrook Newspapers, 1975), p. 98. Further page references are given in the main text.

10 Ibid., p.99

11 'Rupert and the Broken Plate' (1954), in *Rupert: The Daily Express Annual* (London: Beaverbrook Newspapers, 1975), p. 51.

12 M. M. Zimmerman, *The Super Market: A Revolution in Distribution* (New York: Mass Distribution Publications, Inc., 1955), p. 322.

13 George Perry with Alfred Bestall, *Rupert: A Bear's Life* (London: Michael Joseph, 1985), p. 17. Other information about Rupert's history is taken from this book.

14 Charles Vernon, *The Sweet Shop: A Handbook for Retail Confectioners* (London: Sir Isaac Pitman & Sons, Ltd., 1939), p. 81.

15 *Shelf Appeal*, 3:3 (September 1935), 27.

16 John Newsom, *The Education of Girls* (London: Faber and Faber Ltd., 1948), p. 98.

17 Alexander Pope, *The Rape of the Lock*, Canto 1, l.130.

18 John Ruskin, 'Of Queens' Gardens', in *Sesame and Lilies* (1865; London: Dent, Everyman's Library, 1970), p. 59.

19 See John A. Howard and James Hulbert, *Advertising and the Public Interest: A Staff Report to the Federal Trade Commission* (Chicago: Crain Communications, Inc., 1973).

20 *Shelf Appeal*, 5: 6 (December 1937), 14.

## 7 The Supermarket's Beginnings

1 M. M. Zimmerman, *Super Market: Spectacular Exponent of Mass Distribution* (New York: Super Market Publishing Co., 1937), p. v.

2 Zimmerman, pp. v–vi.

3 Zimmerman, pp. 6, 8.

4 Zimmerman, p. 9.

5 Zimmerman, p. 6.

6 Zimmerman, p. 9.

7 Zimmerman, p. vi.

8 René Uhrich, *Super-marchés et usines de distribution: Hier aux Etats-Unis, aujourd'hui en France?* (Paris: Plon, 1962), p. 7.

9 M. M. Zimmerman, *The Super Market: A Revolution in Distribution* (New York: McGraw-Hill Book Company, Inc., 1955), p. 44.

10 Quoted in Uhrich, p. 59.

11 *Shelf Appeal*, 2:5 (November 1934), 208.

12 Carl W. Dipman, *The Modern Grocery Store* (New York: *The Progressive Grocer*, Butterick Publishing Co., 1931), p. iii.

13 Carl W. Dipman (ed.), *Modern Food Stores* (New York: *The Progressive Grocer*, Butterick Publishing Co., 1935), p. 7.

14 Dipman (1931), p. iv.

15 Dipman (1935), p. 10.

16 Carl W. Dipman and John E. O'Brien, *Self-Service and Semi-Self-Service Food Stores* (New York: *The Progressive Grocer*, Butterick Publishing Co., 1940), p. 8.

17 Dipman (1931), p. v.
18 Dipman (1935), p. 11.
19 *Super Market Merchandising*, April 1953, 123.
20 Dipman (1931), p. 142.
21 Dipman (1931), pp. 143–5.
22 Dipman (1931), pp. 145–6.
23 Dipman (1931), p. 148.
24 Dipman (1931), p. 149.
25 Edward A. Brand, *Modern Supermarket Operation* (1963; 2nd edn, New York: Fairchild Publications, Inc., Book Division, 1965), p. 7.
26 Reavis Cox [n.t.], in Albert B. Smith (ed.), *Competitive Distribution in a Free High-Level Economy and its Implications for the University* (Pittsburgh: Pittsburgh UP, 1957), pp. 54–5.
27 Christine Frederick, *Household Engineering: Scientific Management in the Home* (Chicago: American School of Home Economics, 1920), p. 304.

## 8 The Dayton Connection

1 Zimmerman (1955), p. 291.
2 Zimmerman, p. 294.
3 Zimmerman, pp. 289–90.
4 Zimmerman, p. 293.
5 Quoted e.g. in René Uhrich, *Super-marchés et usines de distribution: Hier aux Etats-Unis, aujourd'hui en France* (Paris: Plon, 1962), p. 180.
6 Quoted e.g. in David Powell, *Counter Revolution: The Tesco Story* (London: GraftonBooks, 1991), p. 90.
7 See, for instance, Pierre Benearts, 'Le commerce français a-t-il épousé le siècle?', *Revue Politique et Parlementaire*, vol. 63, no. 717 (novembre 1961), 25–32; C.-J. Gignoux and Bernard Simiot (eds), *Grands magasins, supermarchés . . .* , *Documents de la 'Revue des Deux Mondes'*, 22 (août–septembre, 1962); Eric Langeard and Robert Malsagne, *Les magasins de grande surface: Politique commerciale* (Paris: Dunod Economie, 1971).
8 See Etienne Thil, *Les inventeurs du commerce moderne: Des grands magasins aux bébés-requins* (Paris: Arthaud, 1966), p. 123.
9 Uhrich, p. 8.
10 Uhrich, p. 203.
11 Etienne Thil, *Combat pour la distribution: D'Edouard Leclerc aux supermarchés* (Paris: Arthaud, 1964), p. 122; ellipses in text.
12 Thil, *Les inventeurs*, pp. 105–6.
13 Trujillo, 'Postface', in Thil, *Inventeurs*, p. 293.
14 *Grands magasins, supermarchés . . .* , p. 42.
15 Quoted in Uhrich, p. 139.
16 M. Quétaud, *Etude générale sur les emballages* (Paris: Dunod, 1949), p. 41.
17 Quétaud, p. 42.
18 *Entreprise*, 18 February 1961, quoted in Jean-Marc Villermet, *Naissance de l'hypermarché* (Paris: Armand Colin, 1991), p. 74.

19 Villermet, p. 132.
20 *Magasins* 66 (avril 1968), 7.
21 Villermet, p. 130.
22 Uhrich, p. 59.
23 *Magasins* 72 (décembre–janvier 1968–9), 13.

## 9 The Jungle and Other Post-war Supermarkets

1 Martin H. Perry, *How to Start a Shop* (London: Sidgwick and Jackson Limited, 1947), p. 49.
2 William T. Walsh (ed.), *Salesmanship Simplified: A Short Cut to Success* (Chicago: Opportunity Publishing Co., 1927), p. 184.
3 Paul H. Nystrom, *Retail Selling and Store Management* (New York: D. Appleton and Company, 1925), p. 144.
4 See Virginia Woolf, 'The Leaning Tower' (1940), in *A Woman's Essays* (London: Penguin, 1992), p. 161; and 'Thoughts on Peace in an Air Raid' (1940), in *The Crowded Dance of Modern Life* (London: Penguin, 1993), pp. 168–72.
5 Georges-Marie Tronquet, 'La recherche au service de la publicité', in *Vendre*, 405 (septembre 1963), 43.
6 Randall Jarrell, 'The Taste of the Age' (1953), in *A Sad Heart at the Supermarket: Essays and Fables* (1962; New York: Atheneum, 1967), p. 26.
7 The quotation is from David Karp, *Leave Me Alone* (London: Victor Gollancz, 1957), p. 151.
8 Hannah Arendt, 'Society and Culture', in Norman Jacobs (ed.), *Culture for the Millions? Mass Media in Modern Society* (Boston: Beacon Press, 1961), pp. 46–8.
9 See, for instance, Ernest Dichter, *The Strategy of Desire* (London and New York: T.V. Boardman & Company Limited, 1960), p. 186.
10 D. E. A. Charlton, *The Art of Packaging* (London: The Studio Publications, Inc. [1938]), p. 91.
11 A. Q. Mowbray, *The Thumb and the Scale: Or the Supermarket Shell Game* (Philadelphia: J. B. Lippincott Company, 1967), p. 1.
12 Vance Packard, *The Hidden Persuaders* (1957; Harmondsworth: Penguin, 1960).
13 Mowbray, p. 2.
14 Eirlys Roberts, *Consumers* (London: C. A. Watts & Co. Ltd., 1966), p. 34.
15 'The Original Computer' (1963), reprinted in Mowbray, p. 143.
16 Jennifer Cross, *The Supermarket Trap: The Consumer and the Food Industry* (Bloomington: Indiana UP, 1970), p. viii.
17 Cross, p. viii.
18 Cross, p. 152.
19 Cross, p. 96.
20 Cross, p. 153.
21 Cross, p. 154.
22 *Progressive Grocer*, January 1964, p. C85.
23 Cross, p. 157.

## 10 The Reader in the Supermarket

1 Ian McEwan, *The Child in Time* (1987; London: Picador, 1988), p. 117.
2 Samuel Taylor Coleridge, *Biographia Literaria* (1817), ed. with introduction by George Watson (London: J. M. Dent & Sons Ltd, 1975), p. 28.
3 Q. D. Leavis, *Fiction and the Reading Public* (London: Chatto & Windus, 1932), pp. 16–17.
4 Leavis, p. 19.
5 *Shelf Appeal*, 5:1 (July 1937), 48.
6 Ibid., *loc. cit*
7 See *Shelf Appeal*, 8:5 (January 1941), 10–12.
8 See *Magasins* 53 (septembre–octobre 1965), 53–7.
9 Leslie A. Fiedler, *Waiting for the End: The American Literary Scene from Hemingway to Baldwin* (1964; London: Jonathan Cape, 1965), p. 249. In fact, IBM really did offer a night-school version of the University of Chicago Great Books course to its senior staff at this time.
10 W. G. McLelland, *Studies in Retailing* (Oxford: Basil Blackwell, 1963), p. 46.
11 See Richard Hoggart, *The Uses of Literacy: Changing Patterns in English Mass Culture* (1957; Boston: Beacon Press, 1961).
12 McLelland, p. 10.
13 John Updike, 'A & P' (1960), in *Pigeon Feathers and Other Stories* (London: André Deutsch, 1963), p. 196.
14 Allen Ginsberg, 'A Supermarket in California' (1955), in *Howl* (San Francisco: City Lights, 1956), pp. 23–4.
15 See Betty Friedan, *The Feminine Mystique* (1963; New York: Dell Publishing Co., 1964), chapter 1.
16 Ira Levin, *The Stepford Wives* (1972; New York: Signet, 1994), p. 59. Further page references are given within the main text.
17 Joanna Trollope, *The Rector's Wife* (1991; London: Black Swan, 1994), p. 64. Further page references are given within the main text.
18 Don DeLillo, *White Noise* (1985; New York, Penguin, 1986), p. 81. Further page references are given within the main text.

## 11 The Shopper in the Survey

1 *Progressive Grocer*, 'Consumer Dynamics in the Supermarket', 1965–66, K30, K28. 'K' (for Kroger) is the special pagination adopted for the survey instalments. Further such references are given within the text.
2 Wilfred Burns, *British Shopping Centres: New Trends in Layout and Distribution* (London: Leonard Hill [Books] Limited, 1959), p. 39.
3 Burns, p. 39.
4 Simone de Beauvoir, *Le Deuxième sexe* (1949; Paris: Gallimard, Folio, 1986), vol. II, p. 272.
5 'Shopping', in *Which?*, November 1969, 337.
6 British Market Research Bureau Limited, *Shopping in Suburbia: A Report on Housewives' Reactions to Supermarket Shopping* (London: J. Walter Thompson Company Limited, 1963), pp. 11–12. Further page references

are given in the main text.

7  Mr Peter Firmston Williams, Managing Director of Asda Stores Ltd., 'The case for hypermarkets and superstores', *Hypermarkets and Superstores: Report of a House of Commons Seminar*, Unit for Retail Planning Information Limited, May 1976, p. 10.

8  'Shopping', 336.

9  'Eirlys Roberts writes', *Which?*, November 1969, 323.

10  Margaret Hall, 'The Consumer Sector', in G. D. N. Worswick and P. H. Ady (eds), *The British Economy in the Nineteen-Fifties* (Oxford: Clarendon P, 1962), p. 447.

11  *The Listener*, 27 January 1937, 146.

12  Thos. H. Lewis, MBE (ed.), *Modern Retailing: Stepping-Stones to Success in Retailing* (London: The Caxton Publishing Co. Ltd, 1949), vol. II, p. 78.

13  David Powell, *Counter Revolution: The Tesco Story* (London: GraftonBooks, 1991), p. 118.

14  Powell, p. 62.

## 12  The Deviant, the Checkout and the Future

1  'The Lady and the Layout', *Super Market Merchandising*, June 1957, 56.

2  'The Lady and the Layout', 57.

3  *Consumer Dynamics in the Supermarket*, *Progressive Grocer*, October 1965–October 1966, K85; further page references are given in the main text.

4  *Progressive Grocer, Colonial Study*, part IV (January 1964), C83.

5  L. A. Cherriman and R. Wilson, *The Operation of a Self-Service Store: a limited investigation of the merchandise layout and shelf utilisation in two Co-operative Food Stores, Co-operative College Papers*, 9 (Loughborough: Co-operative Union Education Department, 1962), p. 44. Further page references are given in parentheses in the main text.

6  Valéry Larbaud, *Journal Intime* d' 'A. O. Barnabooth' (1913), in *Œuvres* (Paris: Gallimard, Pléiade, 1957), p. 104.

7  *Vendre* 403 (août 1963), 66.

8  Howard Fox, 'The Grocery Shop of the Future?', *'The Grocer' Centenary Number* (1962), p. 180.

9  René Uhrich, *Super-marchés et usines de distribution: Hier aux Etats-Unis, aujourd'hui en France?* (Paris: Plon, 1962), p. v.

10  Fox, pp. 180–1.

11  Fox, p. 180.

12  *Daily Express*, 8 November 1920; see further chapter 6, p. 126.

# Acknowledgements

I am most grateful to the Rutgers Center for Historical Analysis for a fellowship in 1993, which enabled me to begin work on this book. A number of libraries provided invaluable support: the Mann Library at Cornell; the Bodleian at Oxford; the Bibliothèque Nationale and, especially, the Bibliothèque Forney, in Paris. Shari Steel of York Castle Museum kindly sought out a wonderful selection of interwar chocolate boxes.

Special thanks to Karen Bowie, Jonathan Dollimore, Jeri Johnson, Cora Kaplan, Rhoda McGraw and Sally Mapstone; and to François Cornilliat, Jan Montefiore and Lucy Newlyn for particular suggestions. At Faber, my warm thanks go to Julian Loose and to Sarah Hulbert, whose meticulous collaboration made the last stages of preparation an unexpected pleasure.

# Illustrations

The author and publishers are grateful to the following for permission to reproduce illustrations:

York Castle Museum (p. 111); Bibliothèque Forney, Paris (p. 152); *Which?*, published by the Consumers Association, 2 Marylebone Road, London NW1 4DF (p. 167); W. H. Smith & Son (p. 187); *The Grocer* (p. 235).

# Short Bibliography

Abelson, Elaine S., *When Ladies Go A-Thieving: Middle-Class Shoplifters in the Victorian Department Store*. New York: Oxford UP, 1989.

Adams, Henry Foster, *Advertising and its Mental Laws*. New York: Macmillan, 1916.

Adburgham, Alison, *Shops and Shopping 1800–1914*. 1964; 2nd edn, London: George Allen and Unwin, 1981.

Alexander, Milton, *Display Ideas for Super Markets*. New York: Butterick Publishing Co., *Progressive Grocer*, 1958.

Angot, Christine, *L'Inceste*. Paris: Stock, 1999.

Ardagh, John, *The New France*. Harmondsworth: Penguin, 1970.

Arendt, Hannah, 'Society and Culture'. In Jacobs (1961), 43–52.

Association Française pour l'Acroissement de la Productivité, *Emballages et conditionnements*. Rapport d'un voyage d'études effectué aux Etats-Unis en 1950 par une mission britannique de productivité. Trans. Paris: 1951

Balzac, Honoré de, *Illusions perdues*. 1843; Paris: Garnier-Flammarion, *1966*.

Baster, A. S. J. *Advertising Reconsidered*. London: P. S. King & Son Ltd., 1935.

Beaverbrook Newspapers, 'Rupert and the Broken Plate'. 1954; *Rupert: The Daily Express Annual*. London: Beaverbrook Newspapers, 1975.

– 'Rupert and the Winter Sale'. 1960; *Rupert: The Daily Express Annual*. London: Beaverbrook Newspapers, 1975.

Beeching, C. L. T. 'Window and Shop Dressing'. In Beeching [1922], vol. II, 191–241.

– *The Modern Grocer and Provision Dealer*. 3 vols, new edn, London: Caxton Publishing Company, Limited [1937].

Benearts, Pierre, 'Le commerce français a-t-il épousé le siècle?' *Revue Politique et Parlementaire*, vol. 63, no. 717 (novembre 1961), 25–32.

Benjamin, Walter, *The Arcades Project*. 1982. Trans. Howard Eiland and Kevin McLaughlin, Cambridge: Harvard University Press, 1999.

– *Illuminations*. Trans. Harry Zohn; New York: Schocken Books, 1969.

– *Reflections: Essays, Aphorisms, Autobiographical Writings*. Trans. Edward Jephcott, ed. with an introduction by Peter Demetz; New York: Harcourt Brace Jovanovich, Inc., 1978.

Benson, Susan Porter, *Counter Cultures: Saleswomen, Managers, and Customers in American Department Stores, 1890–1940*. Urbana: U of Illinois P, 1986.

Bishop, F. P., *The Economics of Advertising*. London: Robert Hale Limited, 1944.

Blond, Georges, *J'ai vu vivre l'Amérique de New York à Hollywood*. Paris: Librairie Arthème Fayard, 1957.

Boorstin, Daniel, *The Image: A Guide to Pseudo-Events in America*. 1961; New York: Atheneum, 1971.

Bournville Studio, *Sweet-Shop Success: A Handbook for the Sweet Retailer*.
London: Sir Isaac Pitman & Sons, Ltd., 1949.

Bowlby, Rachel, *Just Looking: Consumer Culture in Dreiser, Gissing and Zola*.
London: Methuen, 1985.

– *Shopping with Freud*. London: Routledge, 1993.

– *Still Crazy After All These Years: Women, Writing and Psychoanalysis*. London:
Routledge, 1992.

Braithwaite, Dorothea, and S. P. Dobbs, *The Distribution of Consumable Goods:
An Economic Survey*. London: George Routledge & Sons Ltd., 1932.

Brand, Edward A., *Modern Supermarket Operation*. 1963. 2nd edn, New York:
Fairchild Publications, Inc., Book Division, 1965.

British Market Research Bureau Limited, *Shopping in Suburbia*. London:
J. Walter Thompson Company Limited, 1963.

Bronner, Simon J. (ed.), *Consuming Visions: Accumulation and Display of Goods
in America, 1880–1920*. New York: W. W. Norton & Company, 1989.

Buckley, Jim, *The Drama of Display: Visual Merchandising and its Techniques*.
New York: Pellegrini and Cudahy, 1953.

Burns, Wilfred, *British Shopping Centres: New Trends in Layout and Distribution*.
London: Leonard Hill [Books] Limited, 1959.

Butler, William L., *How to Make Grocery Windows Pay*. New York: Butterick
Publishing Co., 1932.


Campbell, Colin, *The Romantic Ethic and the Spirit of Modern Consumerism*.
Oxford: Basil Blackwell, 1987.

Carey, John, *The Intellectuals and the Masses: Pride and Prejudice among the
Literary Intelligentsia, 1880–1939*. London: Faber and Faber, 1992.

Casson, Herbert N., *Window Display Above All*. London: The Efficiency
Magazine [1934].

Charlton, D. E. A., *The Art of Packaging*. London: The Studio Publications, Inc.
[1938].

Chase, Stuart, and F. J. Schlink, *Your Money's Worth: A Study in the Waste of the
Consumer's Dollar*. New York: Macmillan, 1927.

Cherriman, L. A., and R. Wilson, *The Operation of a Self-Service Store: A limited
investigation of the merchandise layout and shelf utilisation in two Co-operative
Food Stores. Co-operative College Papers*, 9 (September 1962); Loughborough:
Co-operative Union Ltd., Education Department.

Coleridge, Samuel Taylor, *Biographia Literaria*. 1817; London: J. M. Dent &
Sons Ltd., 1975.

– *Selected Poetry and Prose*. Ed. Elisabeth Schneider. San Francisco: Rinehart
Press, 1971.

Co-operative Wholesale Society Ltd., *A Consumers' Democracy*. Manchester:
C.W.S., 1951.

Copsey, W. G. (ed.), *The Practical Grocer*. London: The Gresham Publishing
Company Ltd. [1933]. 2 vols.

Corina, Maurice, *Pile it High, Sell it Cheap: The Authorised Biography of Sir John
Cohen, Founder of Tesco*. London: Weidenfeld and Nicolson, 1971.

Cross, Jennifer, *The Supermarket Trap: The Consumer and the Food Industry*.
Bloomington: Indiana UP, 1970.

Darby, W. D., *Story of the Chain Store: A Study of Chain Store Policies and Methods, Particularly as they Affect the Independent Merchant in the Dry Goods Field, together with a General Survey of Chain Store Developments*. New York: Dry Goods Economist, 1928.

Davis, Alec, *Package and Print: The Development of Container and Label Design*. London: Faber and Faber, 1967.

Davis, Dorothy, *A History of Shopping*. London: Routledge & Kegan Paul Ltd, 1966.

De Beauvoir, Simone, *Le Deuxième sexe*. 2 vols, 1949; Paris: Gallimard, Folio, 1986.

Debord, Guy, *La société du spectacle*. 1967; Paris: Editions champ libre, 1973.

De Certeau, Michel, *Arts de faire. L'invention du quotidien*, vol. 1. Paris: Union Générale d'Editions, 10/18, 1980.

De Grazia, Victoria, with Ellen Furlough (eds), *The Sex of Things: Gender and Consumption in Historical Perspective*. Berkeley: U of California P, 1996.

DeLillo, Don, *White Noise*. 1985; New York: Penguin, 1986.

Dichter, Ernest, *Handbook of Consumer Motivations: The Psychology of the World of Objects*. New York: McGraw-Hill Book Company, 1964.

– *The Strategy of Desire*. London and New York: T. V. Boardman & Company Limited, 1960.

Dipman, Carl W. (ed.), *Modern Food Stores*. New York: *Progressive Grocer*, Butterick Publishing Co., 1935.

– *The Modern Grocery Store*. New York: *The Progressive Grocer*, Butterick Publishing Co., 1931.

Dipman, Carl W., and John E. O'Brien, *Self-Service and Semi-Self-Service Food Stores*. New York: *The Progressive Grocer*, Butterick Publishing Co., 1940.

Distributive Trades Economic Development Committee, *The Future of the High Street*. London: HMSO, 1988.

Dreiser, Theodore, *Sister Carrie*. 1900; New York: Penguin, 1981.

Elliott, C. J., *The Retail Grocery Trade*. London: Methuen & Co. Ltd., 1938.

Fournials, Gaston, *L'Etalage: Bases théoriques et méthodes pratiques*. 1949; 2nd edn, Paris: Dunod, 1956.

Fox, Howard, 'The Grocery Shop of the Future?' '*The Grocer*' Centenary Number (1962), 180–1.

Franken, Richard B., and Carroll B. Larrabee, *Packages that Sell*. New York: Harper & Brothers Publishers, 1928.

Frederick, Christine, *Household Engineering: Scientific Management in the Home*. Chicago: American School of Home Economics, 1920.

– *The New Housekeeping: Efficiency Studies in Home Management*. New York: Doubleday, Page & Company, 1916.

Freer, Cyril H., *The Inner Side of Advertising: A Practical Handbook for Advertisers, Those Engaged in Advertising, and Students*. 1921; 2nd edn, London: The Library Press Limited, 1925.

Freulon, R., *Pour faire des affaires dans l'alimentation: L'art de vendre, de diriger et d'organiser au service du détaillant, du grossiste, du fabricant*. Paris: Editions Publis, 1924.

Friedan, Betty, *The Feminine Mystique*. 1963; New York: Dell Publishing Co., 1964.

Gabriel, Yiannis, and Tim Lang, *The Unmanageable Consumer: Contemporary Consumption and its Fragmentations*. London: Sage, 1995.
Galbraith, J. K., *The Affluent Society*. 1958; Harmondsworth: Penguin, 1968.
Gardner, Carl, and Julia Sheppard, *Consuming Passion: The Rise of Retail Culture*. London: Unwin Hyman, 1989.
Gaskell, Elizabeth, *Mary Barton*. 1848; Harmondsworth: Penguin, 1970.
Giard, Luce, and Pierre Mayol, *Habiter, cuisiner. L'invention du quotidien*, vol. 2. Paris: Union Générale d'Editions, 10/18, 1980.
Gignoux, C.-J., and Bernard Simiot (eds), *Grands magasins, supermarchés . . . Documents de la 'Revue des Deux Mondes'*, no. 22 (août–septembre, 1962).
Ginsberg, Allen, *Howl and Other Poems*. San Francisco: City Lights, 1954.
Giordan, Marion, *The Consumer Jungle*. London: Fontana, 1974.
Greenly, A. J. *Psychology as a Sales Factor*. 1927; 2nd edn, London: Sir Isaac Pitman & Sons, Ltd., 1929.
Greer, William, *America the Beautiful: How the Supermarket Came to Main St.* Washington: Food Marketing Institute, 1986.
Gruen, Victor, and Larry Smith, *Shopping Towns USA: The Planning of Shopping Centers*. New York: Reinhold Publishing Corporation, 1960.
Gundrey, Elizabeth, *Your Money's Worth: A Handbook for Consumers*. Harmondsworth: Penguin, 1962.

Hall, Margaret, 'The Consumer Sector'. In G. D. N. Worswick and P. H. Ady (eds), *The British Economy in the Nineteen-Fifties*; Oxford: Clarendon P, 1962, pp. 429–60.
Harman, Richard, 'Window and Interior Display'. In Copsey [1933].
Harrison, Major G., and F. C. Mitchell, *The Home Market: A Book of Facts about People*. London: George Allen & Unwin Ltd, 1939.
– *The Home Market: A Handbook of Statistics*. London: George Allen & Unwin Ltd., 1936.
Harman, Richard (ed.), *The Practical Display Instructor*. London: Blandford Press Ltd., 1937.
Haug, W. F., *Critique of Commodity Aesthetics: Appearance, Sexuality and Advertising in Capitalist Society*. 1971; trans. Robert Bock, Cambridge: Polity, 1986.
Henry, Harry, *Motivation Research: Its Practice and Uses for Advertising, Marketing, and Other Business Purposes*. London: Crosby Lockwood & Son, Ltd., 1958.
Herbin, Pierre, *Comment concevoir et rédiger votre publicité*. Paris: Editions de la revue, *La Publicité*, 1938.
– *Manuel Pratique de Publicité*. La Chapelle-Montligeon (Orne): Les Editions de Montligeon, 1949.
Herdeg, Walter (ed.), *International Window Display*. London: Cassell and Company Limited, 1951.
Hine, Thomas, *The Total Package: The Secret History and Hidden Meanings of Boxes,*

*Bottles, Cans, and Other Persuasive Containers*. Boston: Little, Brown, 1995.

Hoggart, Richard, *The Uses of Literacy: Changing Patterns in English Mass Culture*. 1957; Boston: Beacon Press, 1961.

Howard, John A., and James Hulbert, *Advertising and the Public Interest: A Staff Report to the Federal Trade Commission*. Chicago: Crain Communications, Inc., 1973.

Jacobs, Norman (ed.), *Culture for the Millions? Mass Media in Modern Society*. Boston: Beacon Press, 1961.

Jarrell, Randall, *A Sad Heart at the Supermarket: Essays and Fables*. 1962; New York: Atheneum, 1967.

Jeune, M., 'The Ethics of Shopping'. *The Fortnightly Review*, vol. LVII (1895), 123–32.

Jones, Harry, *Planned Packaging*. London: George Allen and Unwin Ltd, 1950.

Kay, William, *Battle for the High Street*. London: Piatkus, 1987.

Ketchum, Morris, Jr., *Shops & Stores*. New York: Reinhold Publishing Corporation, Progressive Architecture Library, 1948.

Kitson, Henry Dexter, *Manual for the Study of the Psychology of Advertising*. Philadelphia: J. B. Lippincott Company, 1920.

– *The Mind of the Buyer: A Psychology of Selling*. New York: The Macmillan Company, 1921.

Kuisel, Richard F., *Seducing the French: The Dilemma of Americanization*. Berkeley: U of California P, 1993.

Langeard, Eric, and Robert Malsagne, *Les magasins de grande surface: Politique commerciale*. Paris: Dunod Economie, 1971.

Larbaud, Valéry, 'A. O. Barnabooth', *Journal intime*. 1913; in *Œuvres*. Paris: Gallimard, Pléiade, 1957. 81–304.

Lears, Jackson, *Fables of Abundance: A Cultural History of Advertising in America*. New York: BasicBooks, 1994.

Leavis, F. R., *Mass Civilisation and Minority Culture*. Cambridge: Minority P, 1930.

Leavis, F. R., and Denys Thompson, *Culture and Environment: The Training of Critical Awareness*. London: Chatto & Windus, 1933.

Leavis, Q. D., *Fiction and the Reading Public*. London: Chatto & Windus, 1932.

Le Bon, Gustave, *Psychologie des foules*. 1895; Paris: PUF, 1983.

Le Clézio, J. M. G., *Les Géants*. Paris: Gallimard, 1973.

Leigh, Ruth, *The Human Side of Retail Selling*. New York: D. Appleton and Company, 1923.

Leinwand, Gerald (ed.), *The Consumer*. New York: Simon and Schuster, Inc., 1970.

Levin, Ira, *The Stepford Wives*. 1972; London: Signet, 1994.

Levy, Hermann, *The Shops of Britain: A Study in Retail Distribution*. London: Kegan Paul, Trench, Trubner & Co. Ltd., 1948.

Lewis, Sinclair, *Babbit*. 1922; London: Granada, 1974.

– *Main Street*. 1920; London: Penguin, 1991.

Lewis, Thomas H., *Modern Retailing: Stepping-Stones to Success in Shopkeeping*, 4 vols. London: The Caxton Publishing Co. Ltd, 1949.

Lynd, Robert S., and Helen Merrell Lynd, *Middletown: A Study in Modern American Culture*. 1929. New York: Harcourt, Brace, Jovanovich, 1956.

McEwan, Ian, *The Child in Time*. 1987; London: Picador, 1988.

McGrath, Raymond, and A. C. Frost, *Glass in Architecture and Decoration*. London: The Architectural Press, 1937.

McLelland, W. G., *Studies in Retailing*. Oxford: Basil Blackwell, 1963.

Mars-Jones, Adam, *The Waters of Thirst*. London: Faber and Faber, 1993.

Martineau, Pierre, *Motivation in Advertising: Motives that Make People Buy*. New York: McGraw-Hill Book Company, Inc., 1957.

Marx, Karl, *Capital: A Critique of Political Economy*, vol. I. 1867. Trans. Ben Fowkes, Harmondsworth: Penguin, 1976.

Mathias, Peter, *Retailing Revolution: A History of Multiple Retailing in the Food Trades*. London: Longmans, 1967.

Mattelart, Armand, *L'internationale publicitaire*. Paris: Editions la Découverte, 1989.

Miller, Daniel, *A Theory of Shopping*. Oxford: Polity, 1998.

Miller, Michael B., *The Bon Marché: Bourgeois Culture and the Department Store, 1869–1920*. Princeton: Princeton UP, 1981.

Morand, Paul, *New York*. Paris: Ernest Flammarion, 1930.

Mowbray, A. Q., *The Thumb and the Scale: Or the Supermarket Shell Game*. Philadelphia: J. B. Lippincott Company, 1967.

Neal, Lawrence E., *Retailing and the Public*. London: George Allen & Unwin Ltd, 1932.

Newsom, John, *The Education of Girls*. London: Faber and Faber Ltd, 1948.

Nietzsche, Friedrich, *Thus Spake Zarathustra*. Trans. R. J. Hollingdale. Harmondsworth: Penguin, 1969.

Nixon, H. K., *Principles of Selling*. 1931; 2nd edn, New York: McGraw-Hill Book Company, Inc., 1942.

Nystrom, Paul H., *Retail Selling and Store Management*. New York: D. Appleton and Company, 1925.

Opie, Robert, *Sweet Memories: A Selection of Chocolate Delights*. London: Pavilion Books Limited, 1988.

Packard, Vance, *The Hidden Persuaders*. 1957; Harmondsworth: Penguin, 1960.
– *The Status Seekers: An Exploration of Class Behaviour in America*. 1959; Harmondsworth: Penguin, 1969.

Pascoe, Charles Eyre, *London of To-day: An Illustrated Book for this Season, and for all Seasons: 1892*. London: Hamish Hamilton, 1892.

Perec, Georges, *Les choses: Une histoire des années soixante*. 1965; Paris: Union Générale d'Editions, 10/18, 1985.

Perry, George, with Alfred Bestall, *Rupert: A Bear's Life*. London: Michael Joseph, 1985.

Perry, Martin H., *How to Start a Shop*. London: Sidgwick and Jackson Limited, 1947.

Pick, Beverley, 'Trends in Window Display in Great Britain'. In Herdeg (1951), 53–6.

Pilditch, James, *The Silent Salesman: How to Develop Packaging that Sells*. 1961; 2nd edn, London: Business Books Limited, 1973.

Pitkin, Walter B., *The Consumer: His Nature and His Changing Habits*. New York: McGraw-Hill Book Company, Inc., 1932.

Plowman, Allan, and K. C. Matthews, *Animated Display and How to Get It Done*. London: Blandford P, 1959.

Pope, Alexander, *The Poems of Alexander Pope*. Ed. John Butt, London: Methuen, 1963.

Powell, David, *Counter Revolution: The Tesco Story*. London: GraftonBooks, 1991.

Powers, Alan, *Shop Fronts*. London: Chatto & Windus, 1989.

*Progressive Grocer. Consumer Dynamics in the Supermarket*. *Progressive Grocer*, October 1965–October 1966.

– *Colonial Study*. *Progressive Grocer*, October 1963–March 1964.

Quétaud, M., *Etude générale sur les emballages*. Paris: Dunod, 1949.

Rachinel, E., and M. Buisson, *Vente et publicité, Agenda Dunod*. Paris: Dunod, 1930.

– *Vente et publicité, Agenda Dunod*. Paris: Dunod, 1936.

Redmayne, Paul, and Hugh Weeks, *Market Research*. London: Butterworth & Co. (Publishers) Ltd., 1931.

Roberts, Eirlys, *Consumers*. London: C. A. Watts & Co. Ltd., 1966.

Ruskin, John, *Sesame and Lilies*. 1865; London: Dent, Everyman's Library, 1970.

Russell, Gilbert, *Advertisement Writing*. London: Ernest Benn Ltd, 1927.

St John, Madeleine, *The Women in Black*. 1993; London: Abacus, 1994.

Sartre, Jean-Paul, *Situations*, III. Paris: Gallimard, 1949.

Schwartz, Frederic, *The Werkbund: Design Theory and Mass Culture Before the First World War*. New Haven: Yale UP, 1996.

Scott, Walter Dill, *Influencing Men in Business: The Psychology of Argument and Suggestion*. 1911; 3rd edn revised and enlarged by Delton T. Howard, New York: The Ronald P Co., 1928.

– *The Psychology of Advertising: A Simple Exposition of the Principles of Psychology in their Relation to Successful Advertising*. 1908; 5th edn, Boston: Small, Maynard & Company, 1913.

*Shelf Appeal, Omnibus of Marketing and Packaging*. London: Creative Journals Ltd., 1938.

– *The Package Omnibus*. London: Creative Journals Ltd., 1936.

Simmat, R., *Personal Salesmanship*. London: Sir Isaac Pitman & Sons Ltd., 1934.

Smith, Albert B. (ed.), *Competitive Distribution in a Free High-Level Economy and its Implications for the University*. Pittsburgh: U of Pittsburgh P, 1957.

Somake, Ellis E., and Rolf Hellberg, *Shops and Stores Today: Their Design, Planning and Organisation*. London: B. T. Batsford Ltd, 1956.

Sparke, Penny, *As Long as it's Pink: The Sexual Politics of Taste*. London: Pandora, 1995.

Strasser, Susan, *Never Done: A History of American Housework*. New York: Pantheon, 1982.

– *Satisfaction Guaranteed: The Making of the American Mass Market*. New York: Pantheon, 1989.

*Style for Men* magazine, *Display for the Man's Shop*. London: The National Trade Press Ltd, 1938.

Sullerot, Evelyne, *La vie des femmes*. Paris: Gonthier, 1965.


Taylor, Lou, *Mourning Dress: A Costume and Social History*. London: George Allen and Unwin, 1983.

Thil, Etienne, *Combat pour la distribution: D'Edouard Leclerc aux supermarchés*. Paris: Arthaud, 1964.

– *Les inventeurs du commerce moderne: Des grands magasins aux bébés-requins*. Paris: Arthaud, 1966.

Tillman, Lynne, *Bookstore: The Life and Times of Jeanette Watson and Books & Co.* New York: Harcourt Brace & Company, 1999.

Trethowan, Harry, et al., *Selling through the Window*. London: The Studio Limited, 1935.

Trollope, Joanna, *The Rector's Wife*. 1991; London: Black Swan, 1994.

Tyler, Anne, *Ladder of Years*. 1995; London: Vintage, 1996.


Uhrich, René, *Super-marchés et usines de distribution: Hier aux Etats-Unis, aujourd'hui en France*. Paris: Plon, 1962.

Unit for Retail Planning, *Hypermarkets and Superstores: Report of a House of Commons Seminar*. London: Unit for Retail Planning Information Limited, May 1976.

Updike, John, 'A & P'. In *Pigeon Feathers and Other Stories*. London: André Deutsch, 1963, pp. 187–96.


Vaughan, Floyd L., *Marketing and Advertising: An Economic Appraisal*. Princeton: Princeton UP, 1928.

Veblen, Thorstein, *The Theory of the Leisure Class: An Economic Study of Institutions*. 1899; New York: Mentor, 1953.

Vernon, Charles, *The Sweet Shop: A Handbook for Retail Confectioners*. London: Sir Isaac Pitman & Sons Ltd, 1939.

Villermet, Jean-Marc, *Naissance de l'hypermarché*. Paris: Armand Colin, 1991.


Walsh, William T. (ed.), *Salesmanship Simplified: A Short Cut to Success*. Chicago: Opportunity Publishing Co., 1927.

Wilde, Oscar, *The Picture of Dorian Gray*. 1891; Harmondsworth: Penguin, 1973.

Williams, Bridget, *The Best Butter in the World: A History of Sainsbury's*. London: Ebury P, 1994.

Woolf, Virginia, *The Crowded Dance of Modern Life: Selected Essays*, vol. 2. Ed. Rachel Bowlby, London: Penguin, 1993.
– *Orlando*. 1928. Ed. Rachel Bowlby, Oxford: Oxford World's Classics, 1992.
– *The Waves*. 1931. Ed. Gillian Beer, Oxford: Oxford World's Classics, 1992.
– *A Woman's Essays: Selected Essays*, vol. 1. Ed. Rachel Bowlby, London: Penguin, 1992.
– *The Years*. 1937. Ed. Hermione Lee, Oxford: Oxford World's Classics, 1992.

Zimmerman, M. M., *Super Market: Spectacular Exponent of Mass Distribution*. New York: Super Market Publishing Co., 1937.
– *The Super Market: A Revolution in Distribution*. New York: McGraw-Hill Book Company, Inc., 1955.
Zola, Emile, *Au Bonheur des Dames*. 1883; Paris: Garnier Flammarion, 1971.

# Index